Leonardo da Vinci
197 Drawings

By Narim Bender

First Edition

*****

I0477253

Leonardo da Vinci: 197 Drawings
*****

Foreword

Leonardo was born on, "Saturday April 15, 1452 at three o'clock in the night". We know this to be correct as the quote is from notes written by Leonardo's grandfather. Leonardo's birthplace was the small village of Vinci located between the Tuscan cities of Pistoia and Empoli. He was the illegitimate son of notary, Ser Piero d'Antonio and a peasant woman named Caterina. Little is known of her, but she probably came from the village of Anchiano and may have been a barmaid. It is almost definite that she had contact with her son throughout her life.

After the baby's birth Ser Piero was quickly convinced to marry into a wealthy family while Caterina was married off to a cowherd. Initially, Leonardo lived with his grandparents on his father's side. After some years had passed Ser Piero realized that his wife could not have children; at this time Leonardo was taken to be raised and educated in his father's house.

Some authors have Leonardo as spending the first five years of his childhood living with his mother, or bearing the brunt of much misery from later arriving legitimate half-brothers. However, his grandfather's notes also show us that the child was baptized and accepted into his father's side of the family immediately. It is known that he could not have been the object of teasing from half-brothers as it was not until Ser Piero's third wife that there were to be any legitimate sons; by this time Leonardo was 24. During that period in history illegitimate and legitimate children were bought up together, even in the most noble of homes. Wives would not register any protest over this and there was no stigma attached.

Even as a young child Leonardo showed extraordinary talent, being quick at music and learning to play the lyre; he could also sing beautifully and was strong in the area of mathematics. At a young age he was often to be found out sketching plants and animals.

When, in 1468, his paternal grandfather died the family moved to Florence. It was at this stage that his father decided the boy had unusual artistic talents and decided to send him to study with the most sought after Florentine master of the time. Andrea Verrocchio was a renown sculptor, painter and goldsmith, all areas Leonardo would study while apprenticed to him. Little remains of Verrocchio's painted works and not much is known of Leonardo's activities during this stage though his apprenticeship would have been the same as those available to all of Verrocchio's students. This involved grinding and mixing pigments, learning geometry and the mixing of colours, preparing panels correctly so they could receive paintings, the actual act of painting itself and the working of clay and casting bronze.

In 1472, Leonardo was enrolled as a master in the Company of Painters; this indicates that his actual apprenticeship to Verrocchio had probably ended by this time, though he stayed at his master's workshop. Although he is best remembered for his paintings, very few artists painted as little and drew as much as Leonardo. While very limited numbers of paintings have survived their creator, Leonardo's drawings of people, places and things are very numerous with over 10,000 being found in various parts of the world. He always wrote extensive notes on his subject and these were obviously never thought of by him as being for publication as they were often written in codes and mirror writing.

There are no records of Leonardo's activities between 1476-1478 and no documents to place him either in Florence or anywhere else.

In 1480 Leonardo became a member of the garden of San Marcos run under the patronage of Lorenzo the Magnificent. This was also the year that he was commissioned to paint the Adoration of the Magi for the church of San Donato Scopeto, just outside of Florence. But Leonardo was ready to move on; exactly why unknown but it is may have been due to his disappointment at not being one of the four masters chosen to decorate the walls of the Sistine Chapel.

1482 saw him writing to the Duke of Milan, Ludovico Sforza listing his capabilities as a designer of both civil and military machines. Italy was being afflicted by wars between the various city-states; this was followed by a French invasion. This was a time of rapid development of firearms and explosives and military engineers were important figures. Leonardo's had many ideas for fortifications, bridges, weapons, and river diversions to flood the enemy. Leonardo was summoned to court one day where it is said he was the least nervous of the pair.

In 1500, after many years serving in Milan, Leonardo returned to Florence. By this stage he was a celebrated genius in both painting and engineering. He was also known for a number of celebrated failures, including an overly ambitious design for a bronze equestrian statue. It was here that Leonardo met up with another great genius in the form of Michelangelo. He mocked Leonardo about the unfinished statue and Leonardo was deeply hurt. This would lead to a never ending rivalry between the two, although they had much in common.

In 1503, both were commissioned to produce major murals for the great council hall in the Palazzo Vecchio. Neither finished. Both would also help lead a revolution in anatomy. At that stage in history doctors still relied upon text books and tradition. Artists, as well as doctors, changed everything by beginning to dissect bodies and recording the results accurately. The work of artists and doctors during the Renaissance was often very similar.

Starting about this time, Leonardo developed his dreams of flying and over the next two years he filled a notebook with sketches and studies of bird flight. He also designed a parachute and a helicopter, amongst other flying machines.

Leonardo went to Rome in 1513 where he worked for Giuliano de' Medici and occupied rooms in the Belvedere Palace of the Vatican. The next two years involved much illness for the artist and he was often frustrated during this period. He experimented with flight a little by attempting to attach homemade wings to a lizard; other than this most of his time was spent working on geometric and optical puzzles or creating new types of art oils and varnishes. There is little evidence that Leonardo painted actively after he left Rome.

In 1516, the move was made to France where Leonardo was to work for Francois I. The King provided him with lodgings in a house called Cloux which still stands and has been carefully restored. Though still able to draw Leonardo was already a very sick man and his right hand was partially paralysed due to a stroke.

Most of his time was spent organizing his notebooks and the King did not require he carry out commissions, though Leonardo had to suffer frequent royal visits and produce plans for festivals and plays. The King would enter the manor house of Cloux via a stretch of tunnel connected to the castle at Amboise. One of the items Leonardo made for him during this period was a mechanical lion with a breast that opened to reveal lilies.

Leonardo died quietly on the 2nd May, 1519 just a few weeks after his 67th birthday. He was buried in the Church of St Florentine, but his remains were scattered during the Wars of Religion. Three centuries later the French artist Jean Auguste Dominique painted a romantic deathbed picture showing the King of France leaning over the dying Leonardo and cradling him in his arms. In reality, the king was not present at the death, but was off celebrating the birth of his second son.

Leonardo had many friends who are now renowned either in their fields or for their historical significance. They included the mathematician Luca Pacioli, with whom he collaborated on a book in the 1490s, as well as Franchinus Gaffurius and Isabella d'Este. Leonardo appears to have had no close relationships with women except for his friendship with the two Este sisters, Beatrice and Isabella. He drew a portrait of Isabella while on a journey which took him through Mantua, and which appears to have been used to create a painted portrait, now lost.

Beyond friendship, Leonardo kept his private life secret. His sexuality has been the subject of satire, analysis, and speculation. This trend began in the mid-16th century and was revived in the 19th and 20th centuries, most notably by Sigmund Freud.

Giorgio Vasari, in the enlarged edition of Lives of the Artists, 1568, introduced his chapter on Leonardo da Vinci with the following words:

"In the normal course of events many men and women are born with remarkable talents; but occasionally, in a way that transcends nature, a single person is marvellously endowed by Heaven with beauty, grace and talent in such abundance that he leaves other men far behind, all his actions seem inspired and indeed everything he does clearly comes from God rather than from human skill. Everyone acknowledged that this was true of Leonardo da Vinci, an artist of outstanding physical beauty, who displayed infinite grace in everything that he did and who cultivated his genius so brilliantly that all problems he studied he solved with ease."

Others also displayed their admiration of Leonardo at various times during and after his life. Italian painter Raphael depicted Leonardo as the Greek philosopher Plato in his famed work School of Athens.

His genius, perhaps more than that of any other figure, epitomized the Renaissance humanist ideal. Leonardo has often been described as the archetype of the Renaissance Man, a man of "unquenchable curiosity" and "feverishly inventive imagination". He is widely considered to be one of the greatest painters of all time and perhaps the most diversely talented person ever to have lived.

Fifteen works are generally attributed either in whole or in large part to him, most of them paintings on panel but including a mural, a large drawing on paper and two works in the early stages of preparation. A further six paintings are disputed, there are four recently attributed works, and two are copies of lost work. None of Leonardo's paintings are signed, and this list draws on the opinions of various scholars. The small number of surviving paintings is due in part to Leonardo's frequently disastrous experimentation with new techniques, and his chronic procrastination. Nevertheless, these few works together with his notebooks, which contain drawings, scientific diagrams, and his thoughts on the nature of painting, comprise a contribution to later generations of artists rivaled only by that of his contemporary, Michelangelo.

Drawings

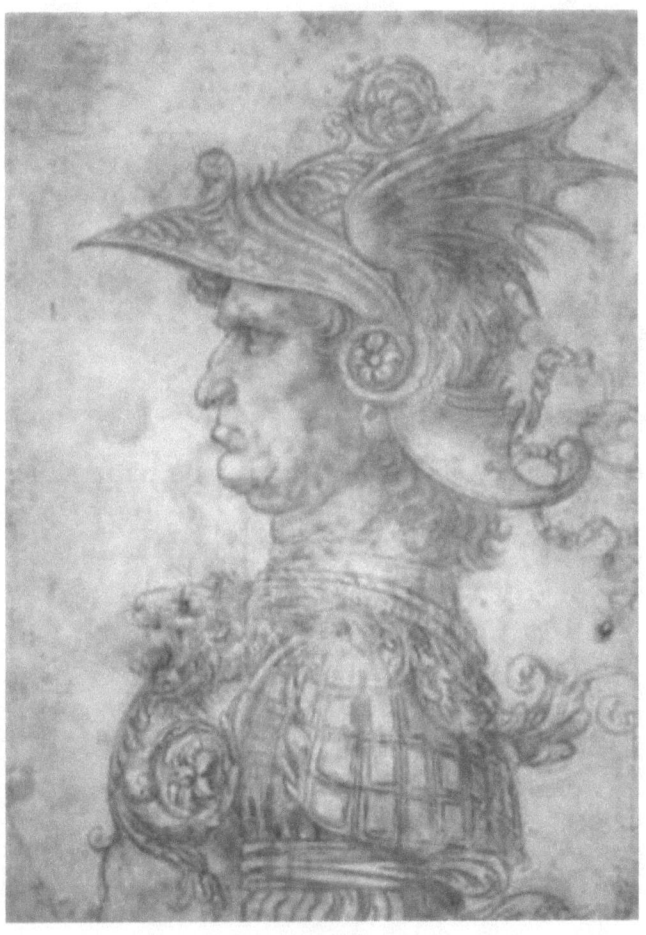

Profile of a warrior in helmet, 1472, metalpoint, 28.5 x 20.7 cm, British Museum, London

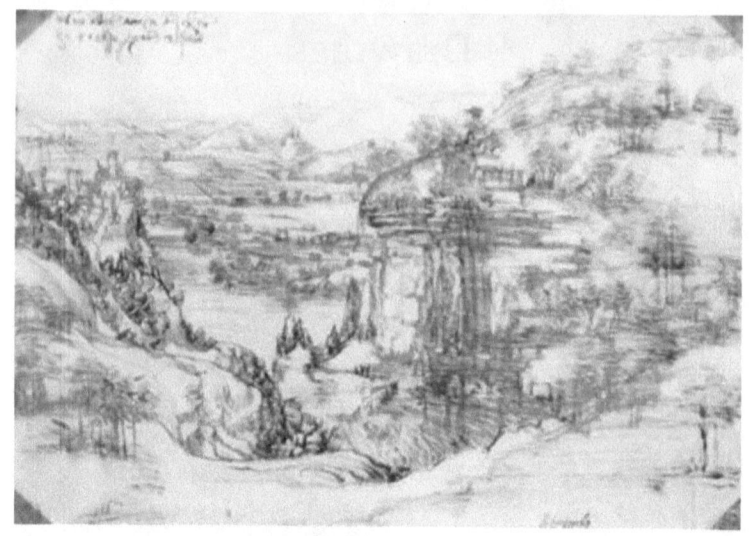

Arno Landscape, 1473, Pen and ink on paper. 19 x 28.5 cm. Uffizi Gallery, Florence, Italy

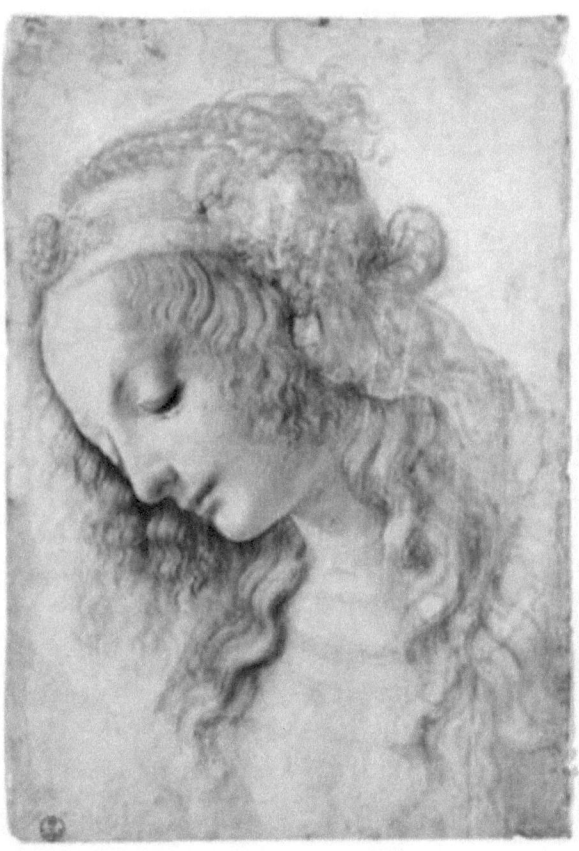

Woman's Head, 1474, Pen, ink and white pigment on paper, 28.2 x 19.9 cm. Uffizi Gallery, Florence, Italy

The detailed drawing of a girl's head contains elements typical of the school of Verrocchio, such as the diagonally placed eyes with the considerably rounded pupils and hair painted in meticulous detail. A relationship between this drawing and the Mary in the Annunciation predella in the Louvre has quite rightly been established. The attribution of the drawing to Leonardo is now just as disputed as its dating.

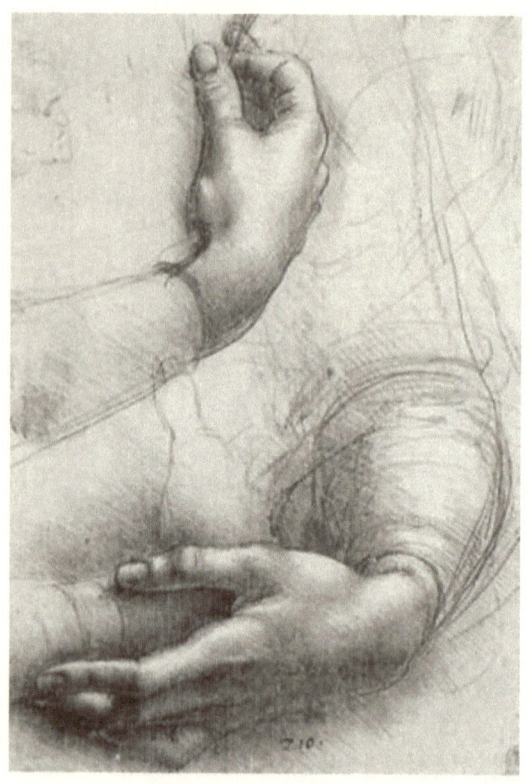

**Study of hands, c. 1474, Silverpoint and white
highlights on pink prepared paper, 21.4 x 15 cm,
Royal Library, Windsor**

This study is remarkable in the amount of life it brings
to a simple drawing. The image may have been a
source of inspiration for Escher's famous drawing of a
hand drawing another hand; there has also been
unsubstantiated speculation that this may have served
as a study for hands in the Mona Lisa. This seems
unlikely, but the sketch is striking.

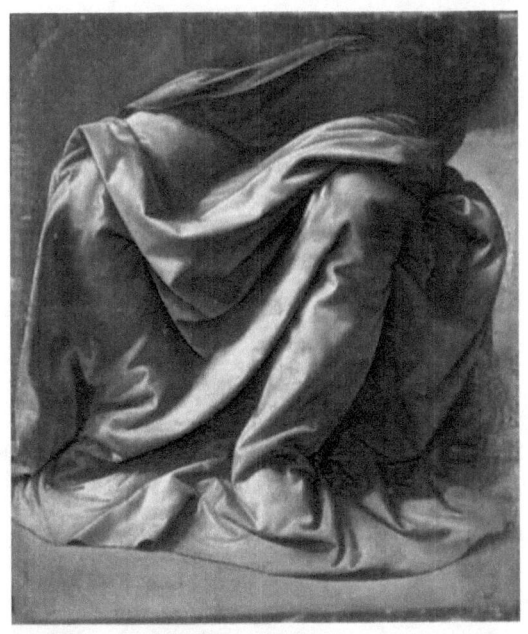

Garment study for a seated figure, 1470-84, Brush and grey distemper on grey canvas, 26.6 x 23.3 cm, Louvre, Paris

Garment studies were part of the training of every painter. It is likely that prepared materials were used for this in the workshops in Florence. On them, the students were above all able to study the depiction of light and shade, which is why these works appear to have been carried out primarily in one colour. Several such garment studies at different levels of artistic ability survive, though their attribution is disputed. It is above all the fineness of this study that has led to its being attributed to Leonardo.

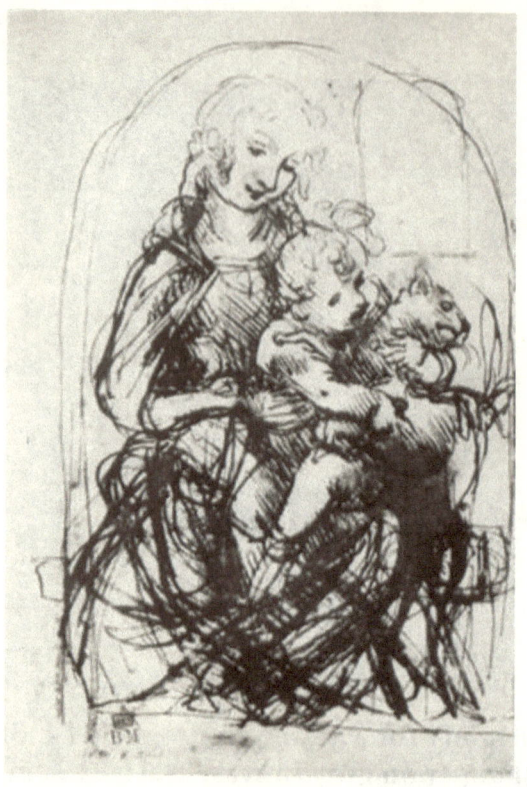

**Study of the Madonna and Child with a Cat, c. 1478,
Pen and ink on paper, 28.1 x 19.9 cm, British Museum,
London**

The compositional drawing is connected with the
painting of the Benois Madonna, as indicated by the
head of Mary and the sketched window in the
background. Leonardo traced the composition from the
rear side, worked out the mirror image version with
additional variations, and then applied a wash. There is
no record of a painting of this composition by
Leonardo. The motif of the Madonna with a cat was
later depicted in a student's painting that is now in the
Brera in Milan.

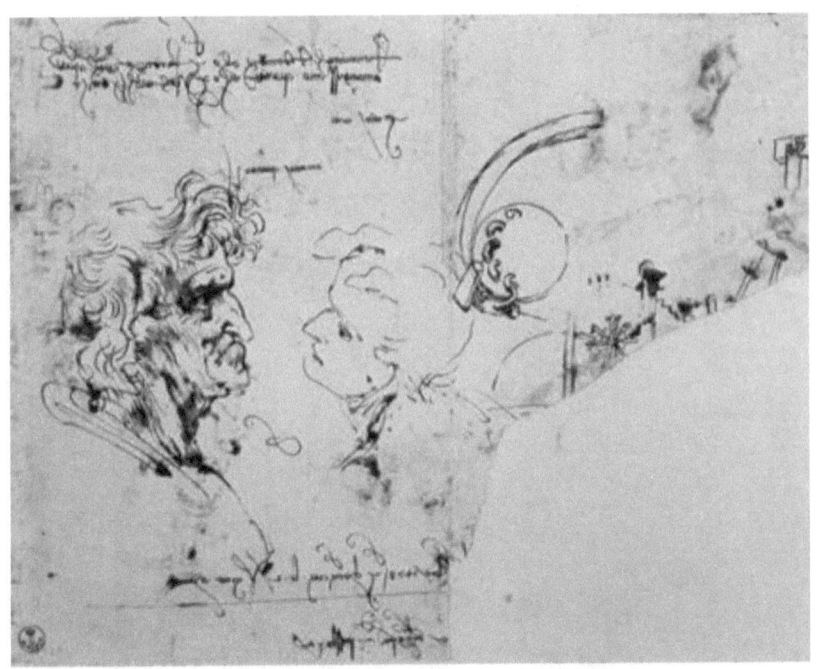

Study sheet, 1478, Pen and ink on paper, 20.2 x 26.6 cm, Galleria degli Uffizi, Florence

In addition to sketches of two profile heads, there are also mechanical and military drawings on the sheet. Due to a comment which Leonardo notes down in his characteristic mirror writing, to the effect that he is working on two pictures of Mary in 1478, the sheet is important for the artist's early work. The mirror writing was not intended to hide any secrets, as had so frequently been thought, but probably only had the simple practical reason of not wanting to smear the ink when writing with his left hand.

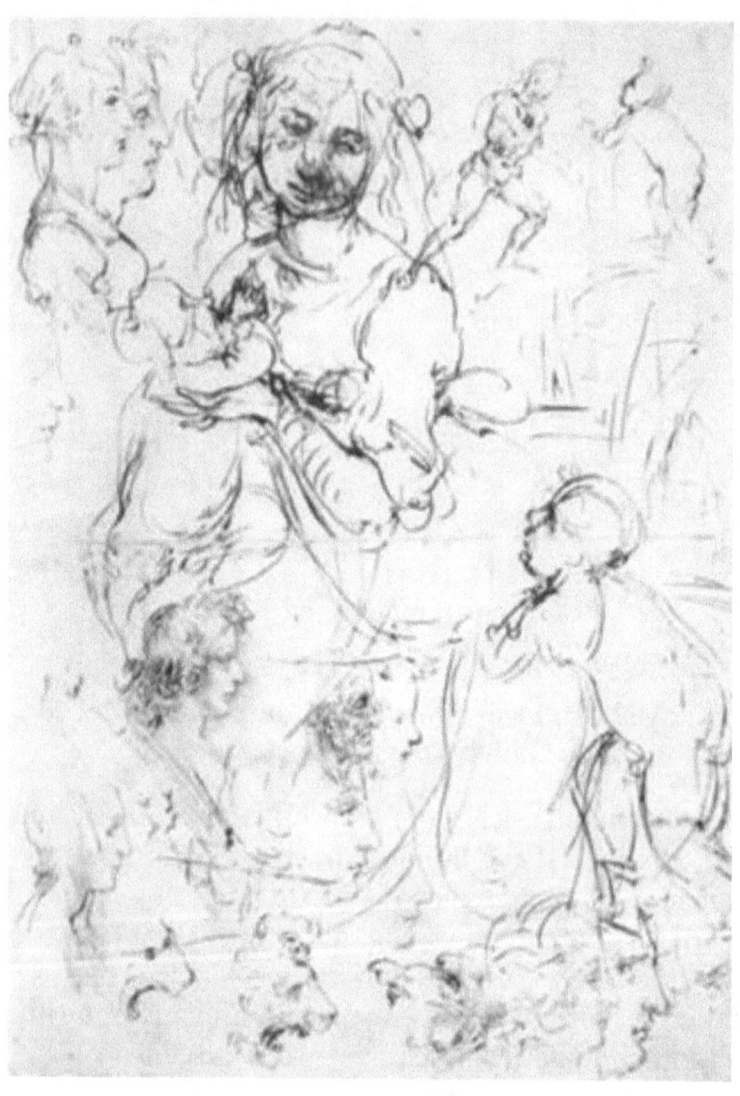

Study of nursing Madonna and profile heads, c.1480, ink, 40.5 x 29 cm, Royal Collection, Windsor Castle, London,

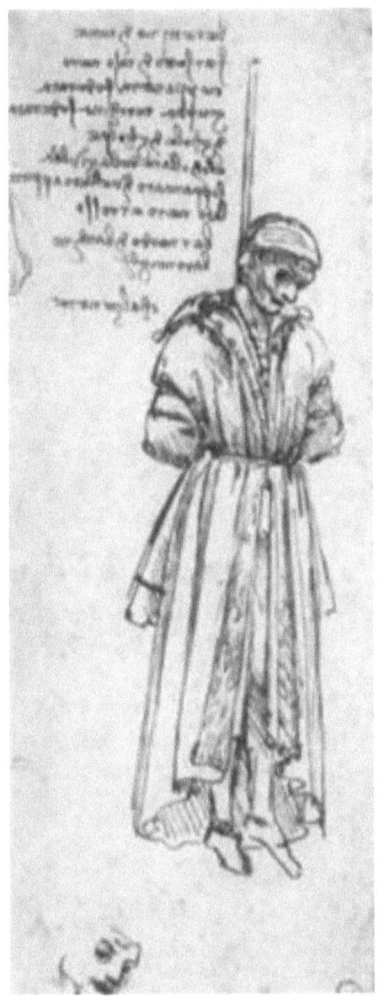

**Study of the Hanged Bernardo di Bandino Baroncelli,
assassin of Giuliano de Medici, 1479, ink, 7.3 x 19.2
cm, usee Bonnat, Bayonne, France**

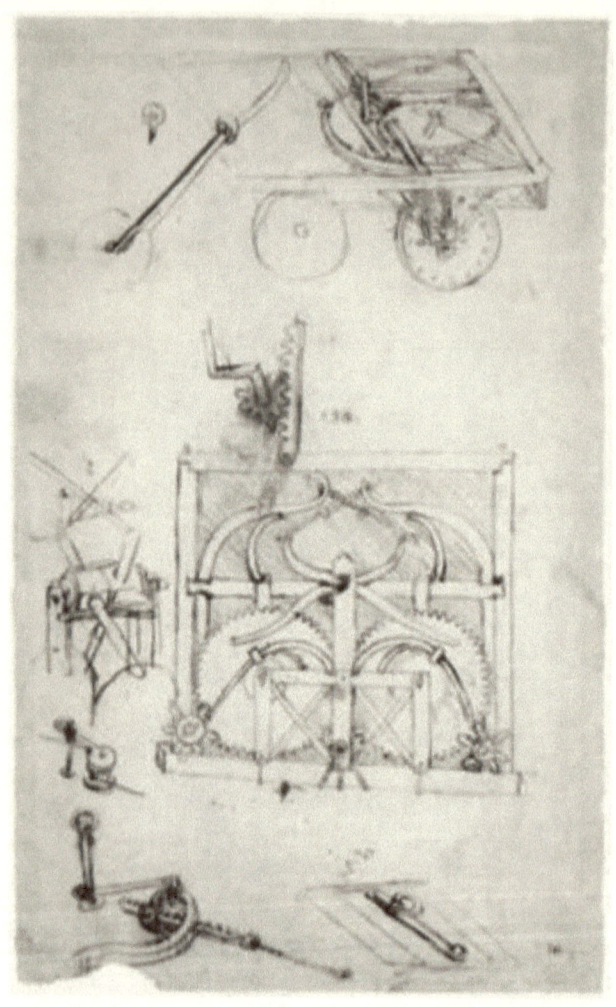

Automobile, 1480, ink, 20 x 27 cm, Biblioteca Ambrosiana, Milan, Italy

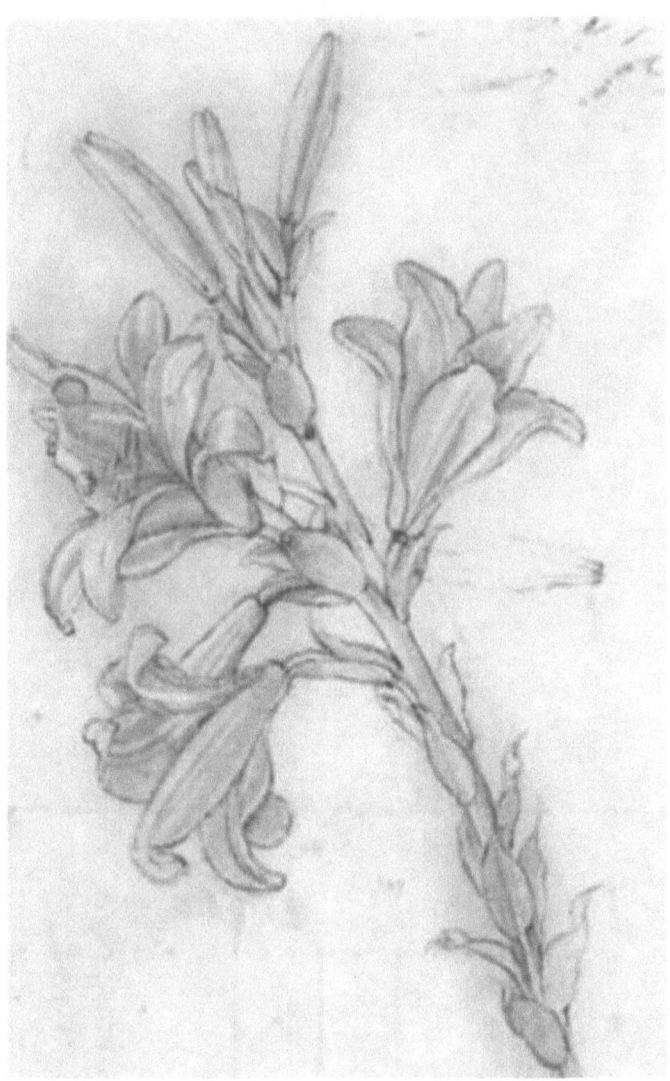

**Lily, c.1480, chalk, ink, 31.4 x 17.7 cm, Royal
Collection, Windsor Castle, London**

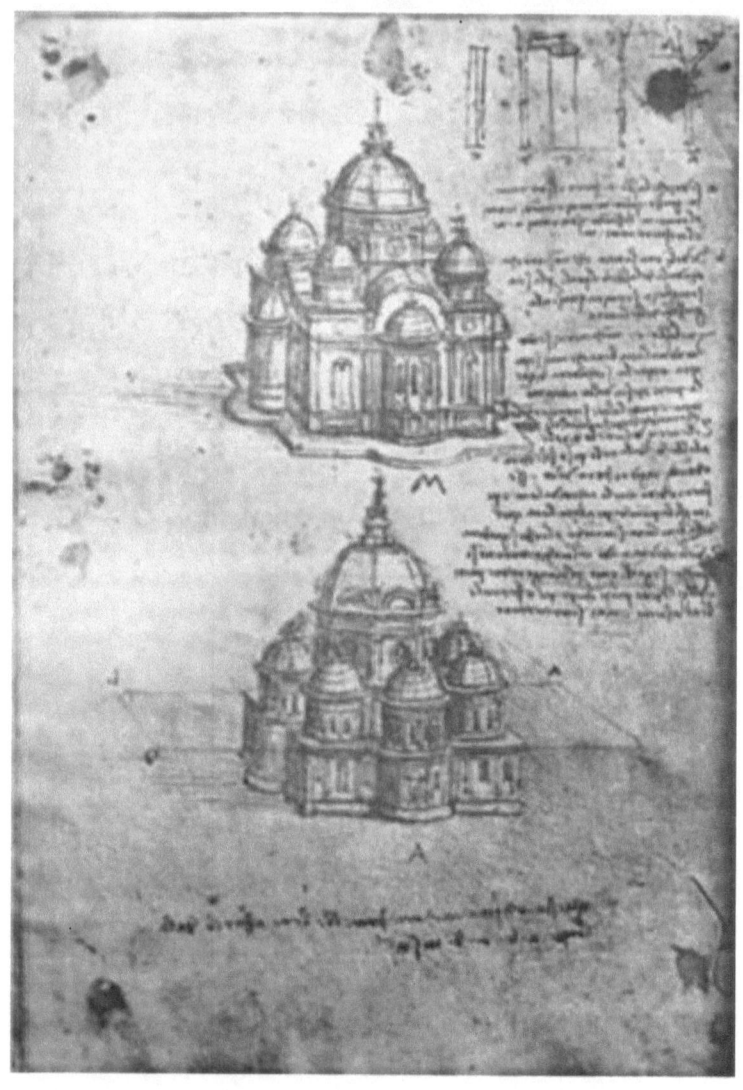

Studies of central plan buildings, 1480, ink, 16 x 22 cm, Bibliotheque de l'Institut de France, Paris, France

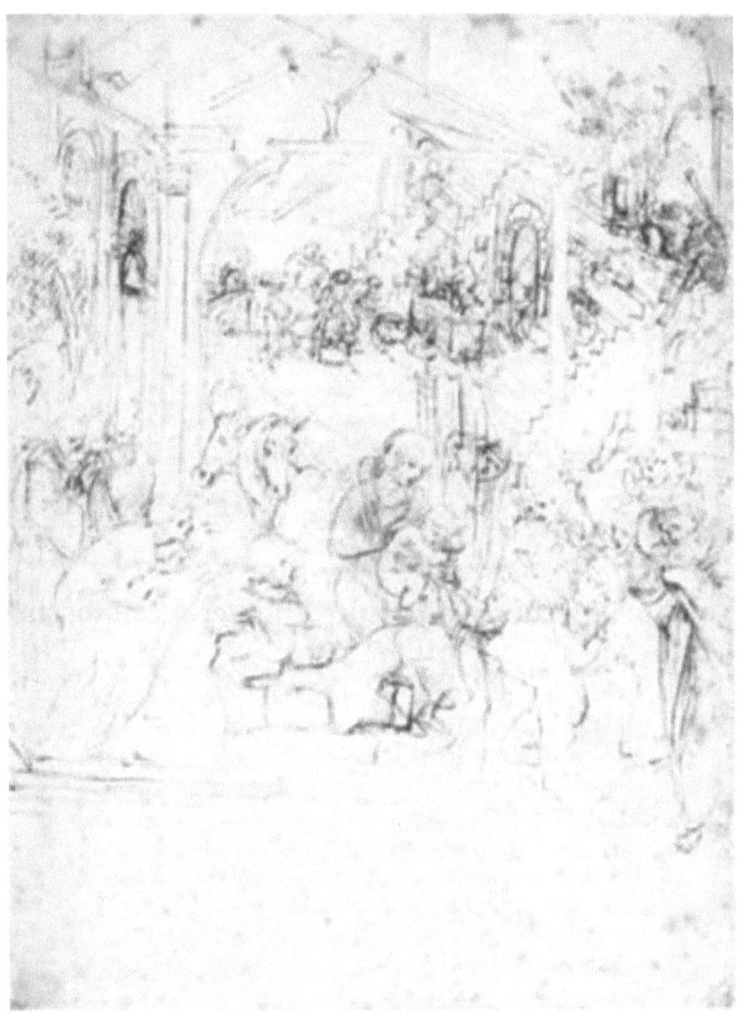

Study for the Adoration of the Magi, 1480, ink, 28.5 x
21.5 cm, Musée du Louvre, Paris,

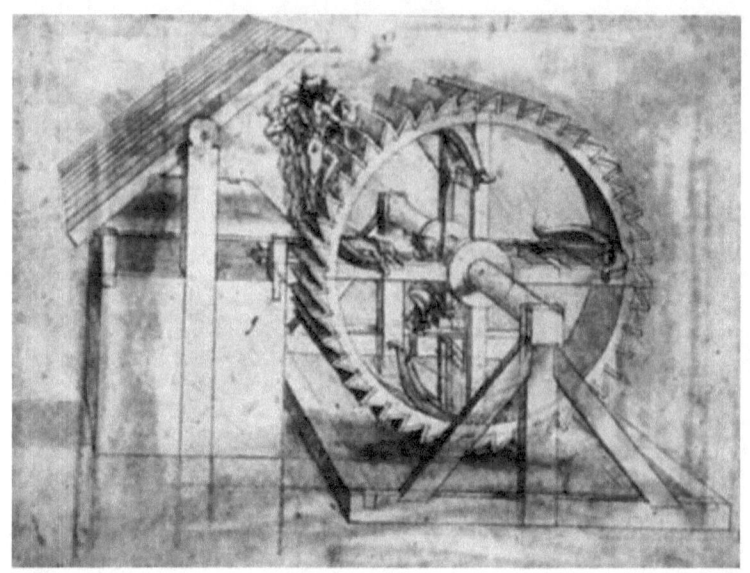

Crossbow Machine, 1481, ink, Biblioteca Ambrosiana, Milan, Italy

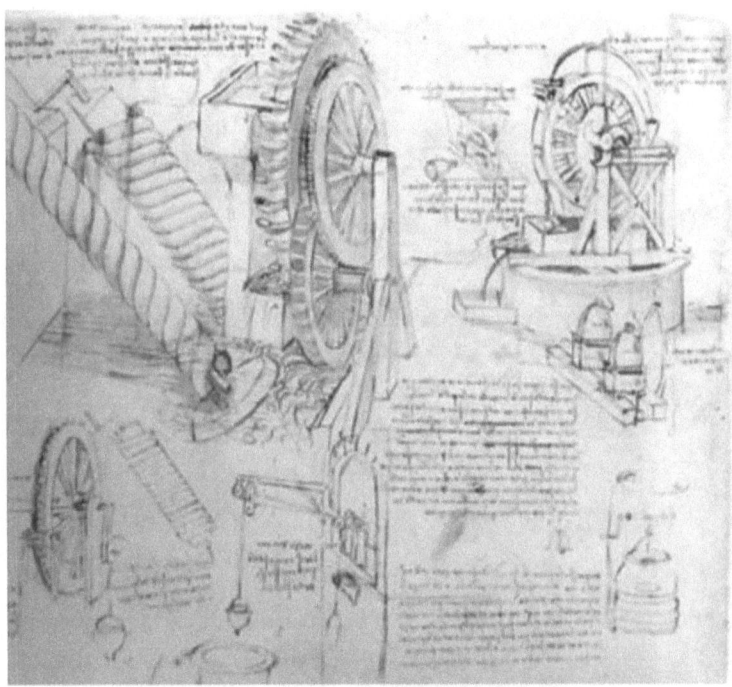

Drawings of Water Lifting Devices, c.1481, ink,
Biblioteca Ambrosiana, Milan, Italy

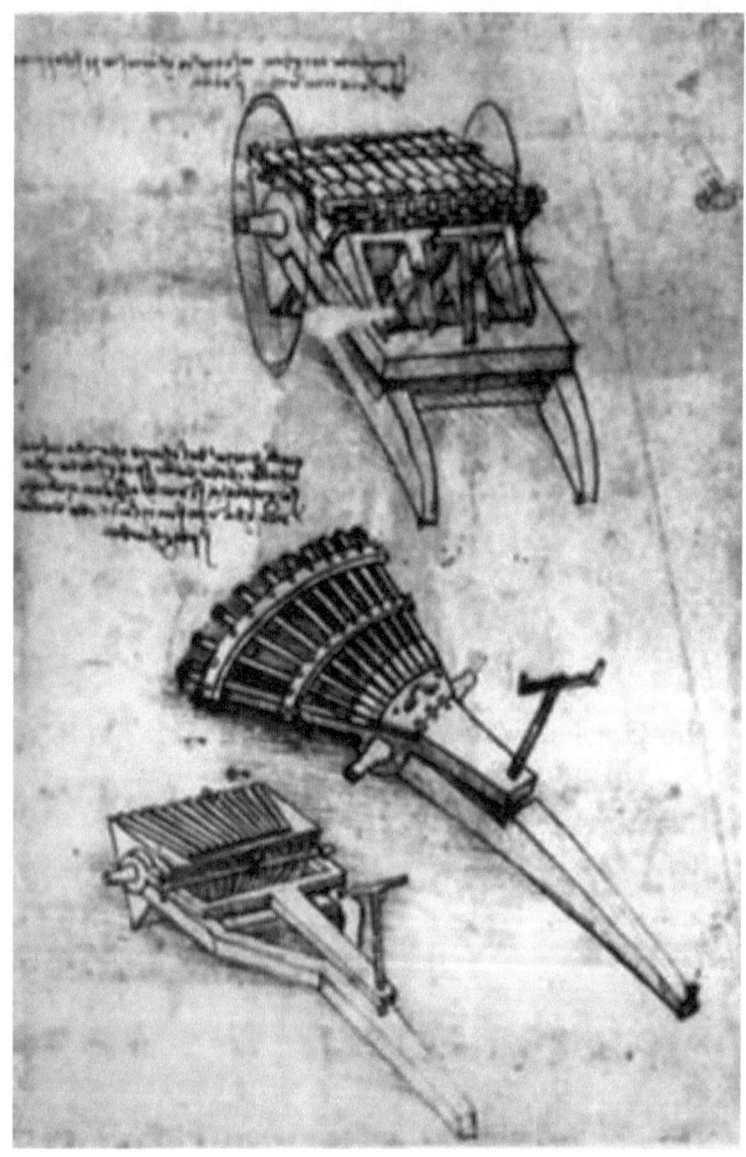

Multi Barrel Gun, c.1481, ink, Biblioteca Ambrosiana, Milan, Italy

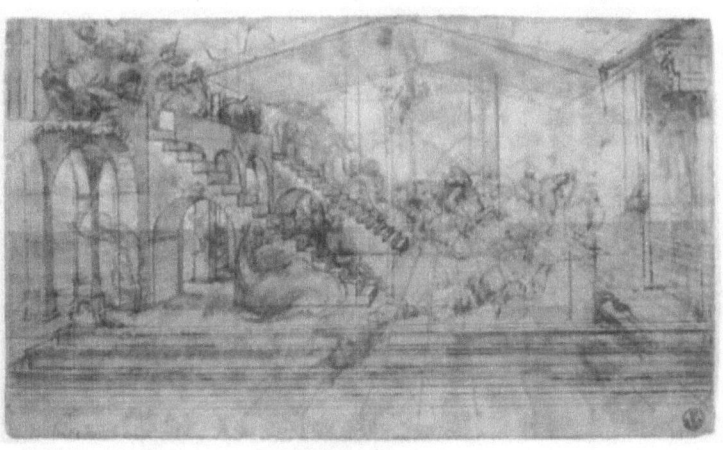

Perspectival study of the Adoration of the Magi, c.1481, ink, 16.3 x 29 cm, Galleria degli Uffizi, Florence, Italy

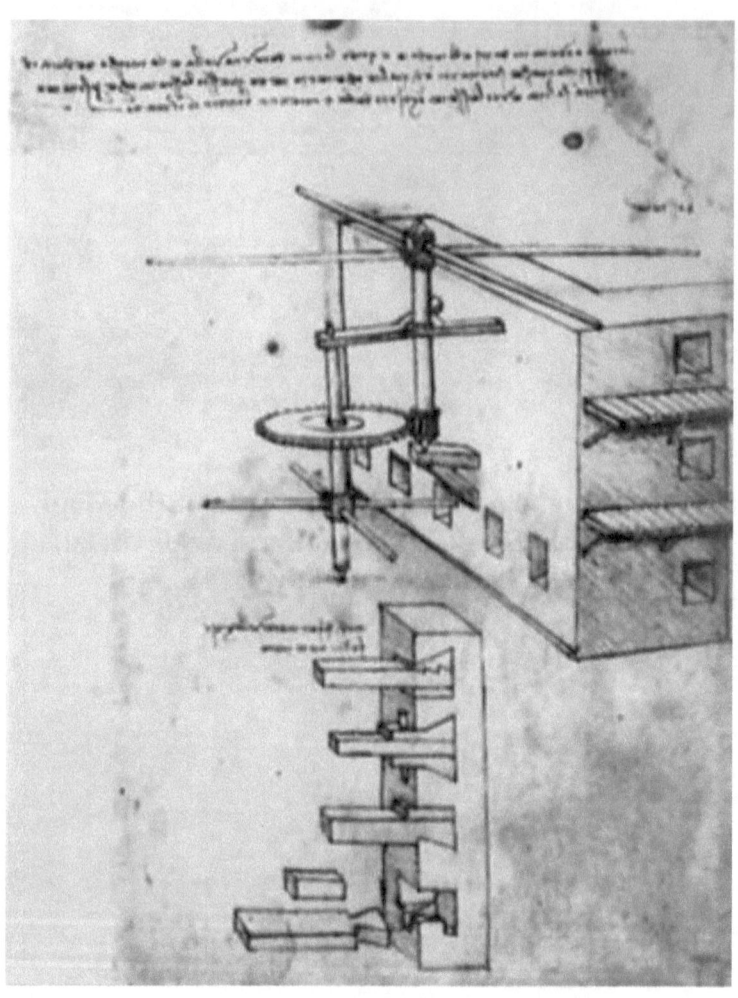

Siege Defenses, c.1481, ink, Biblioteca Ambrosiana, Milan, Italy

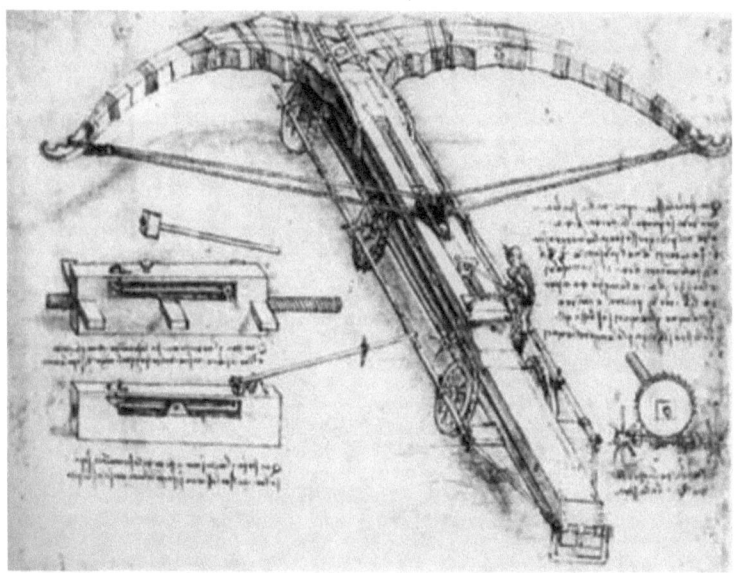

Design for a Giant Crossbow, 1482, ink, Biblioteca
Ambrosiana, Milan, Italy

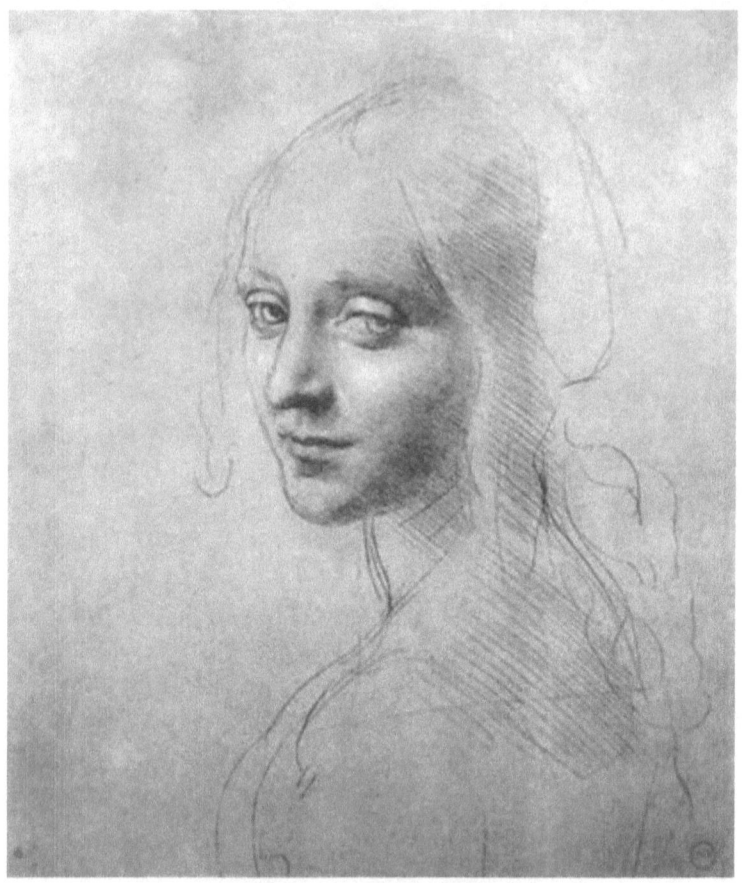

**Head of a Girl, c. 1483, Silverpoint and white
highlights on prepared paper, 18.1 x 15.9 cm,
Biblioteca Reale, Turin**

The eminent art expert Bernhard Berenson called this
sheet "the most beautiful drawing in the world." It is
thought to be a study for the angel in the Virgin of the
Rocks in the Louvre, Paris.

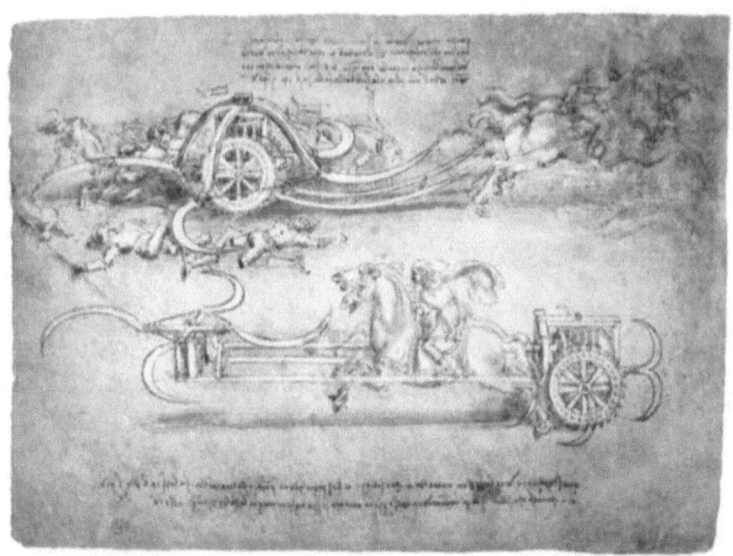

Scythed Chariot, c.1483, ink, Palazzo Reale, Turin, Italy

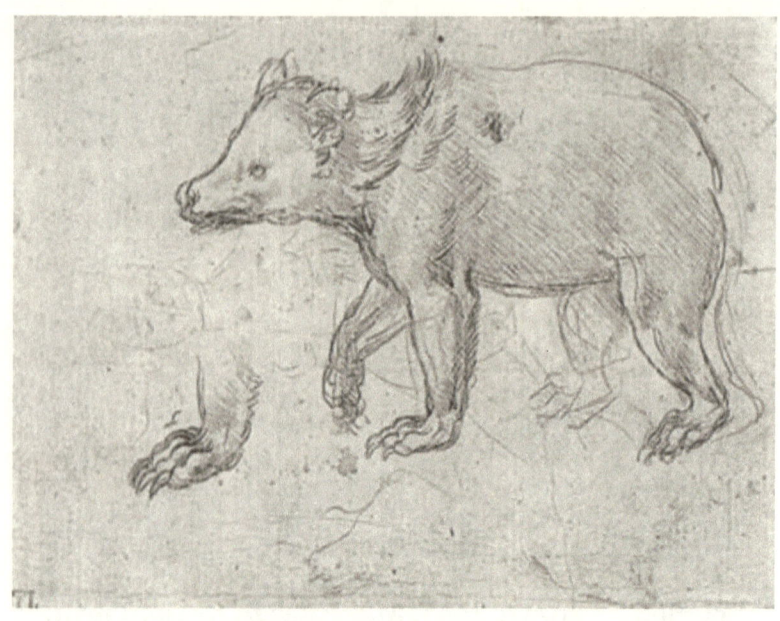

**Studies of a Bear Walking, c.1484, ink, 10.3 x 13.4 cm,
Metropolitan Museum of Art, New York City**

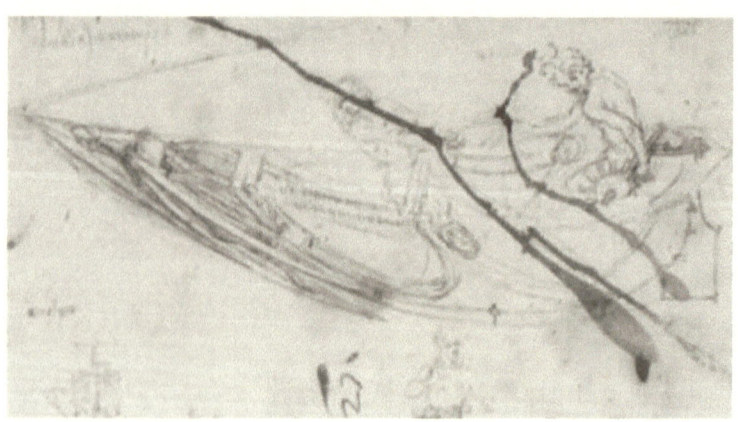

Designs for a Boat, 1485, ink, private collection

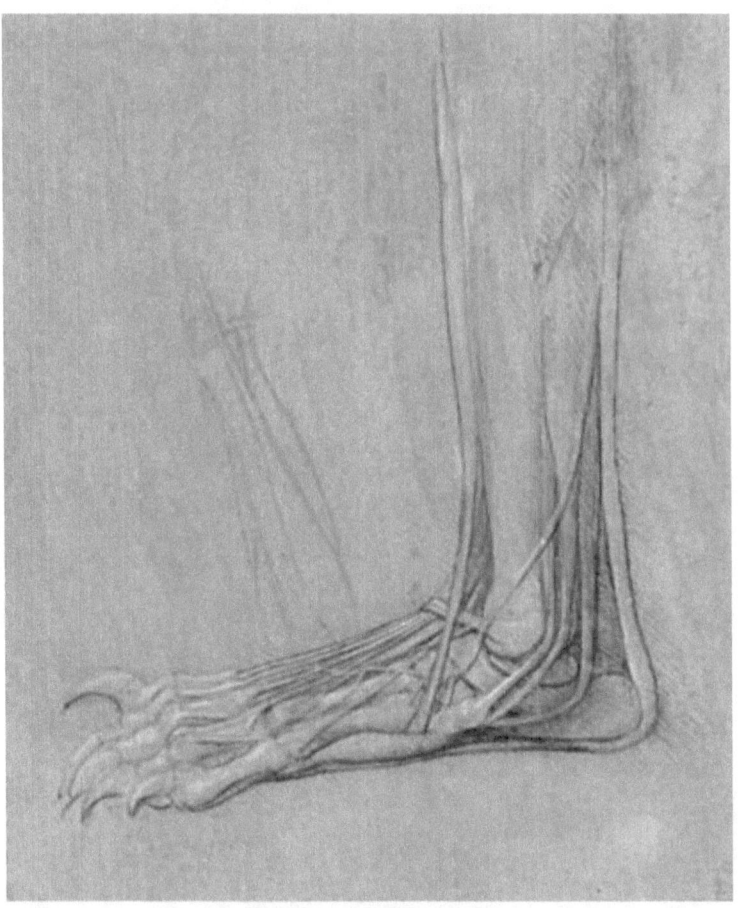

The anatomy of a foot, c.1485, metalpoint, ink, 13.7 x
16.1 cm, Royal Collection, Windsor Castle, London,
UK

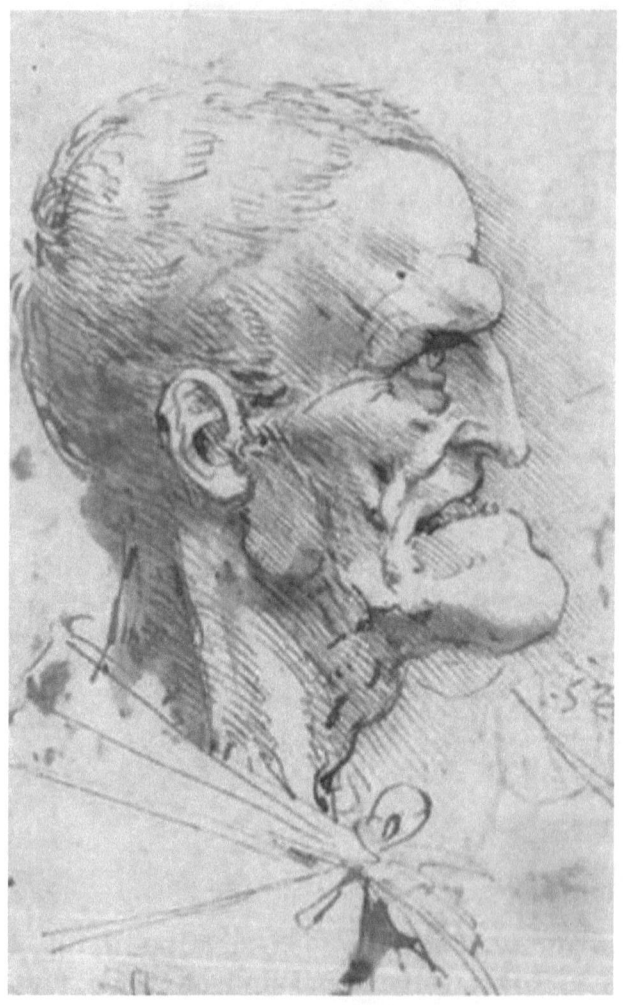

Grotesque Profile, c.1487, Pen and brown ink

The comic intent of this type of representations is obvious. At the root of these drawings lie Leonardo's curiosity about unusual faces and features, his interest in the variety of types of expression and his physiognomic investigations of old age.

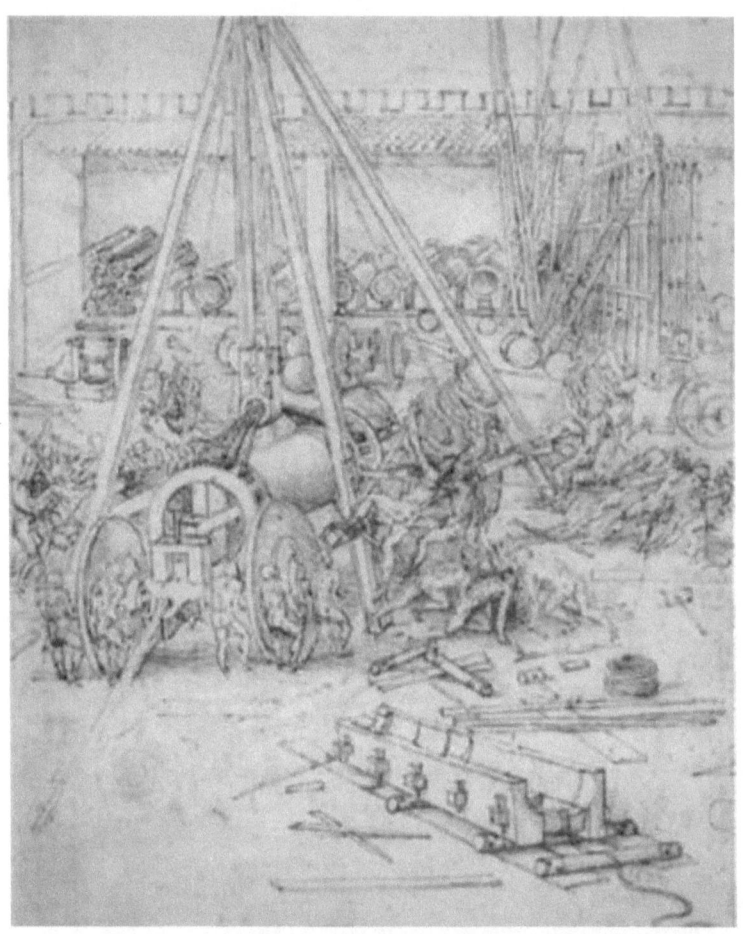

An Artillery Park.jpg, 1487, pencil

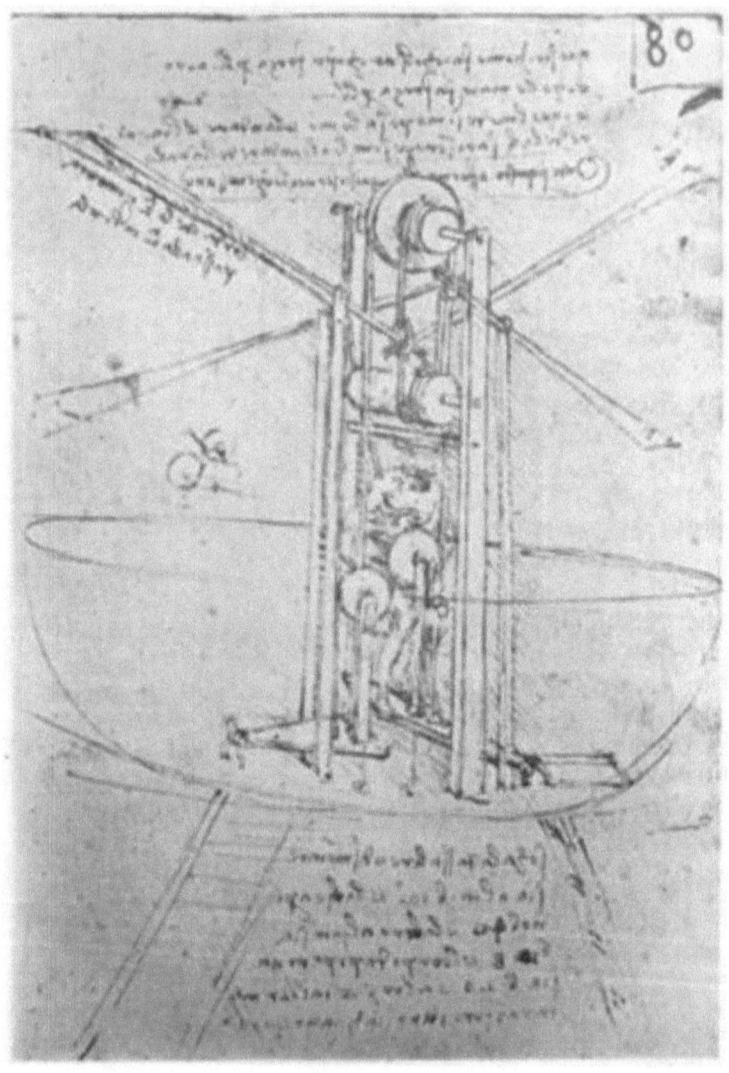

**Flying machine, c.1487, metalpoint, ink, 23.5 x 17.6 cm,
Insritut de France, Paris, France**

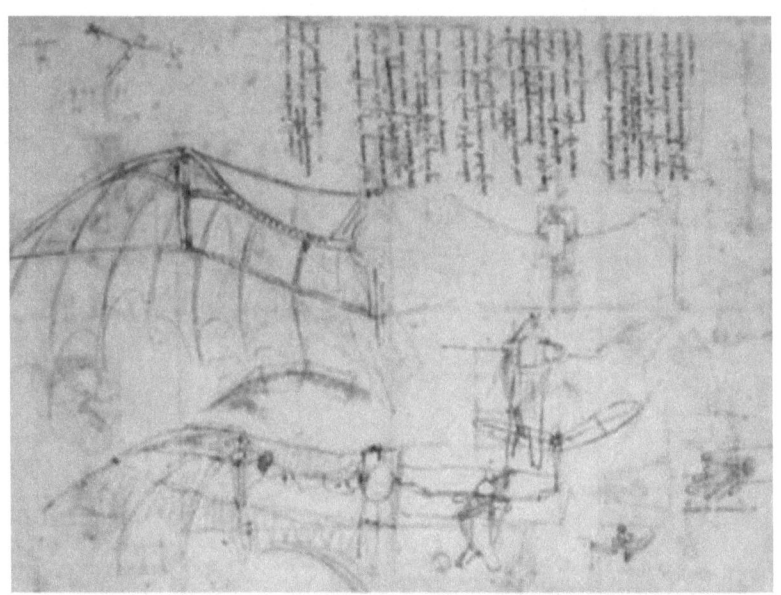

Design for a Flying Machine, 1488, chalk

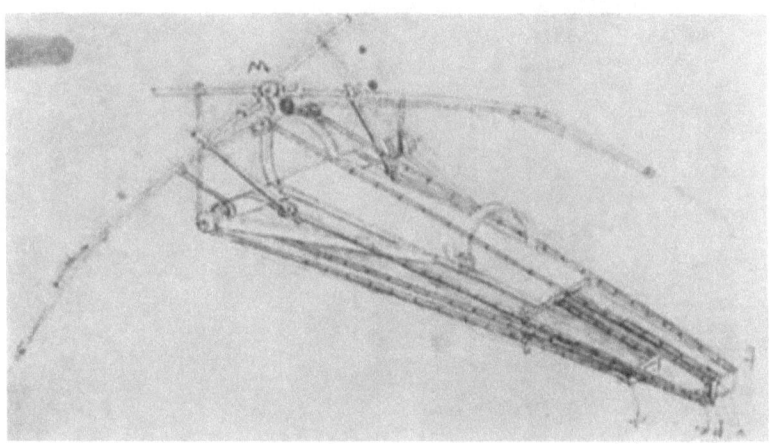

Design for a flying machine, c.1488, ink, Bibliotheque de l'Institut de France, Paris

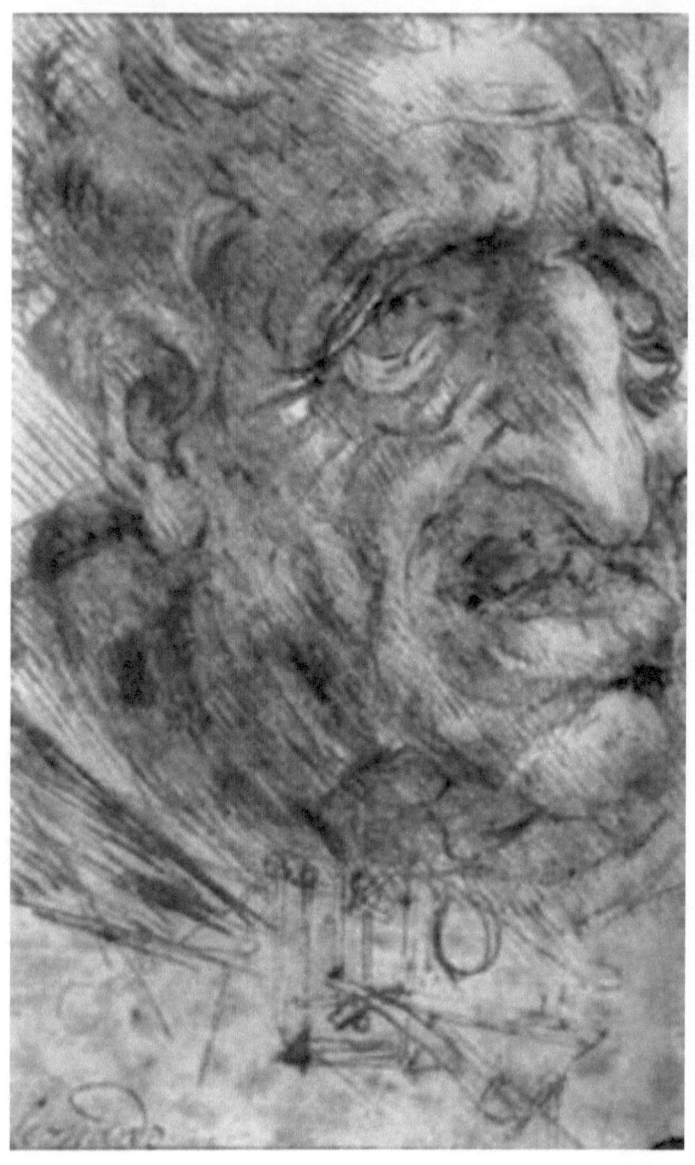

Head of an Old Man, 1488, ink, 11.2 x 7.5 cm

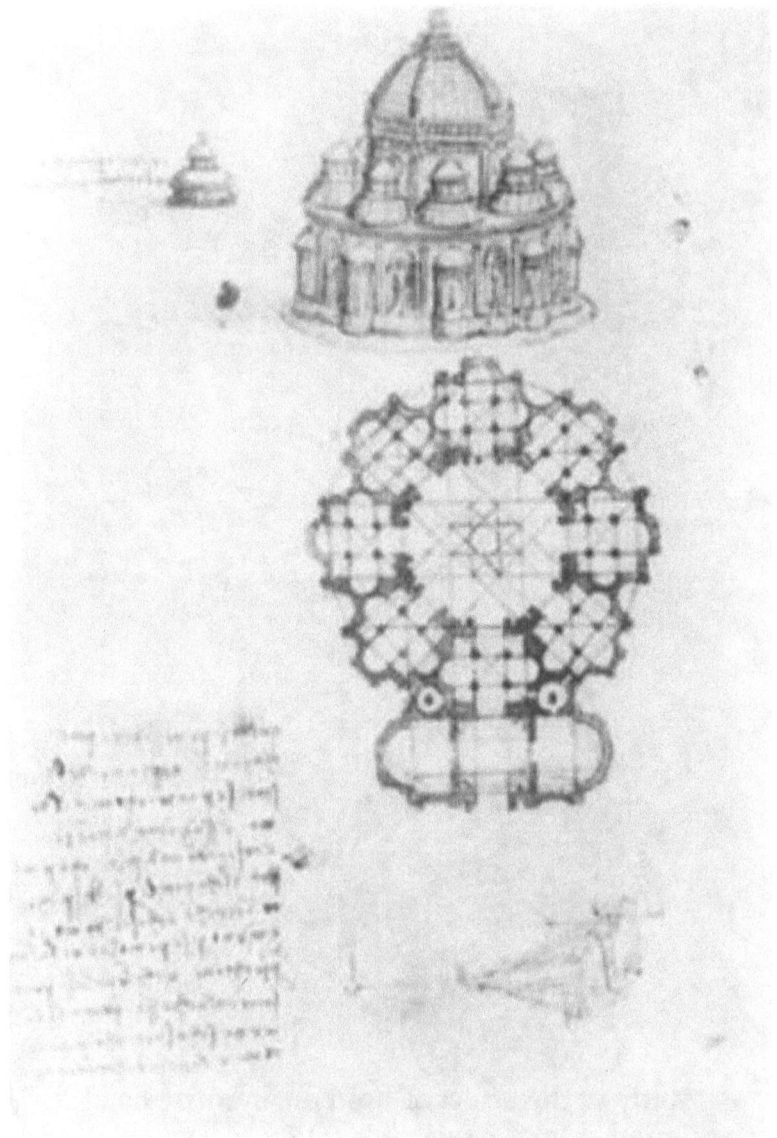

**Study of a central church, 1488, chalk, ink, 24 x 19 cm,
Bibliotheque de l'Institut de France, Paris**

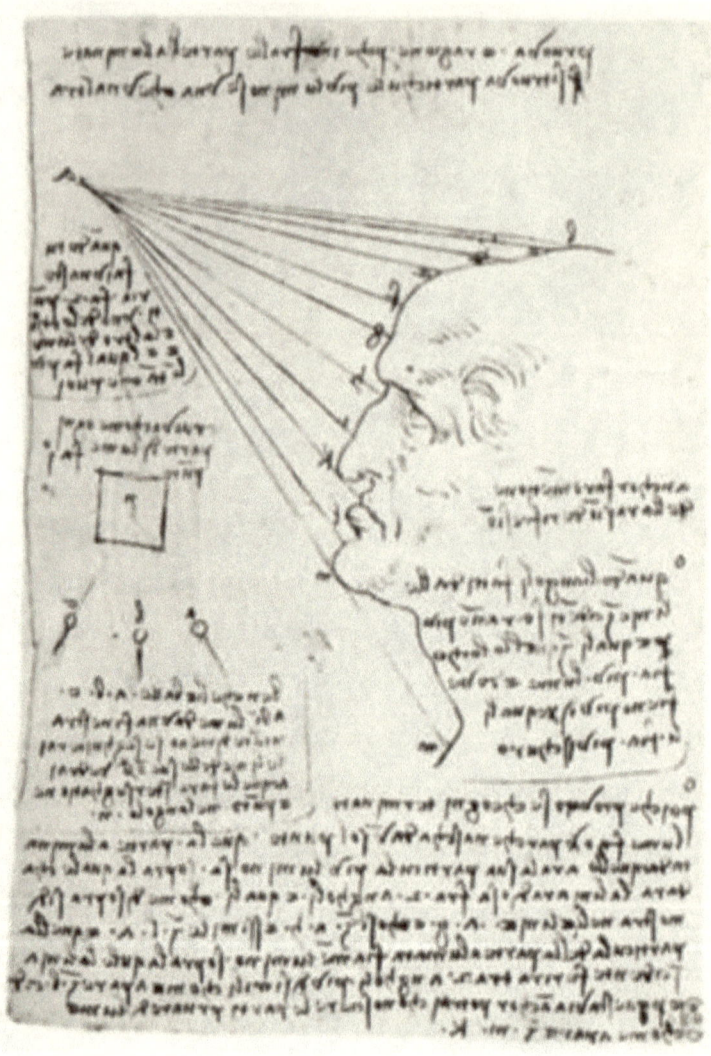

**Study of the effect of light on a profile head
(facsimile), c.1488, chalk, ink, 20.3 x 14.3 cm, Galleria
degli Uffizi, Florence, Italy**

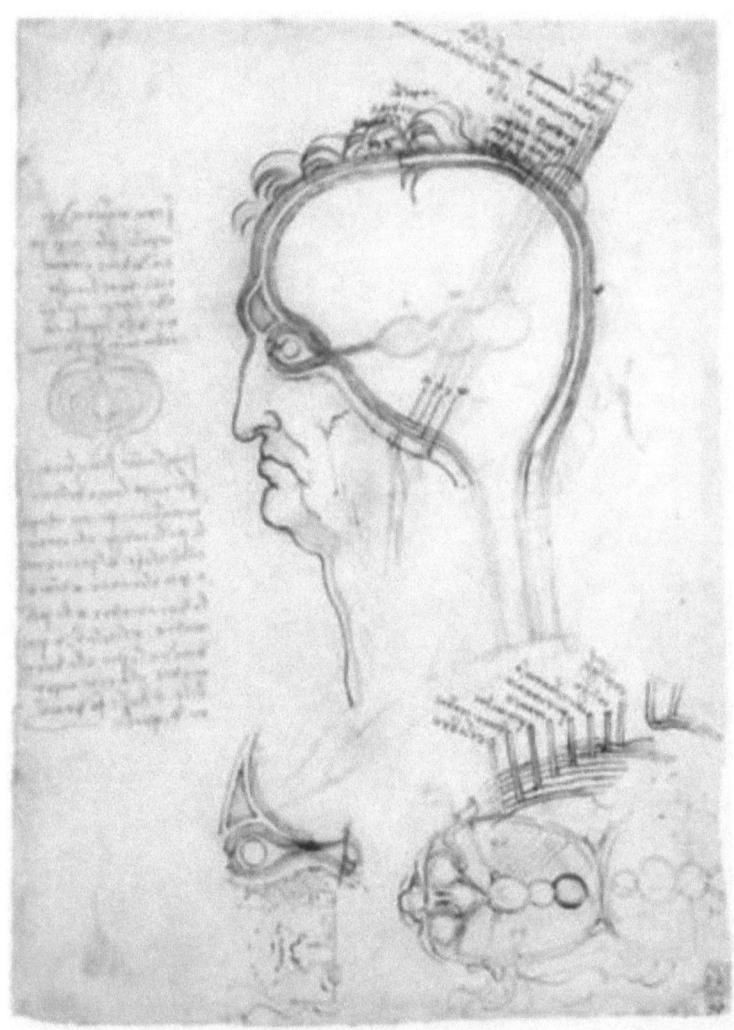

Comparison of scalp skin and onion, 1489, chalk, ink,
20.3 x 15.2 cm, Royal Collection, Windsor Castle,
London, UK

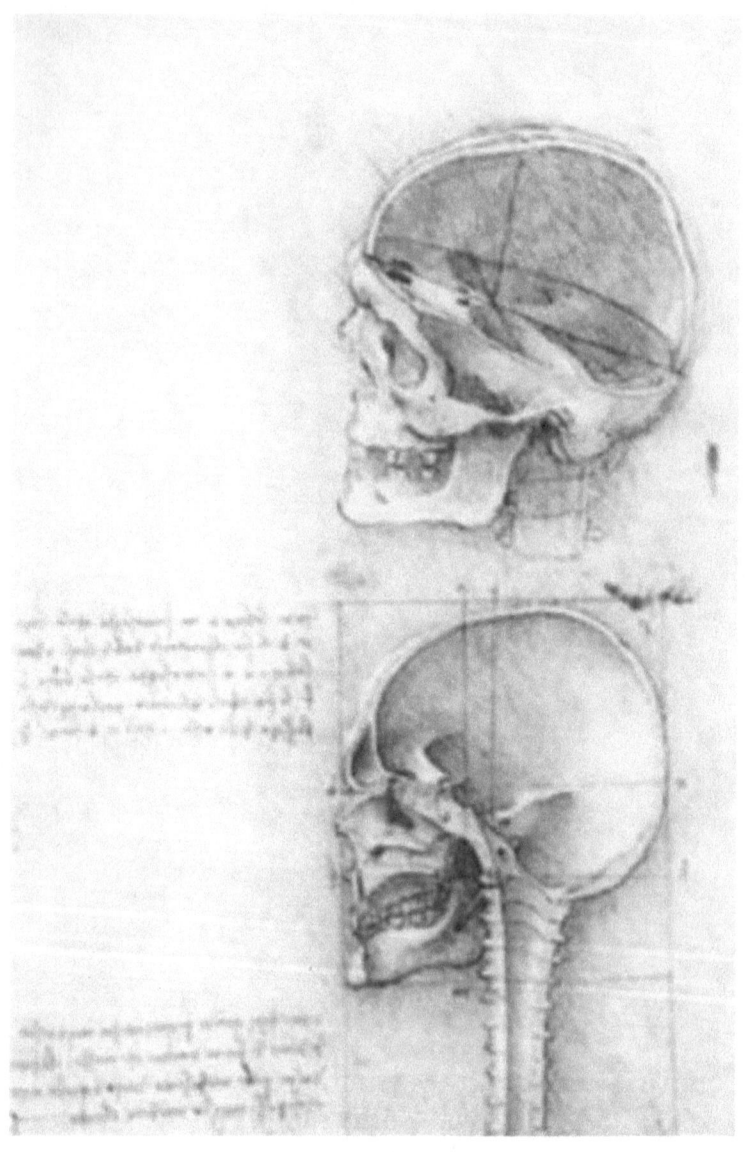

Studies of human skull, 1489, chalk, ink, 18.8 x 13.4 cm, Royal Collection, Windsor Castle, London, UK

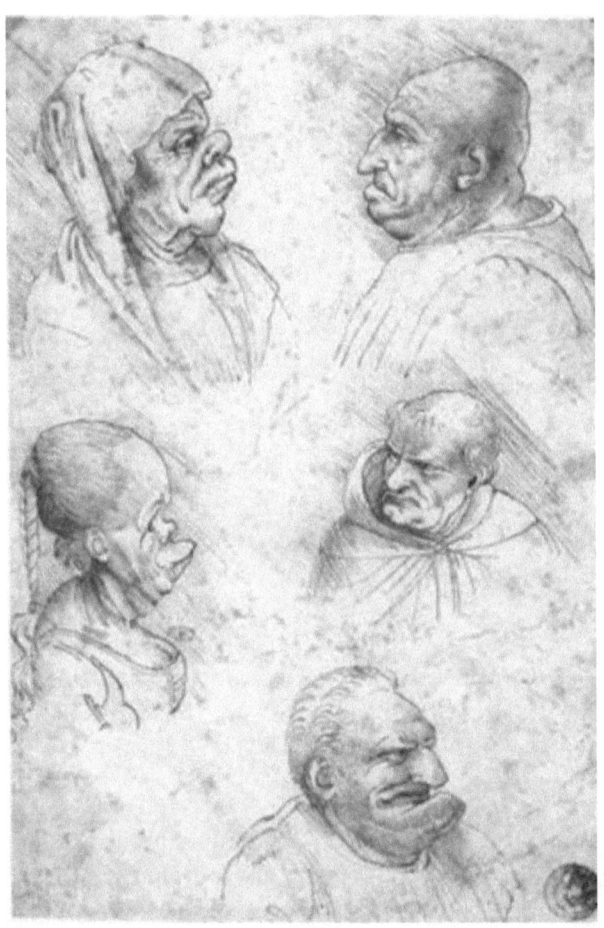

**Five caricature heads, c. 1490, Pen and ink on paper,
18 x 12 cm, Gallerie dell'Accademia, Venice**

Several such drawings still exist in which Leonardo
either portrays or invents pronounced facial features,
exaggerating them like a caricature. The five caricature
heads are thought to be a copy made by an artist who
had access to Leonardo's drawings. The strokes lack the
vividness that characterized Leonardo's drawings.

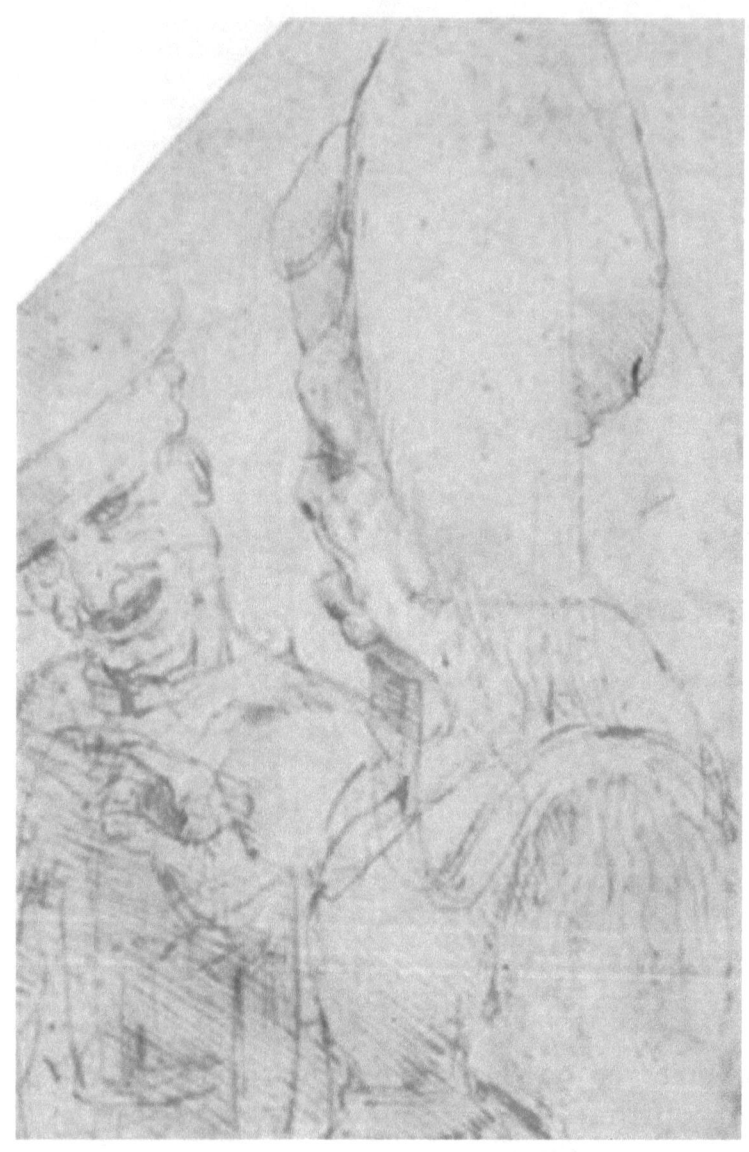

Matched Couple, c.1490, ink

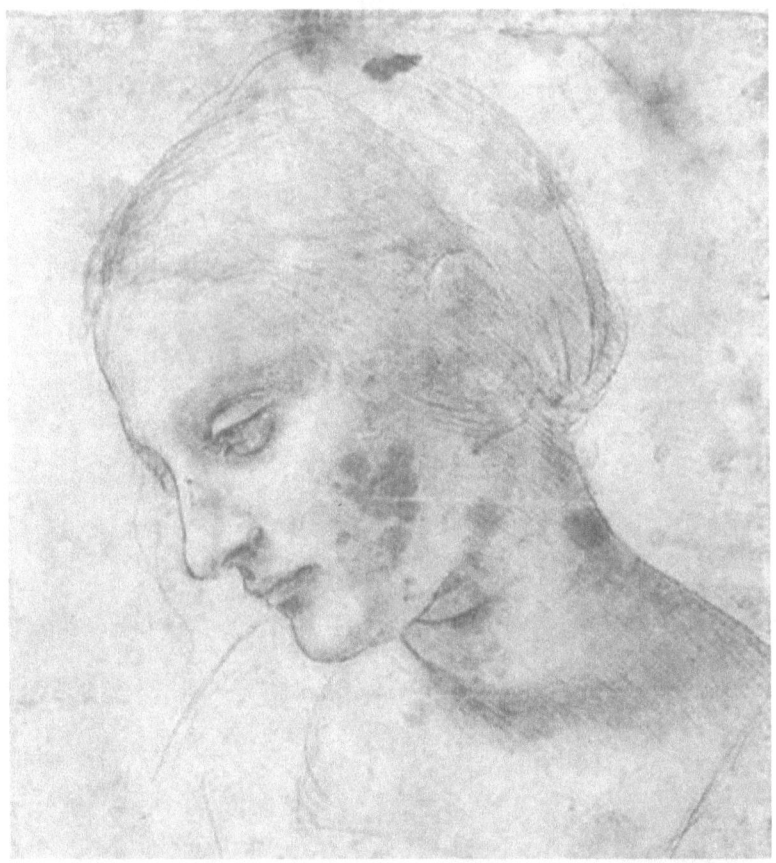

Study of a woman's head, c. 1490, Silverpoint on greenish prepared paper, 18 x 16.8 cm, Louvre, Paris

The drawing is a study for the Madonna Litta.

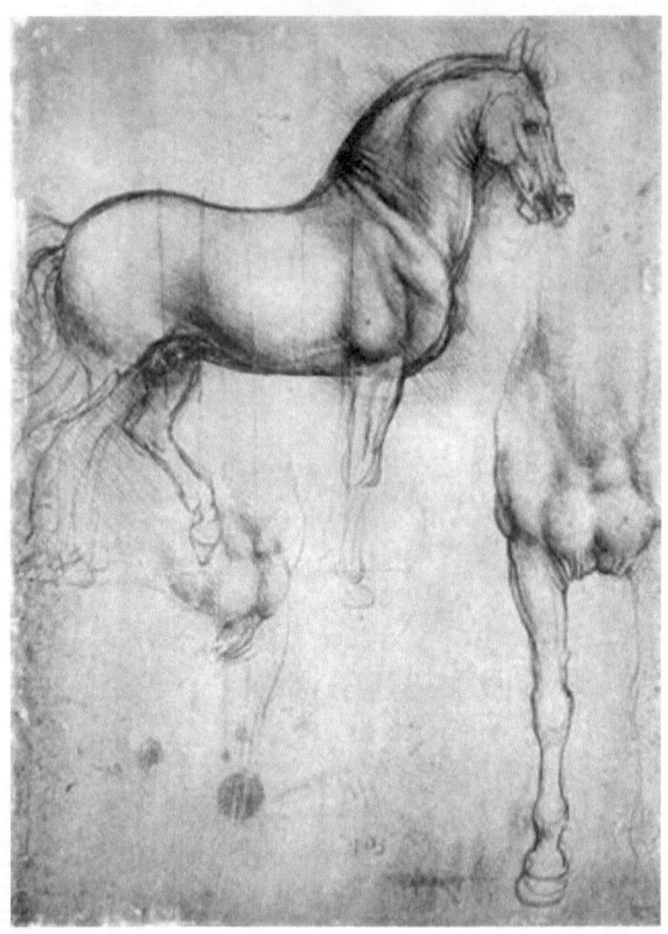

Study of horses, c. 1490, Silverpoint on prepared paper, 25 x 18.7 cm, Royal Library, Windsor

Leonardo displays considerable delicacy in the modelling of the outer surface of the horse, and this combines with a confidence in its figural design. Since the Adoration of the Magi Leonardo had become particularly interested in horses, and this is documented by a large number of studies of their proportions and movements.

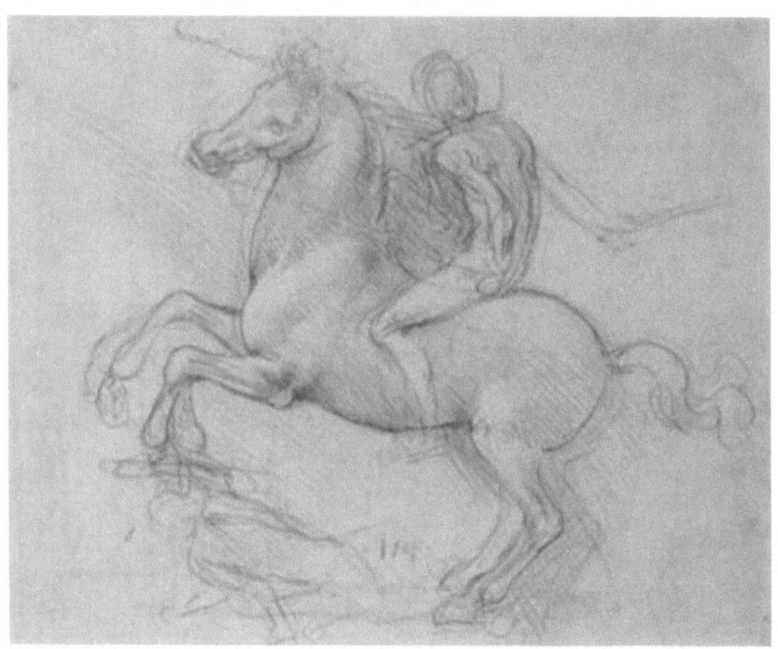

A study for an equestrian monument, c.1490,
metalpoint, 18.8 x 15.2 cm, Royal Collection, Windsor
Castle, London, UK

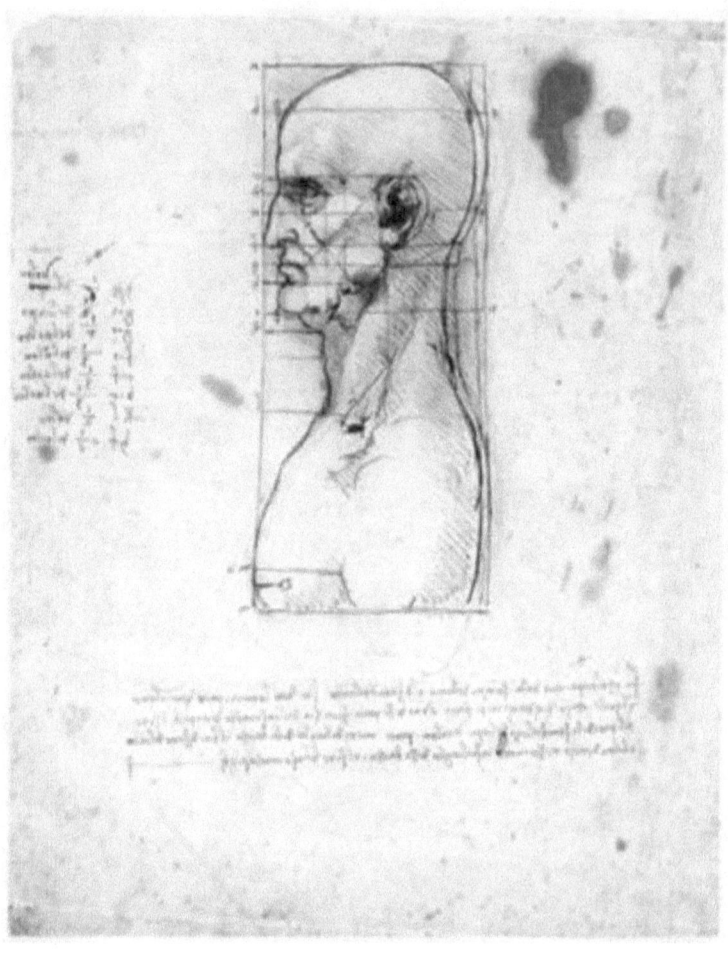

Bust of a man in profile with measurements and notes, c.1490, ink, Gallerie dell'Accademia, Venice, Italy

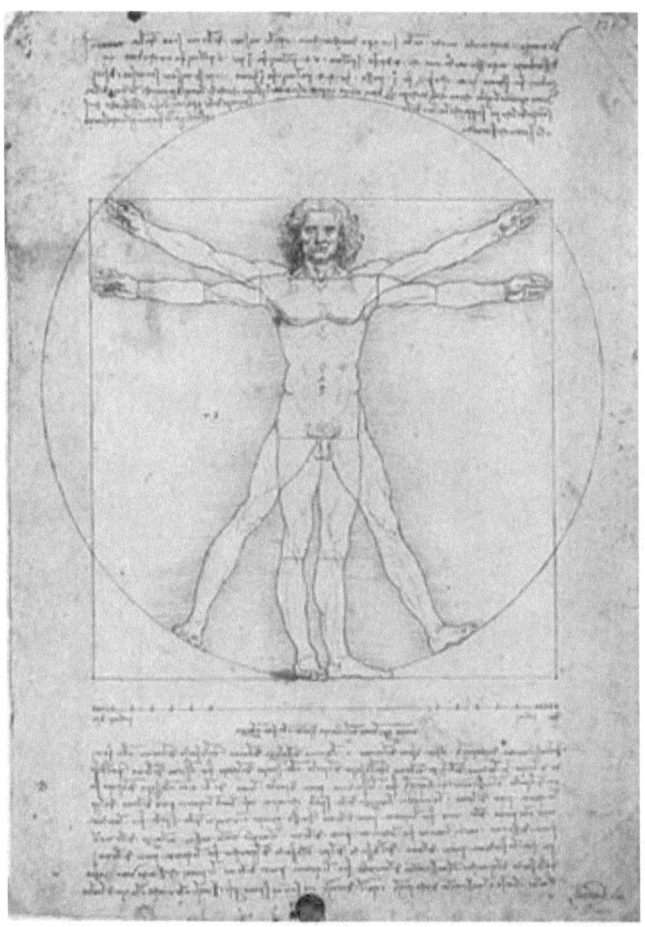

Vitruvian Man, 1492, Pen, ink, watercolour and metalpoint on paper, 34.3 x 24.5 cm, Gallerie dell'Accademia, Venice

This celebrated drawing, probably the most famous by Leonardo, of a man with an athletic physique inscribed within a circle and a square illustrates the measurements of the ideal human body according to the rules of the Roman architect Vitruvius's De Architectura (first century B.C.).

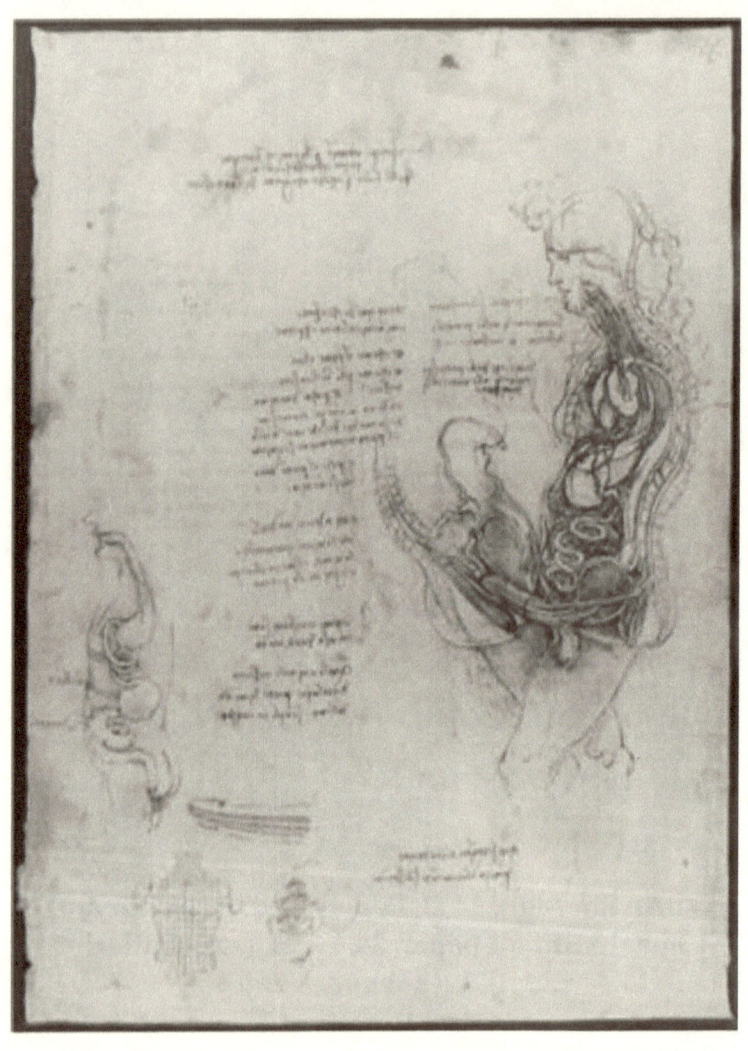

Coition of a Hemisected Man and Woman, 1492, ink

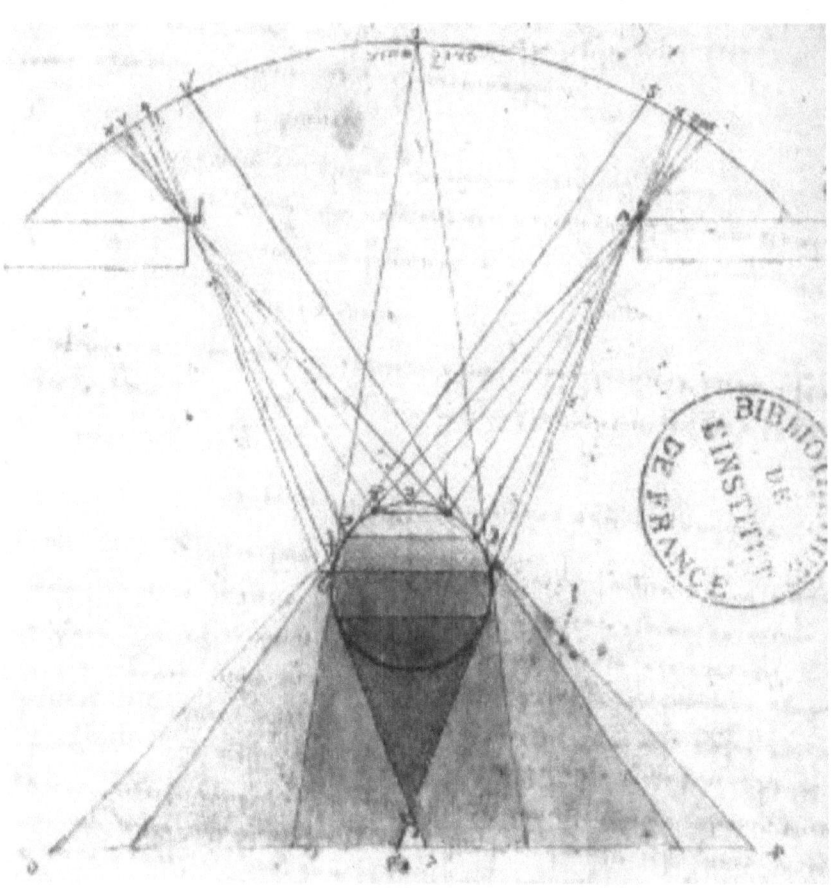

Study of the Graduations of Shadows on Spheres,
c.1492, ink

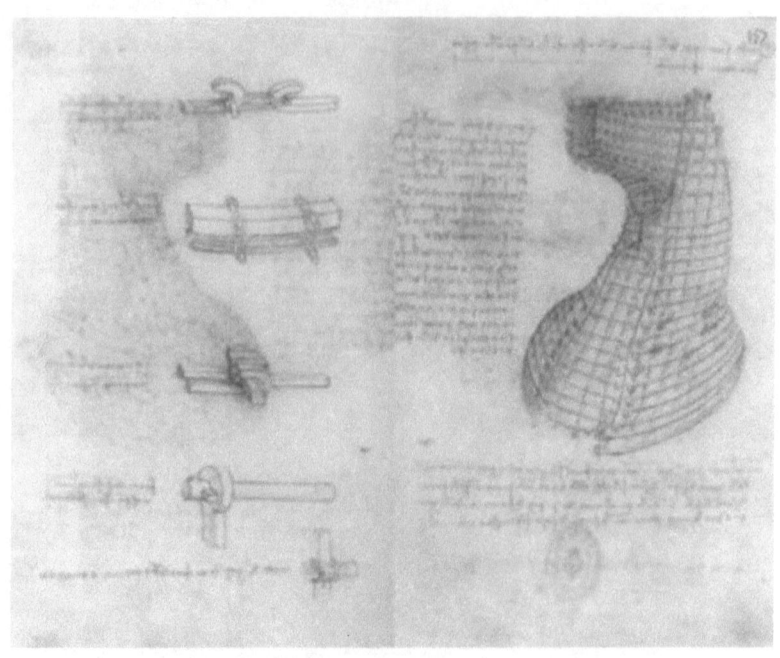

Double manuscript page on the Sforza monument (Casting mold of the head and neck), c.1493, chalk , 21 x 30 cm, Biblioteca Nacional, Madrid, Spain

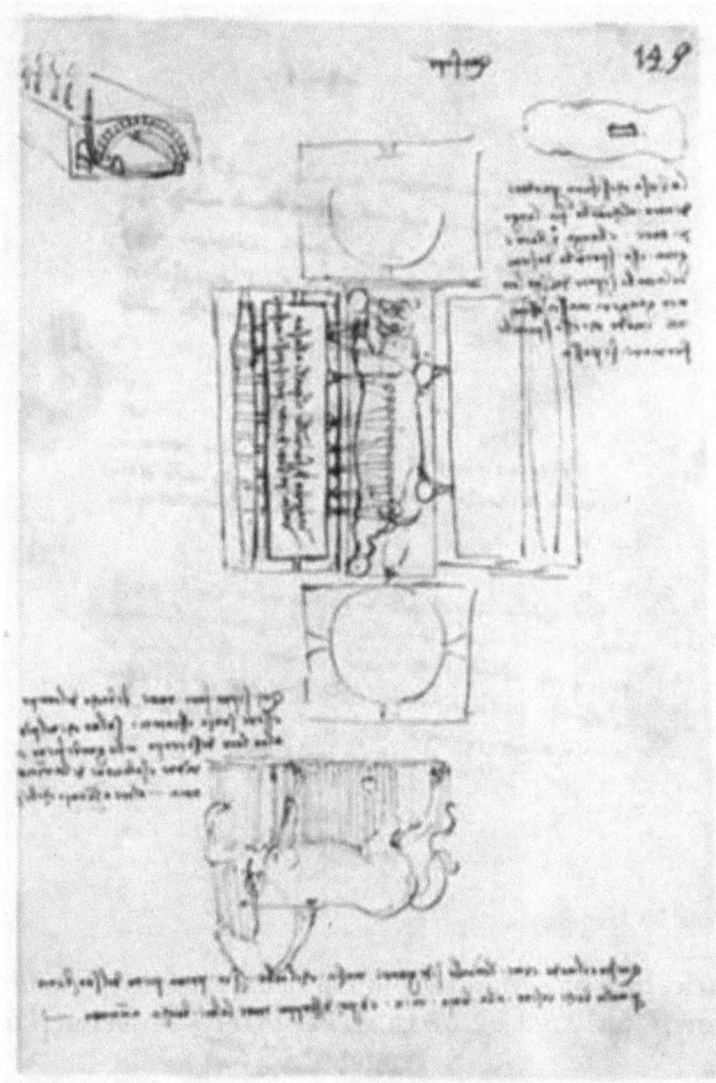

Manuscript page on the Sforza monument, c.1493,
ink, 21 x 15 cm, Biblioteca Nacional, Madrid, Spain

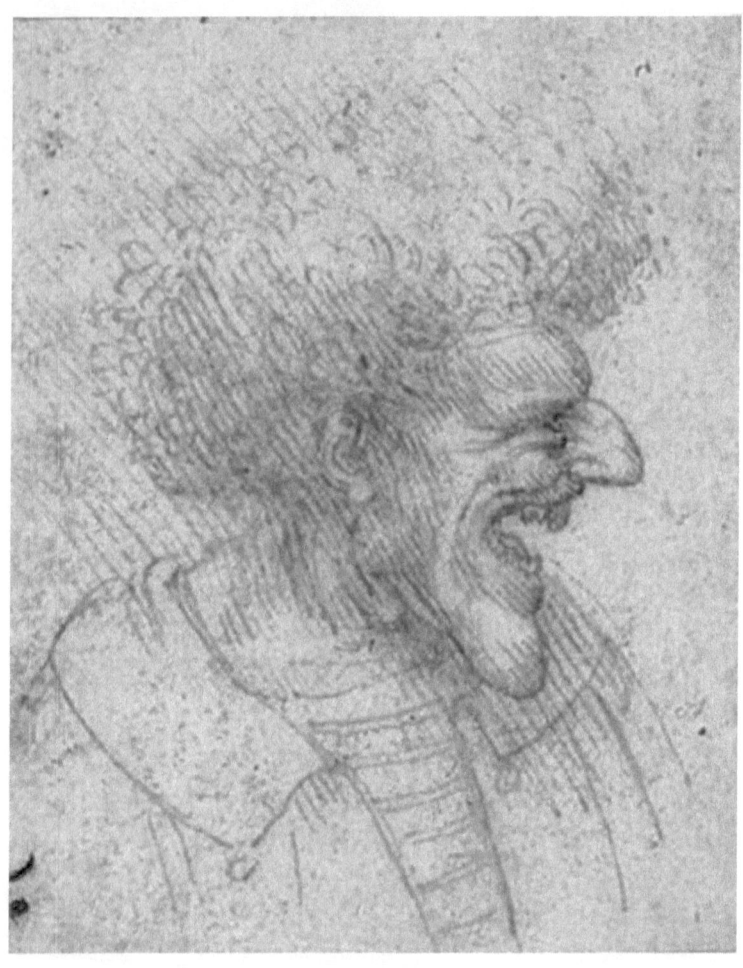

Caricature of a Man with Bushy Hair, c. 1495, Pen and brown ink, 2 5/8 x 2 1/8 in., J. Paul Getty Museum, Los Angeles

According to artist and biographer Giorgio Vasari, Leonardo da Vinci was "so delighted when he saw curious heads, whether bearded or hairy, that he would follow anyone who had thus attracted his attention for a whole day, acquiring such a clear idea of him that when he went home he would draw the head as well as if the man had been present."

Leonardo depicted the man's hair with his characteristic sfumato. The hatching lines slant downward from left to right, running in the natural direction for the left-handed artist. He made this caricature as one of a large series of head studies created in pairs. Years after the artist's death, collectors cut the pairs into individual drawings. Many later artists admired and copied Leonardo's caricatures, both in drawings and prints.

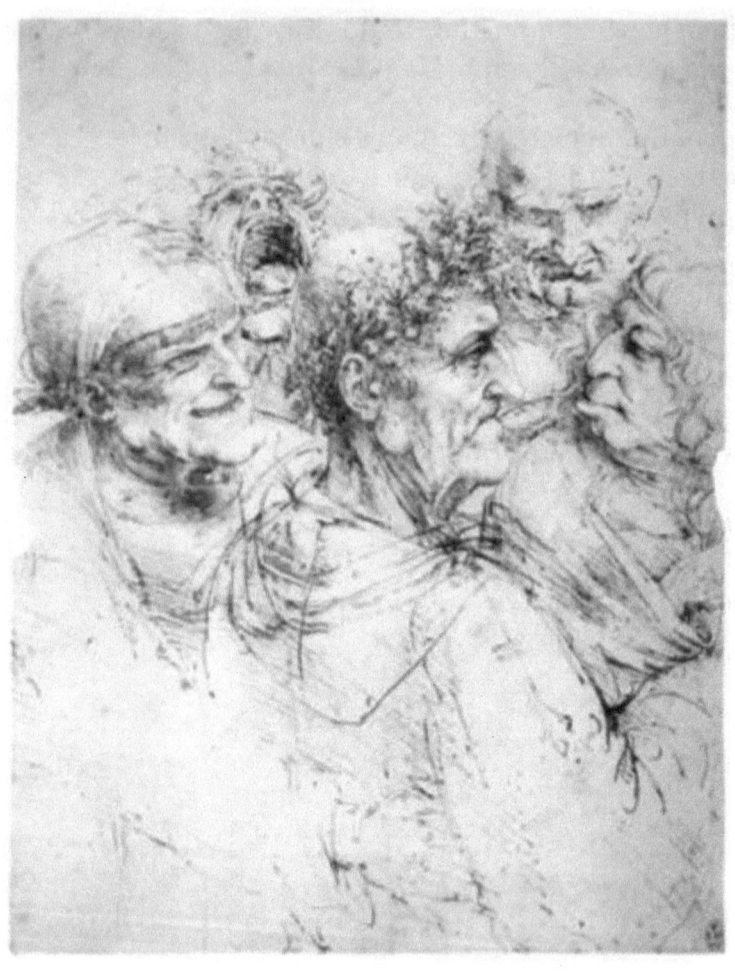

Study of five grotesque heads, c.1495, ink, 26.1 x 20.6 cm, Royal Collection, Windsor Castle, London, UK

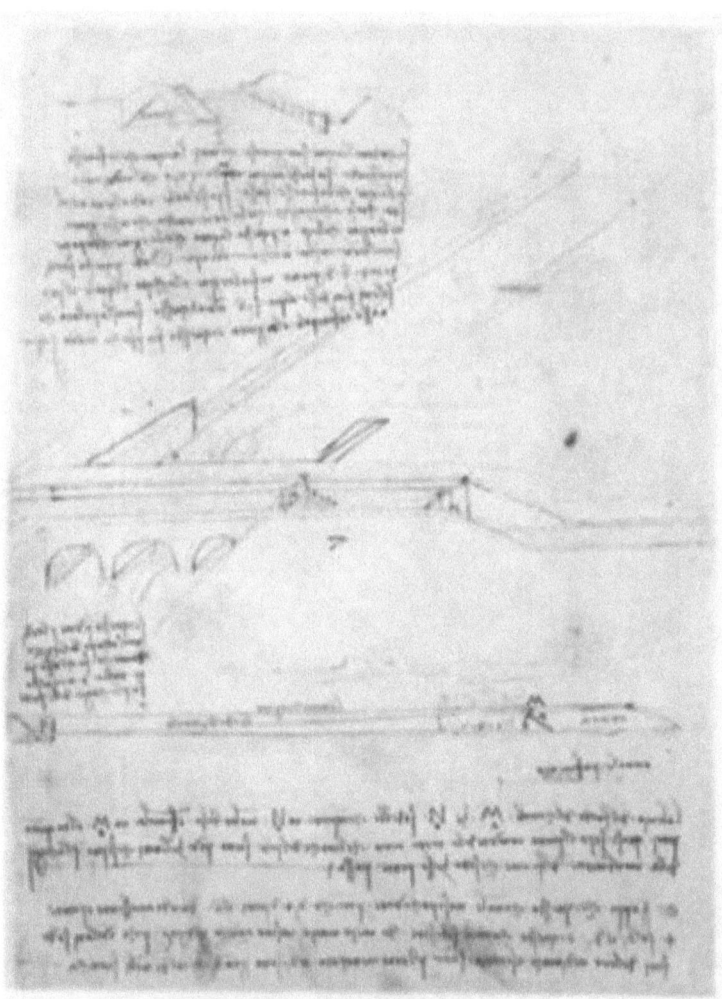

Canal bridge, 1495, 27 x 20 cm, ink, Biblioteca
Ambrosiana, Milan, Italy

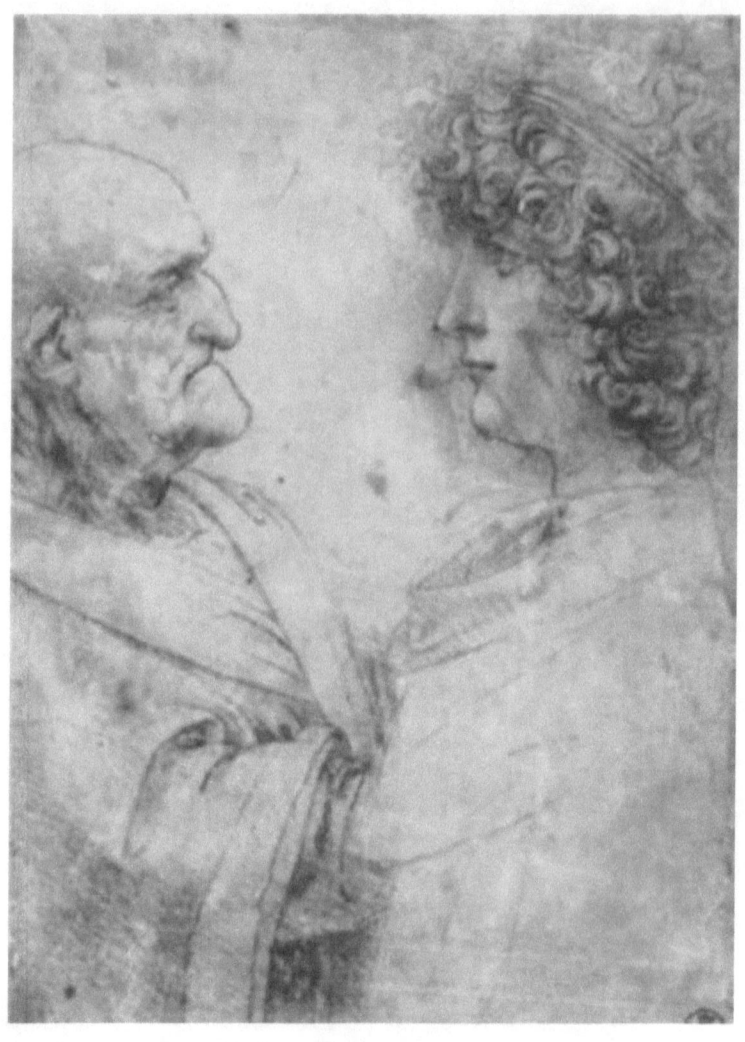

Heads of an old man and a youth, 1495, ink, 20.8 x 15 cm, Galleria degli Uffizi, Florence, Italy

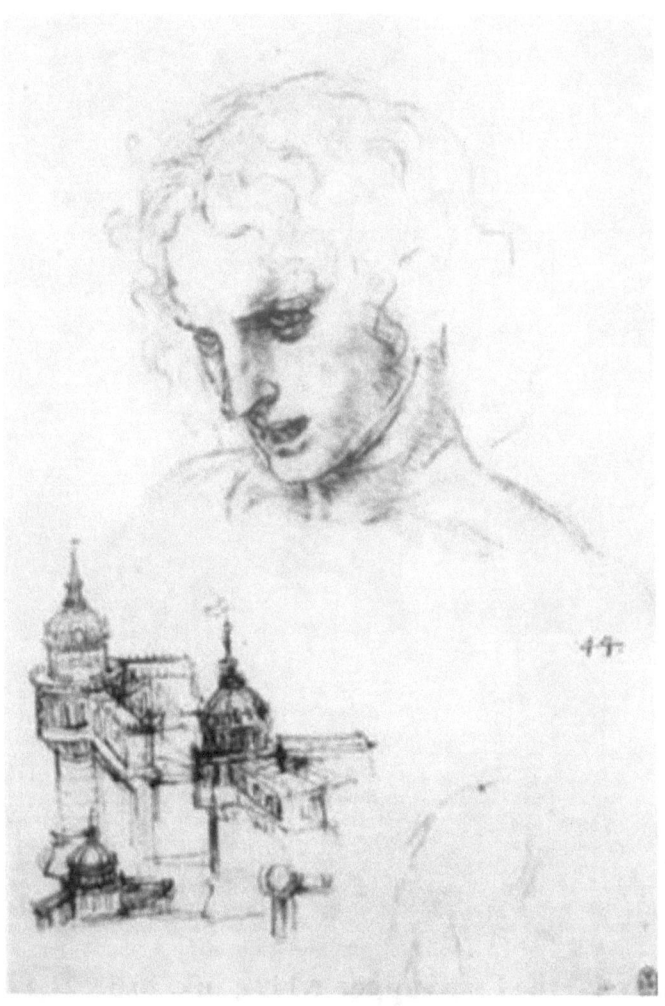

Study of an apostle's head and architectural study,
c.1496, chalk, ink, 25.2 x 17.2 cm, Royal Collection,
Windsor Castle, London, UK

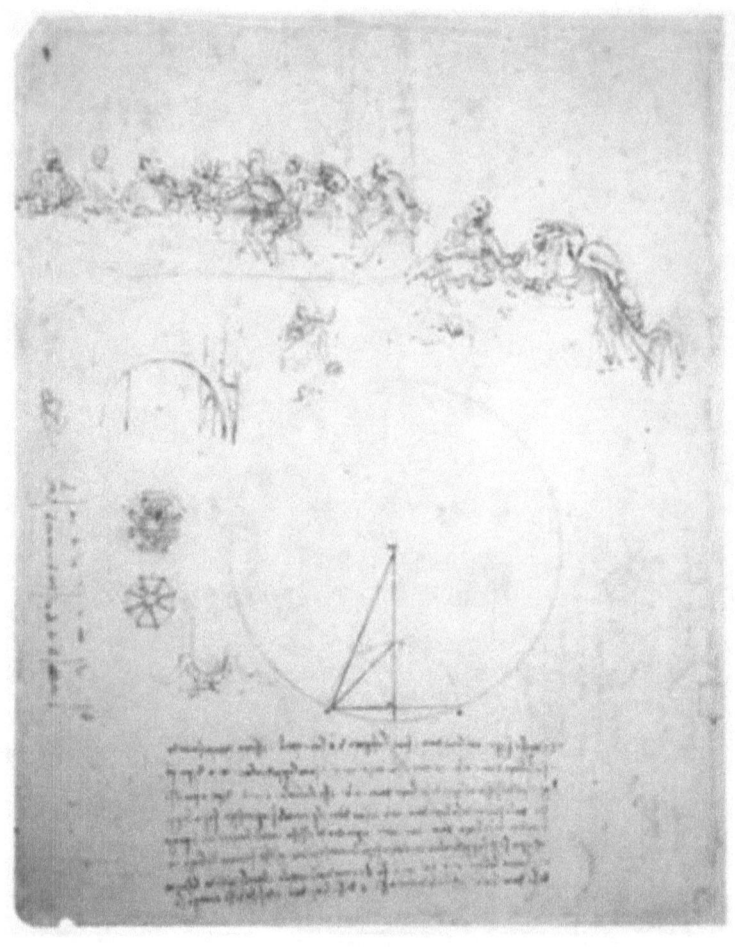

Study for the Last Supper, c.1494, ink, 26.6 x 21.4 cm, Royal Collection, Windsor Castle, London, UK

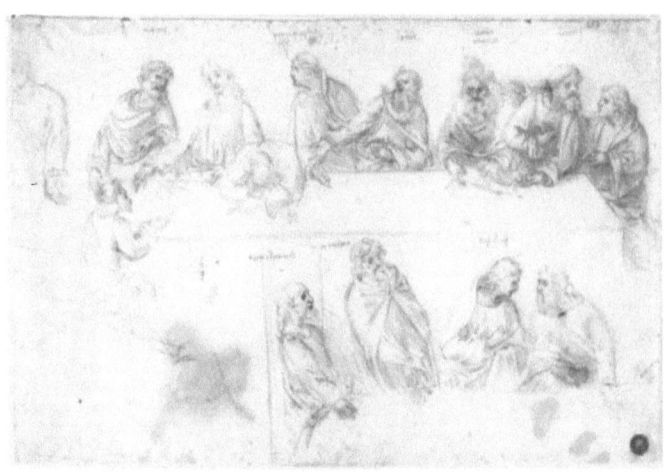

**Study for the Last Supper, c.1494, chalk, 26 x 39.2 cm,
Galleria degli Uffizi, Florence, Italy**

Experienced artist will probably be able to do it in 2 or
3 months, maybe even less than that, but, of course,
Leonardo was not very experienced. Normal approach
would be to copy the preliminary drawings on wet
plaster method called tingling, tracing a sketch on
plaster. You should have been enough to plaster on one
day, and then the clock starts ticking. We had wet paint
pigment in the plaster, which you must paint, while it
is still active. This is completely unacceptable, that we
understand the psychology of Leonardo actually. Here
the idea with good painting is he to plan ahead. As we
know, the situation is not in the best to Leonardo, but
he found a solution. He decided not to make a picture
in the usual way. Instead, he invented a type of plaster
he can write about when dry. This allowed him to take
his time. Unfortunately, the Duke insisted on regular
reports on progress. But Leonardo was hard at work.
He was on the streets of sketches find the right person,
the right gestures to animate each individual follower.

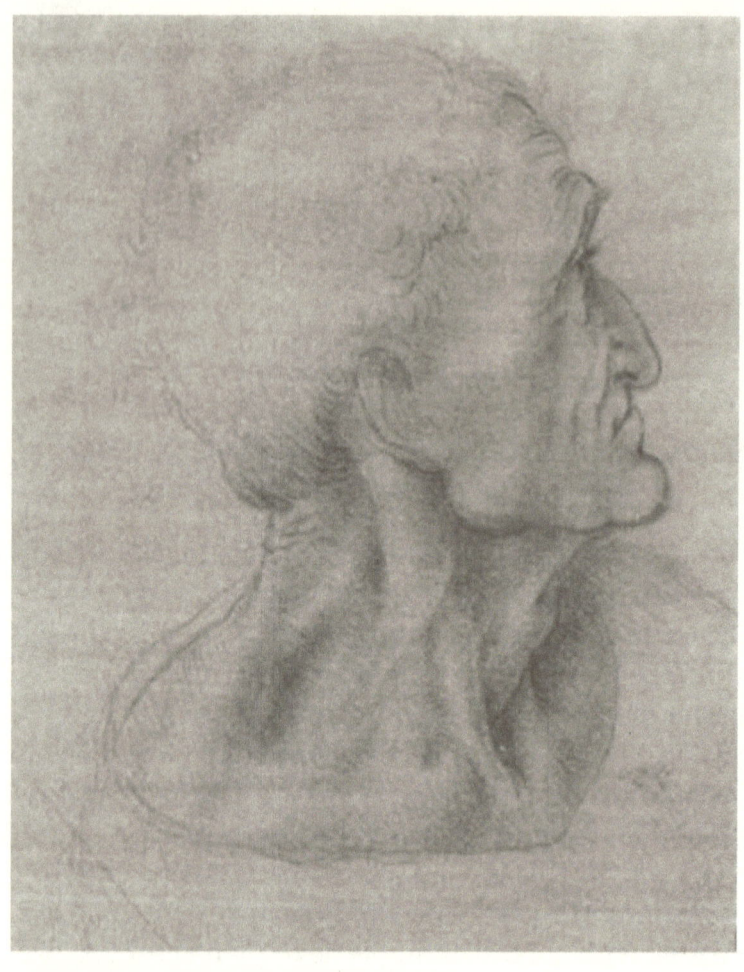

Study for the Last Supper: Judas, c.1495, chalk on paper, 18 x 15 cm, Royal Collection, Windsor Castle, London, UK

The Last Supper specifically portrays the reaction given by each apostle when Jesus said one of them would betray him. All twelve apostles have different reactions to the news, with various degrees of anger and shock.

The apostles are identified from a manuscript (The Notebooks of Leonardo Da Vinci p. 232) with their names found in the 19th century. Before this, only Judas, Peter, John and Jesus were positively identified. From left to right, according to the apostles heads: Bartholomew, James, son of Alphaeus and Andrew form a group of three, all are surprised.Judas Iscariot, Peter and John form another group of three. Judas is wearing green and blue and is in shadow, looking rather withdrawn and taken aback by the sudden revelation of his plan.

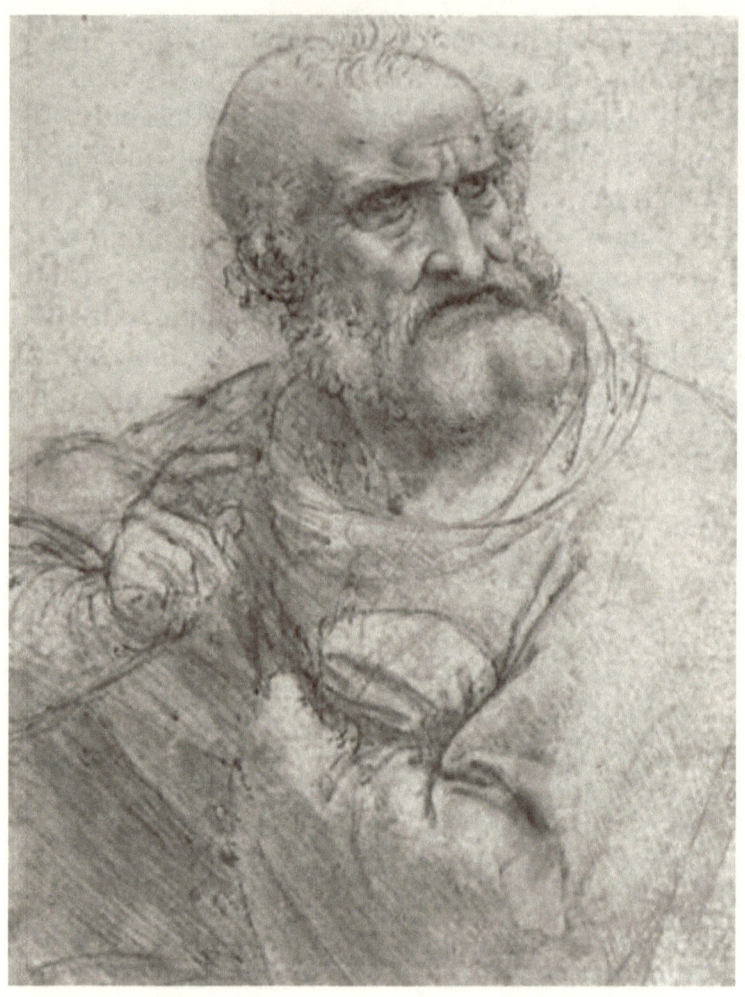

Study for the Last Supper, c.1495, metalpoint, ink on paper, 14.5 x 11.3 cm, Albertina, Vienna, Austria

He is clutching a small bag, perhaps signifying the silver given to him as payment to betray Jesus, or perhaps a reference to his role within the 12 disciples as treasurer. He is also tipping over the salt shaker. This may be related to the near-Eastern expression to "betray the salt" meaning to betray one's Master. He is the only person to have his elbow on the table and his head is also horizontally the lowest of anyone in the painting. Peter looks angry and is holding a knife pointed away from Christ, perhaps foreshadowing his violent reaction in Gethsemane during Jesus' arrest. The youngest apostle, John, appears to swoon. Apostle Thomas, James the Greater and Philip are the next group of three. Thomas is clearly upset; James the Greater looks stunned, with his arms in the air. Meanwhile, Philip appears to be requesting some explanation. Matthew, Jude Thaddeus and Simon the Zealot are the final group of three. Both Jude Thaddeus and Matthew are turned toward Simon, perhaps to find out if he has any answer to their initial questions. In common with other depictions of The Last Supper from this period, Leonardo seats the diners on one side of the table, so that none of them have their backs to the viewer. Most previous depictions excluded Judas by placing him alone on the opposite side of the table from the other eleven disciples and Jesus or placing halos around all the disciples except Judas.

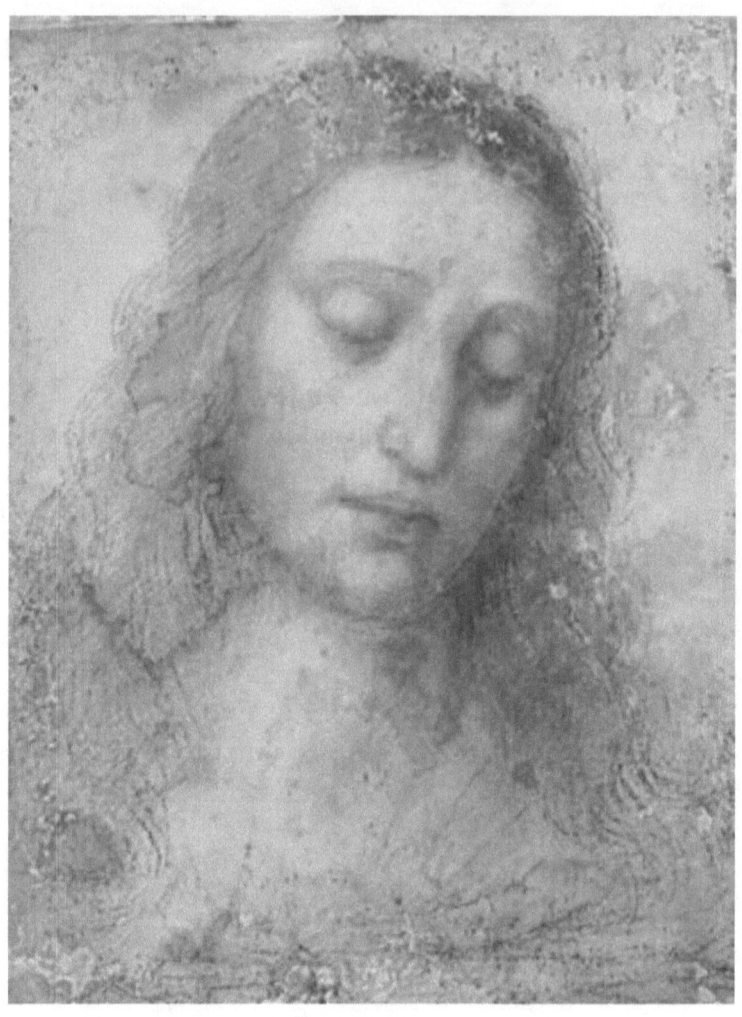

Head of Christ, c.1495, pencil, wash on paper, Musee des Beaux Arts Strasbourg (France)

Leonardo instead has Judas lean back into shadow. Jesus is predicting that his betrayer will take the bread at the same time he does to Saints Thomas and James to his left, who react in horror as Jesus points with his left hand to a piece of bread before them. Distracted by the conversation between John and Peter, Judas reaches for a different piece of bread not noticing Jesus too stretching out with his right hand towards it (Matthew 26: 23). The angles and lighting draw attention to Jesus, whose head is located at the vanishing point for all perspective lines.

The painting contains several references to the number 3, which represents the Christian belief in the Holy Trinity. The Apostles are seated in groupings of three; there are three windows behind Jesus; and the shape of Jesus' figure resembles a triangle. There may have been other references that have since been lost as the painting deteriorated.

Despite warnings from Ludavico, the Last Supper was to take another year of work and constant complaints from Leonardo asked to repay. But in the end he found his Judas, and, finally, in early 1498 the Last Supper was over. Tragically the experimental techniques of painting on dry plaster, which give the time to obtain the image just right, almost lead to this masterpiece lost forever. A few years after the work was finished the tiny, almost imperceptible cracks under the surface of the paint appeared. Deep in plaster moisture rises and damages. Since then there have been many attempts at restoration, some of which have done more harm than good. But something about the strength of the original remains. It is a ghost, but it's a great ghost.

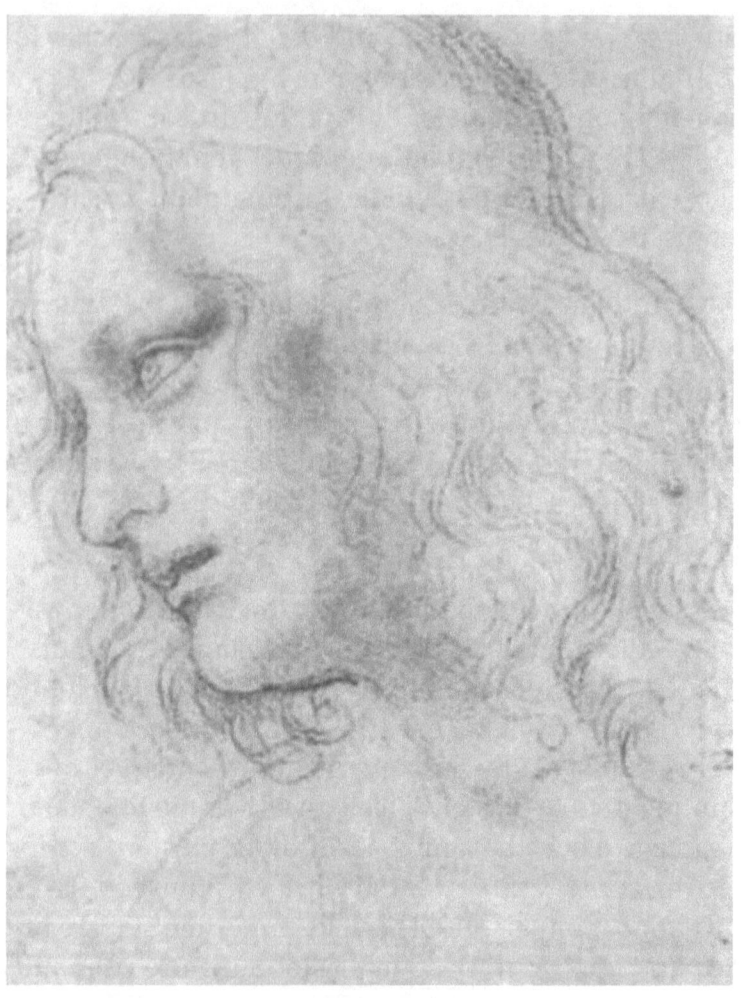

Study for the Last Supper: James, c.1495, chalk on paper, 19 x 14.9 cm, Royal Collection, Windsor Castle, London, UK

When everything seems hitch for Leonardo, something unexpected happened. Massing at the border thousands of French troops were preparing to invade Milan. Within a few months, Leonardo will be forced to flee from town to safe himself.

In 1499, Leonardo da Vinci was 38 years old and enjoying a golden period in his life. He recently finished painting the Last Supper scene for his powerful patron Sforza, Duke of Milan. The picture that captures the moment when Jesus tells his disciples that one of them would betray him, added to his growing reputation as one of the greatest artists of his time. But at that moment, that must have seemed to him the greatest artistic triumph it all went wrong. French invaded Milan, Leonardo's patron was imprisoned and Leonardo was forced to leave Milan in search of work and money.

Two early copies of The Last Supper are known to exist, presumed to be work by Leonardo's assistants. The copies are almost the size of the original, and have survived with a wealth of original detail still intact. One accurate copy, by Giampietrino, is in the collection of the Royal Academy of Arts, London, and the other, with some alterations to the background design, by Cesare da Sesto, is installed at the Church of St. Ambrogio in Ponte Capriasca, Switzerland.

The Last Supper has been the target of much speculation by writers and historical revisionists alike, usually centred around supposed purported hidden messages or hints found within the painting. Some have identified the person to Jesus' right (left of Jesus from the viewer's perspective), not as John the Apostle, but a woman, often purported to be Mary Magdalene. This speculation plays a central role in Dan Brown's fiction novel The Da Vinci Code.

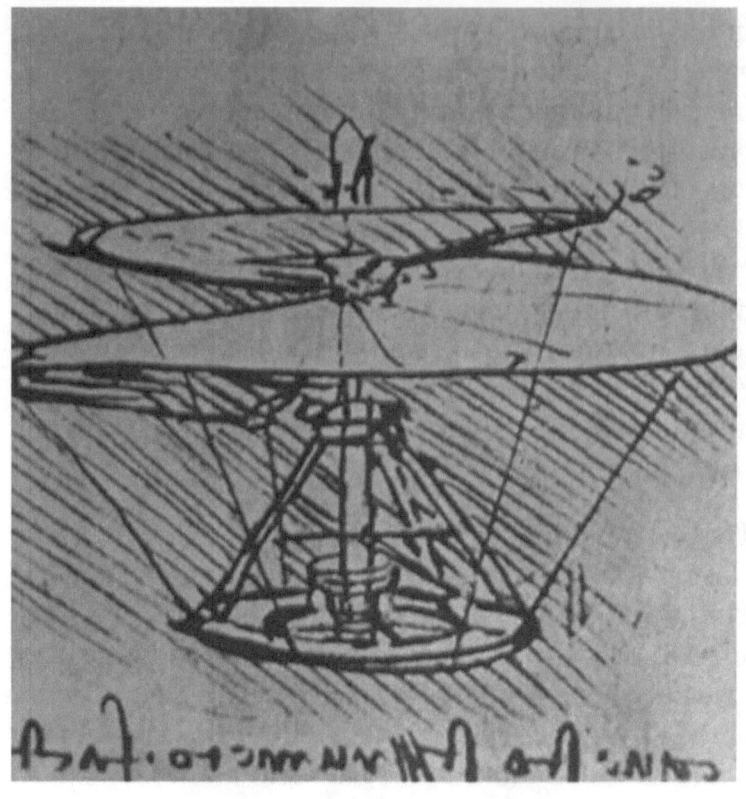

Design for a helicopter, 1500, ink

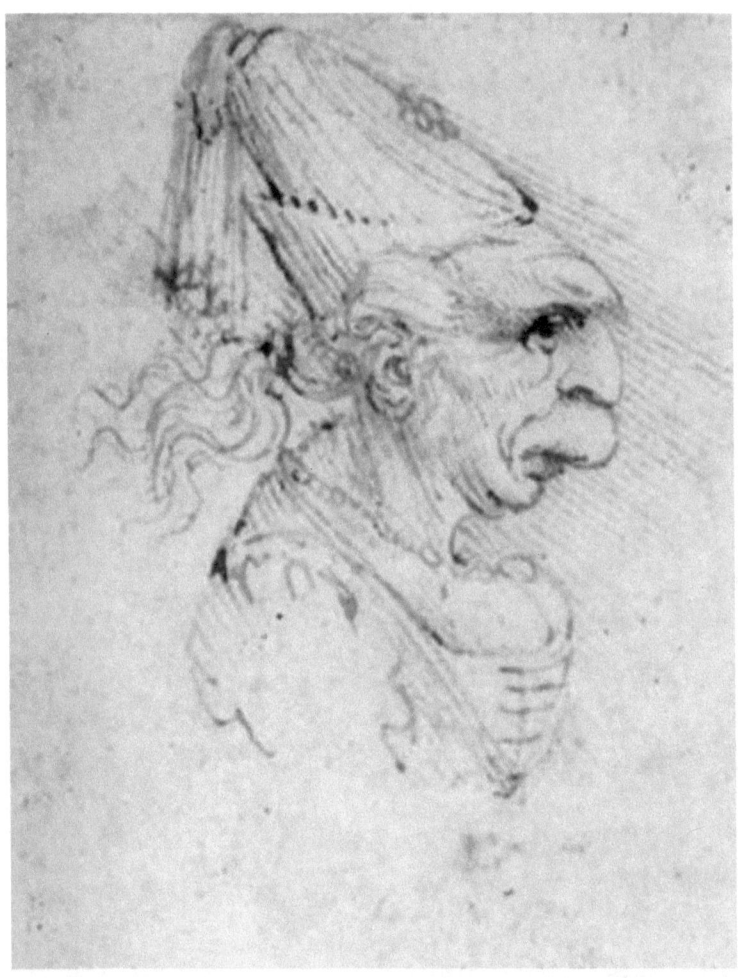

Caricature, 1500, ink, 56 x 69 cm, Private Collection

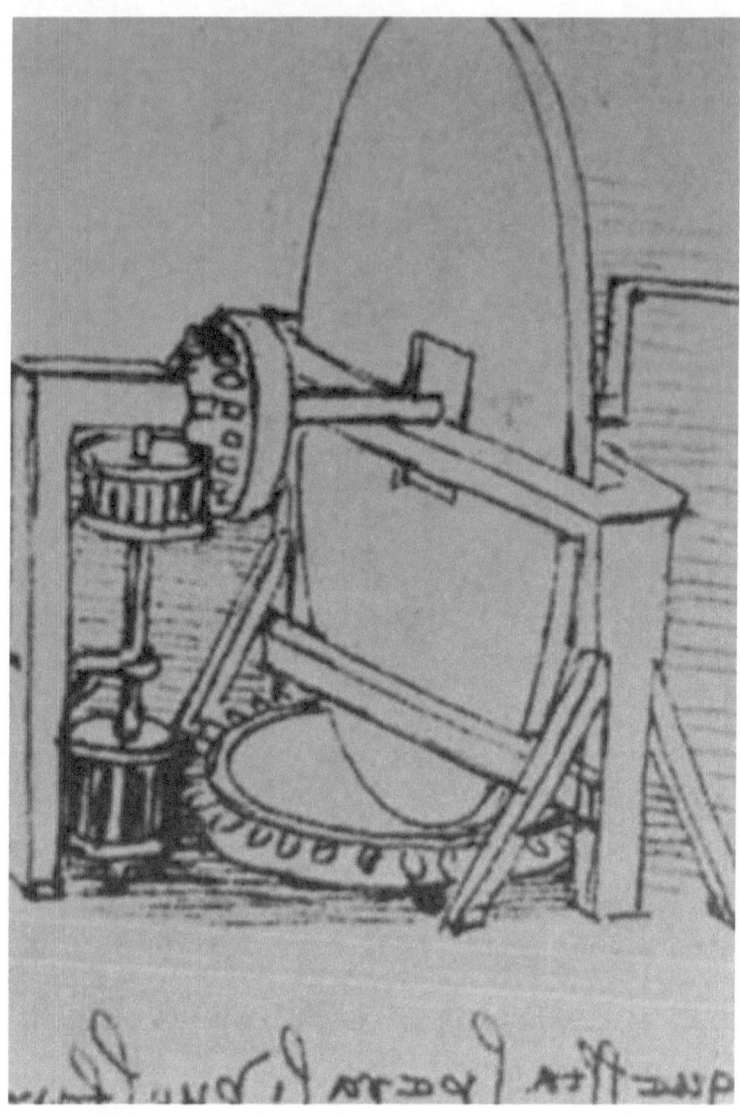

**Design for a machine for grinding convex lenses,
c.1500, ink**

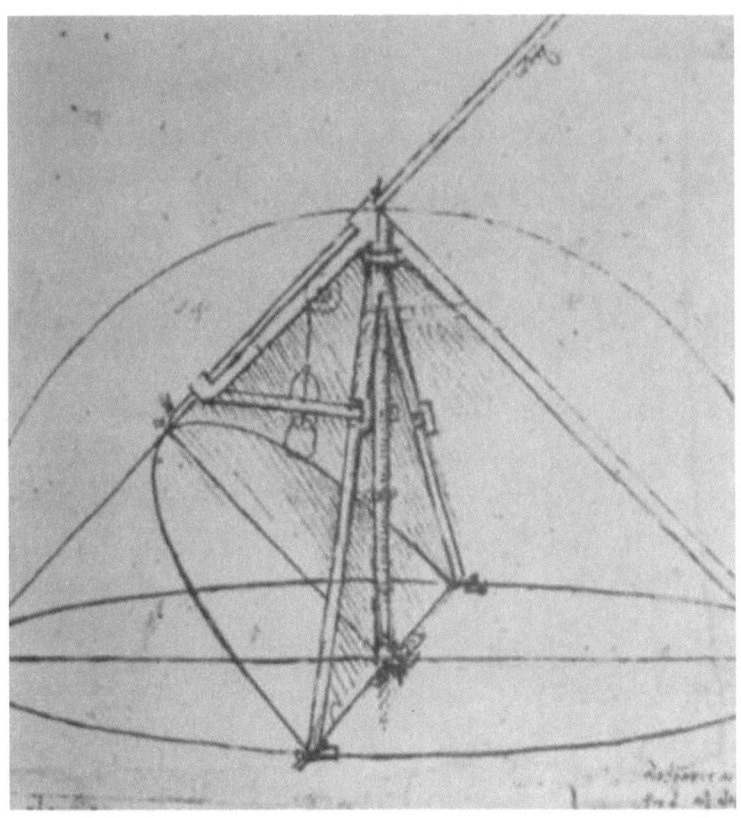

Design for a parabolic compass, c.1500, ink

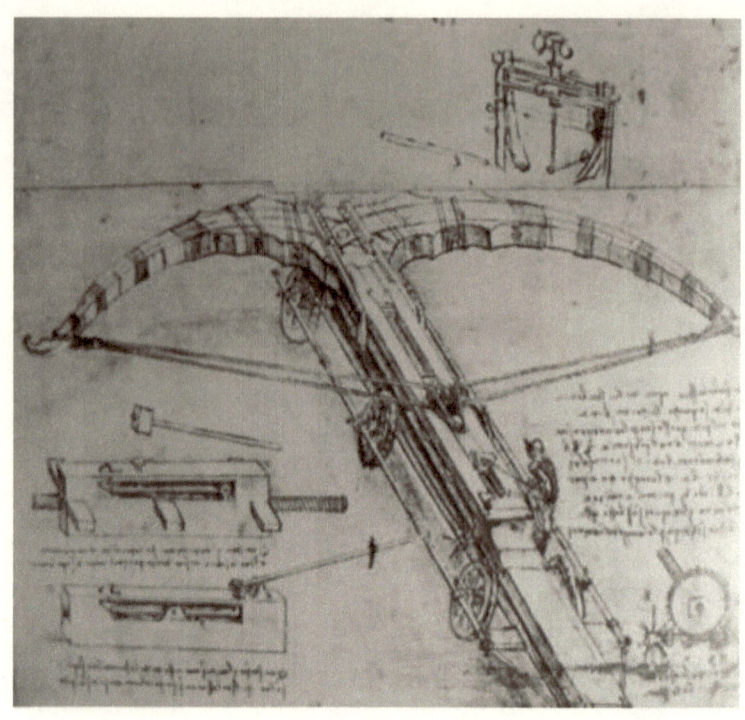

Design for an enormous crossbow, c.1500, ink

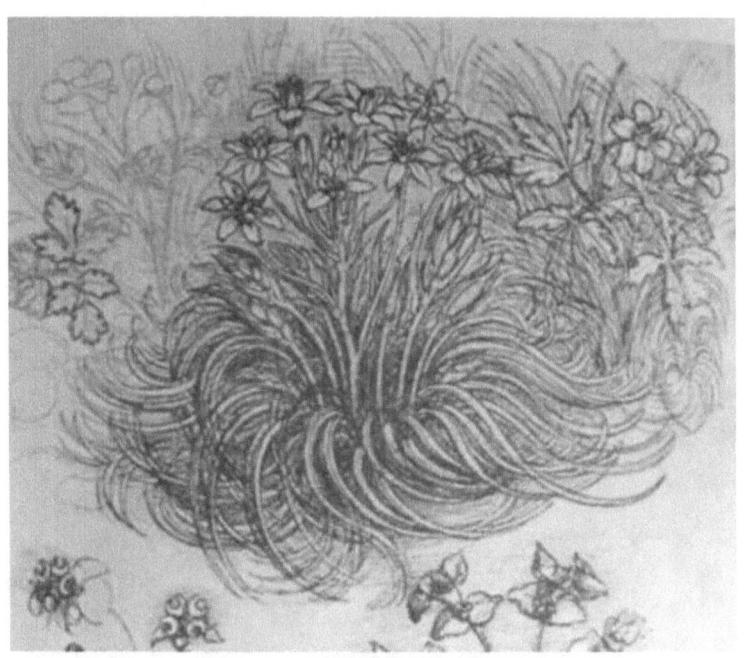

Drawing of a botanical study, c.1500, ink

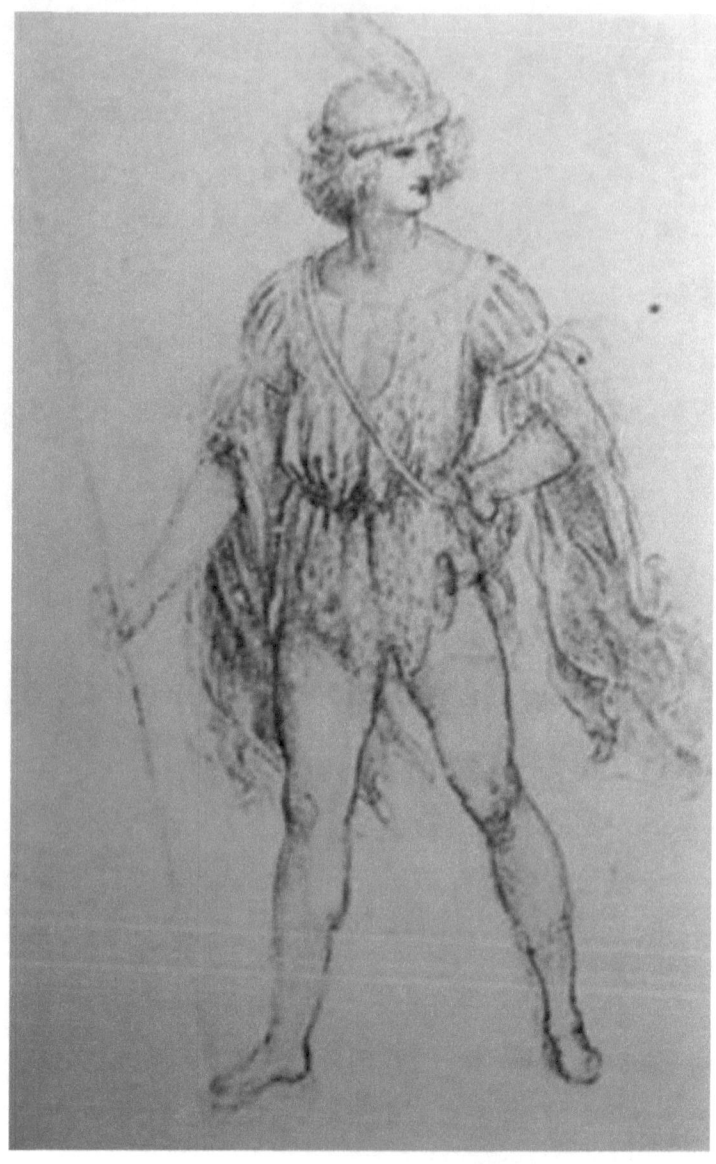

Drawing of a fancy dress costume, 1500, ink

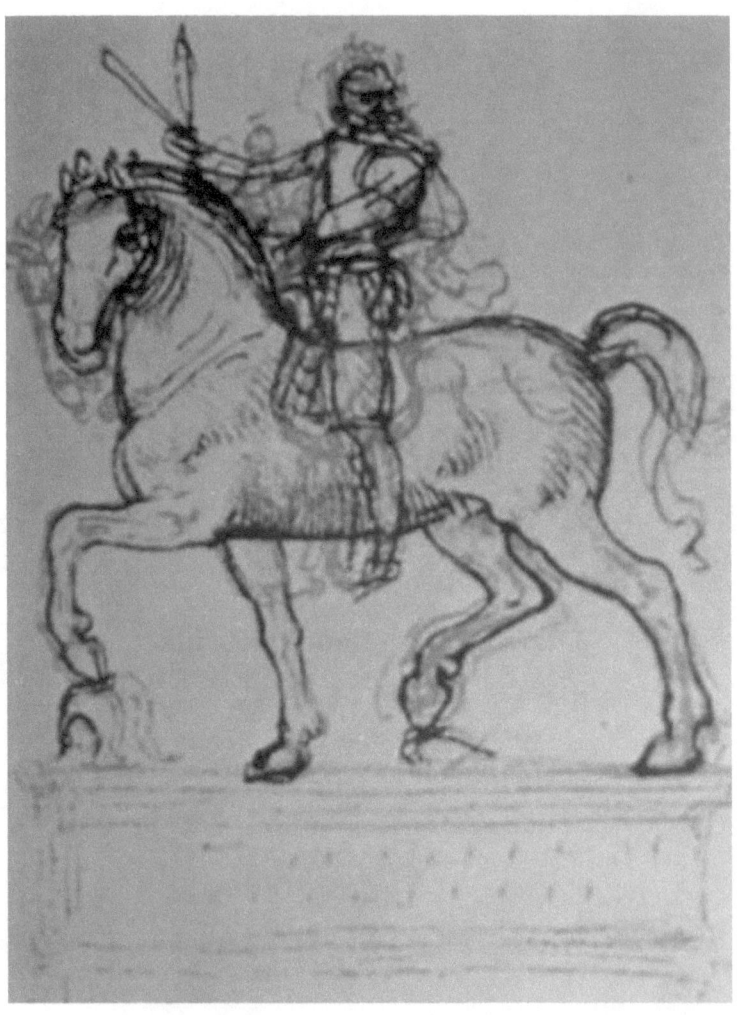

Drawing of an equestrian monument, 1500, ink

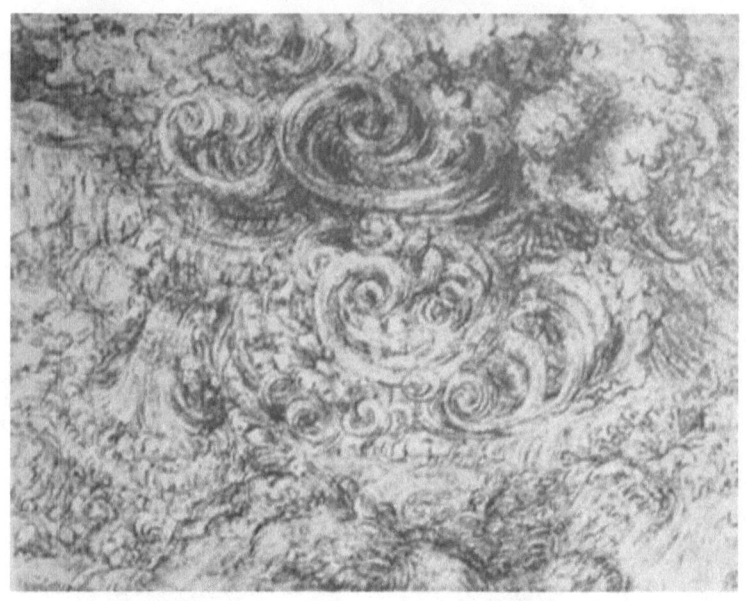

Drawing of an flood, 1500, ink

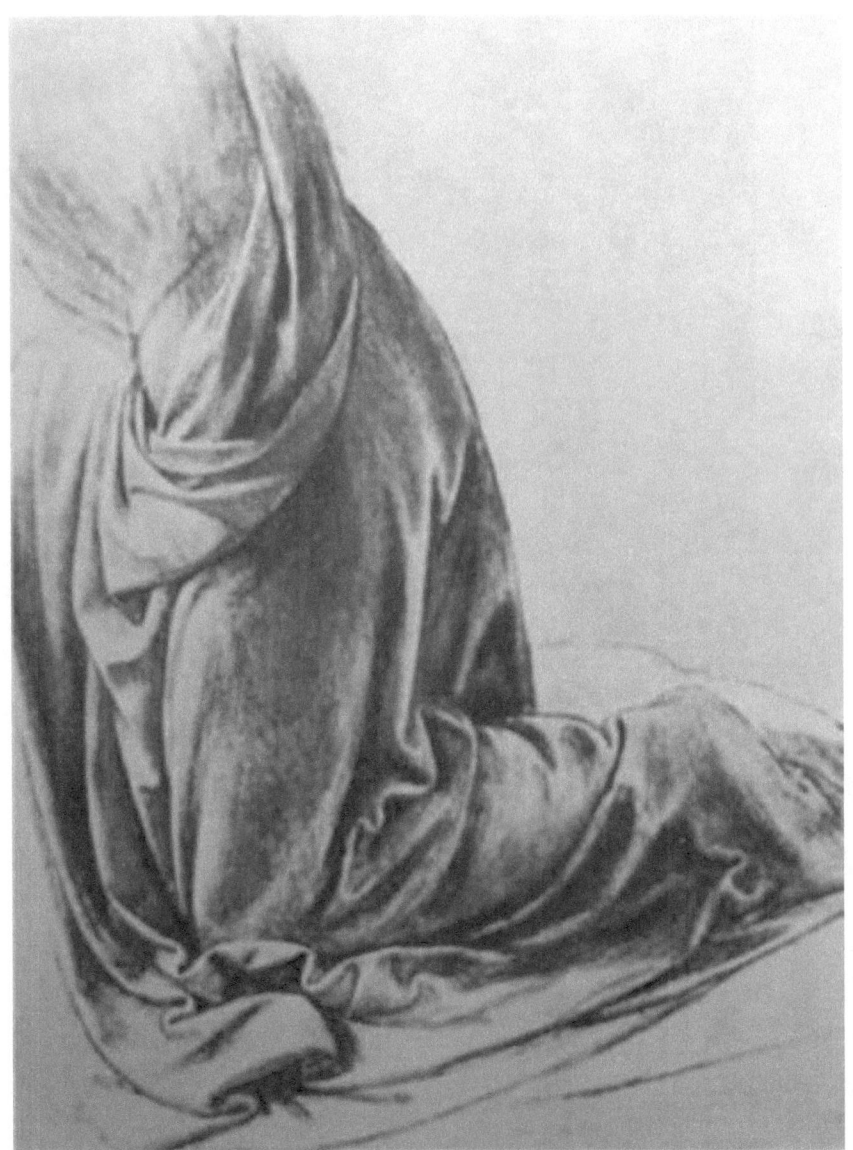

Drawing of drapery, 1500, chalk

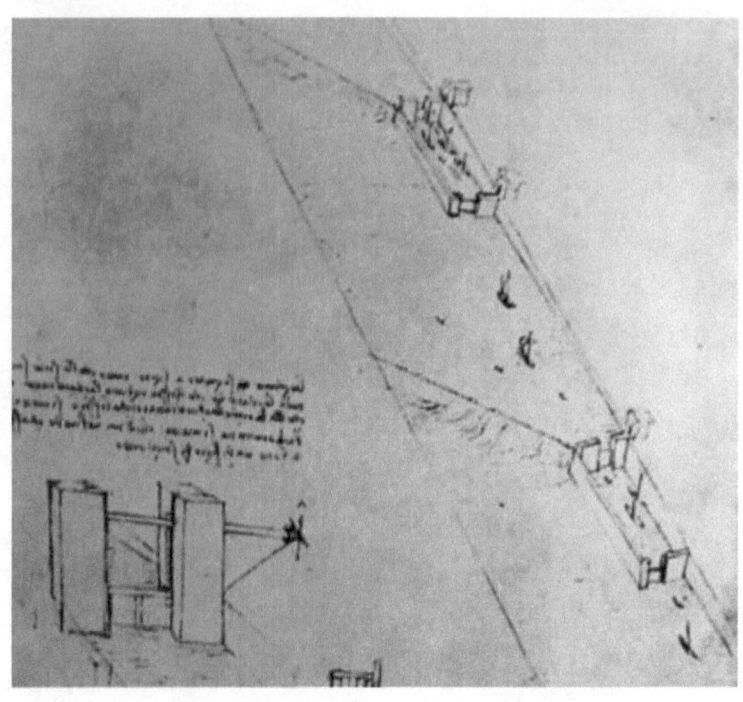

Drawing of locks on a river, 1500, ink

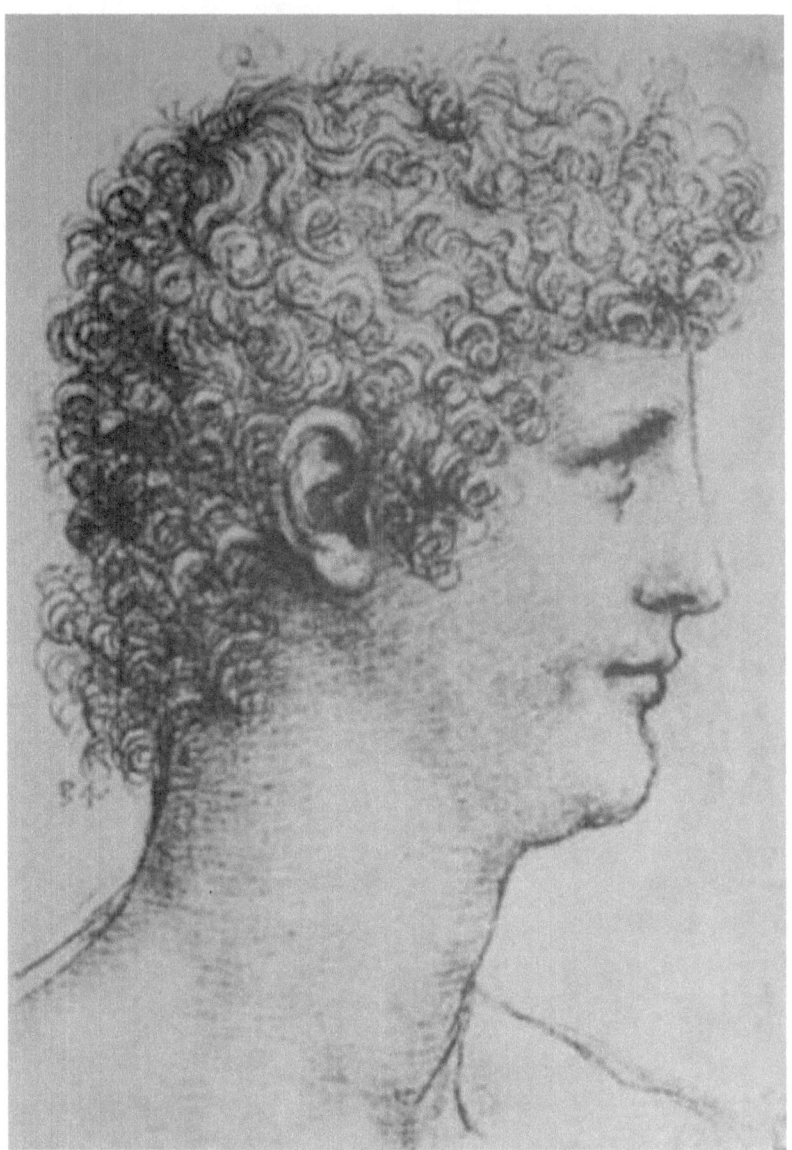

Drawing of Salai, c.1500, ink

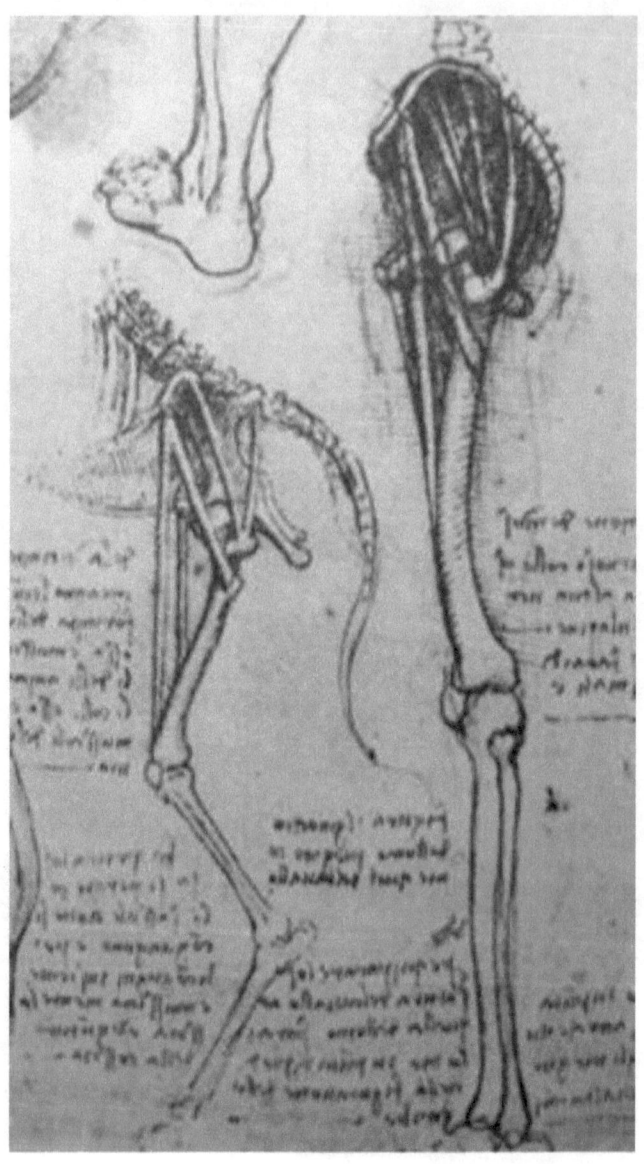

Drawing of the comparative anatomy of the legs of a man and a dog, c.1500, ink

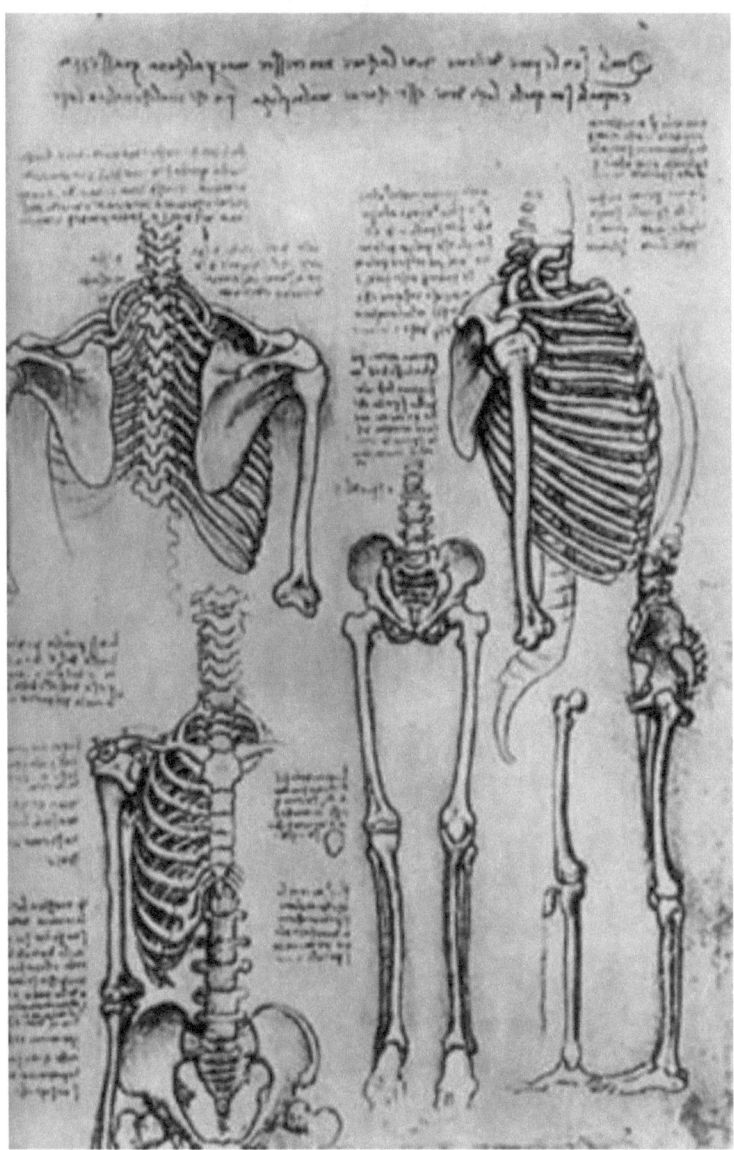

Drawing of the Torso and the Arms, 1500, ink

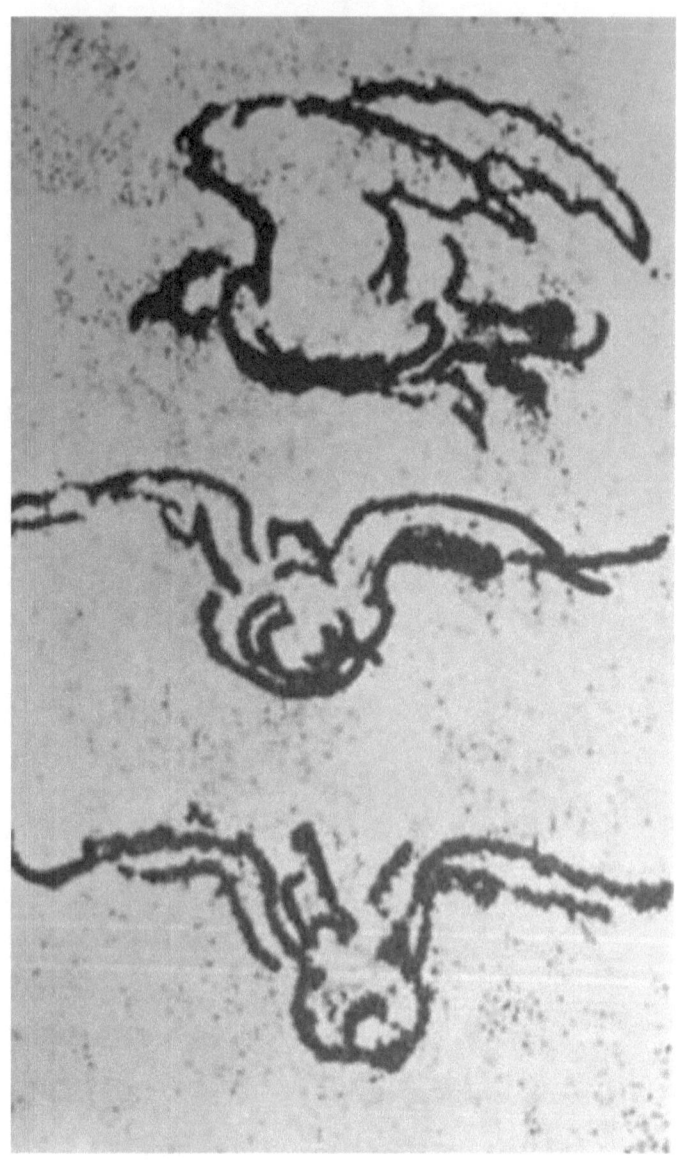

Drawings of a bird in flight, 1500, ink

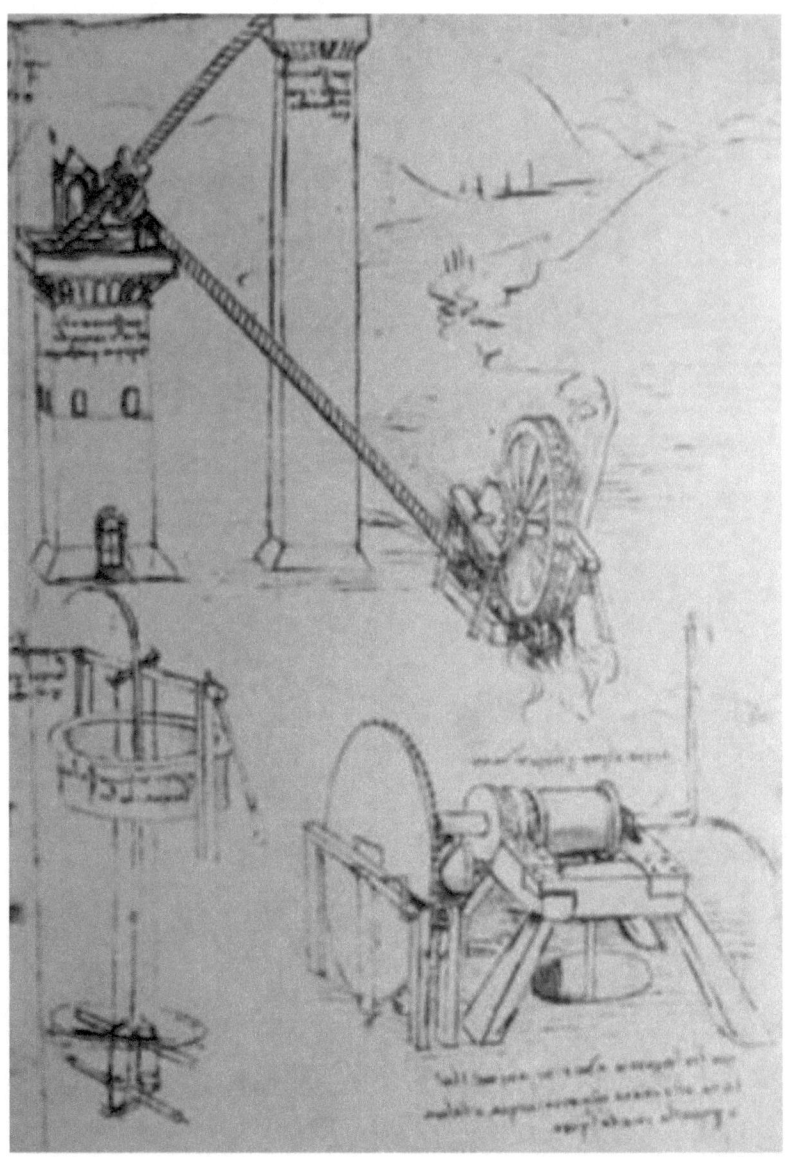

Drawings of machines, c.1500, ink

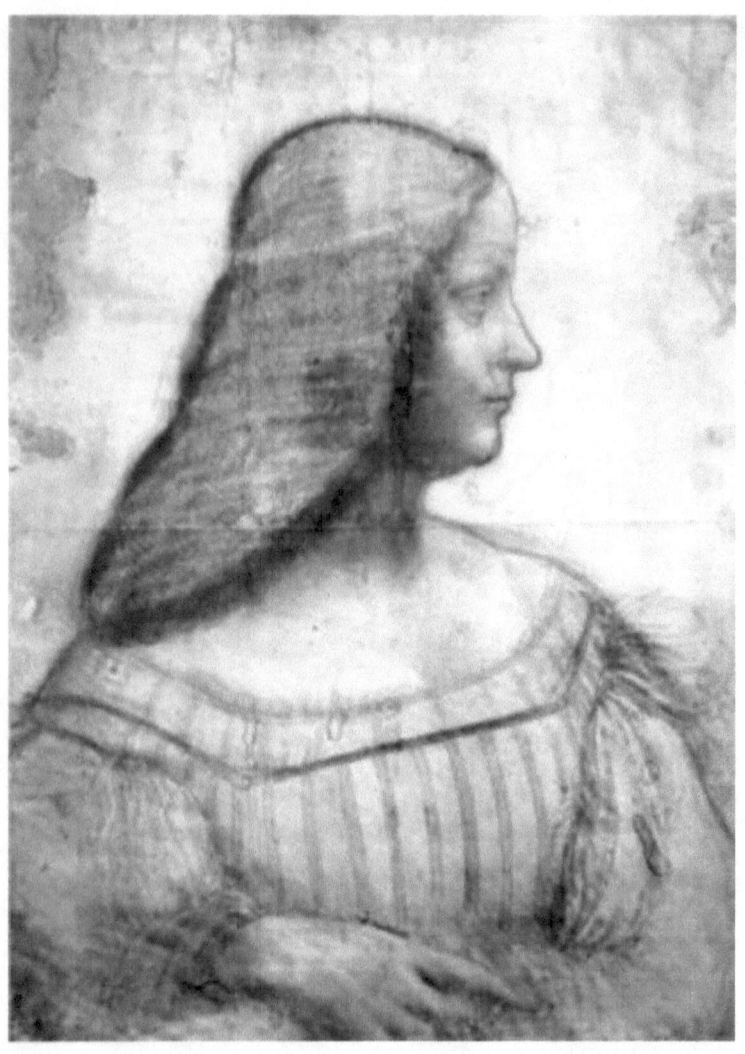

Isabella d'Este, 1500, chalk, 63 x 46 cm, Musée du Louvre, Paris, France

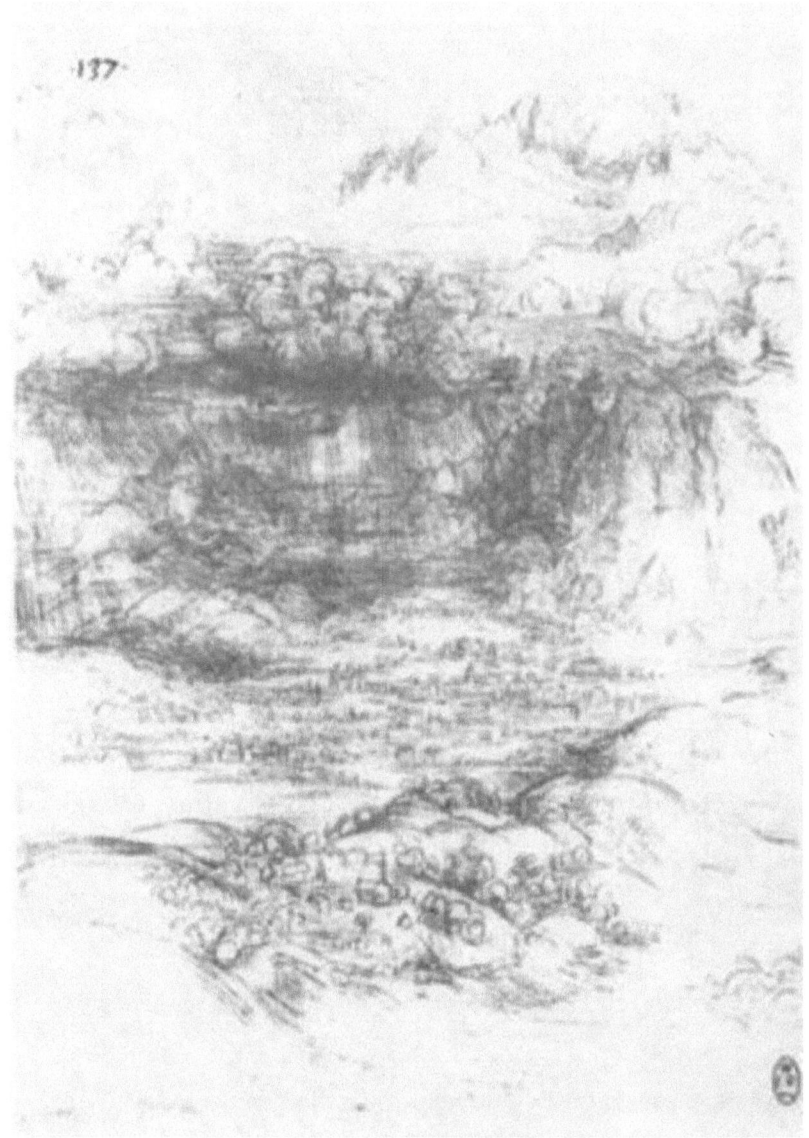

**Storm over a landscape, c.1500, chalk, 20 x 15 cm,
Royal Collection, Windsor Castle, London**

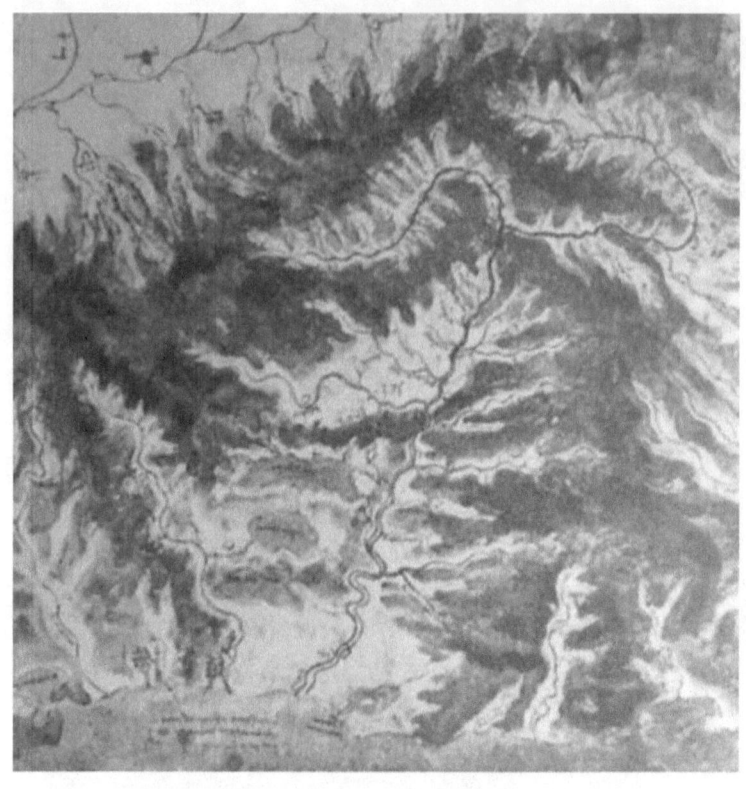

Topographical drawing of a river valley, c.1500

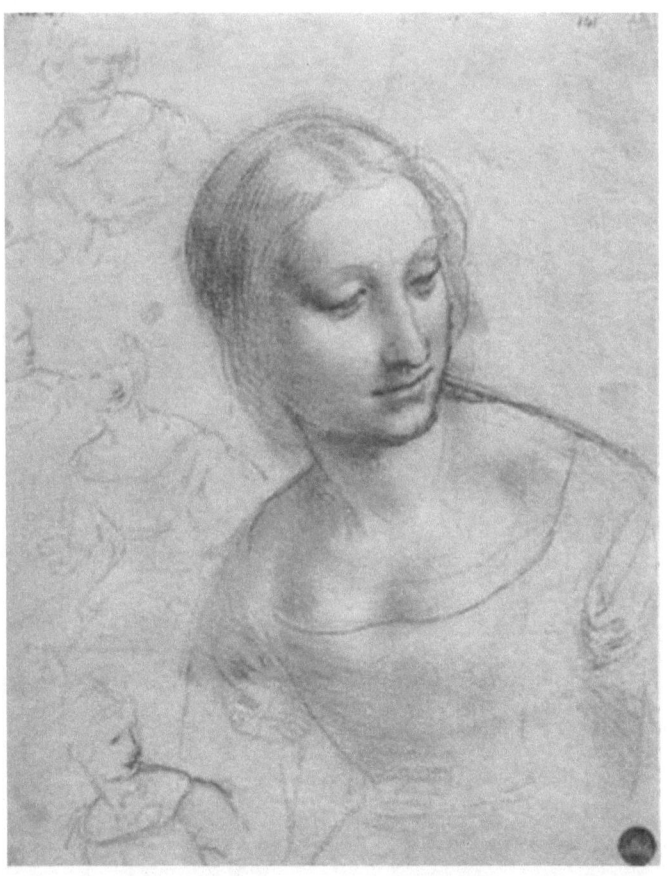

Study for Madonna with the Yarnwinder, c. 1501, Red chalk and silverpoint on rose-colored prepared paper, 25.7 x 20.3 cm, Gallerie dell'Accademia, Venice

The red chalk drawing is generally connected with the Madonna with the Yarnwinder, as the female figure has a posture similar to that of the Mary depicted in that painting. There is, however, a clear difference between the turnings of the bodies of the two figures, so that the dating of the page remains a matter for debate.

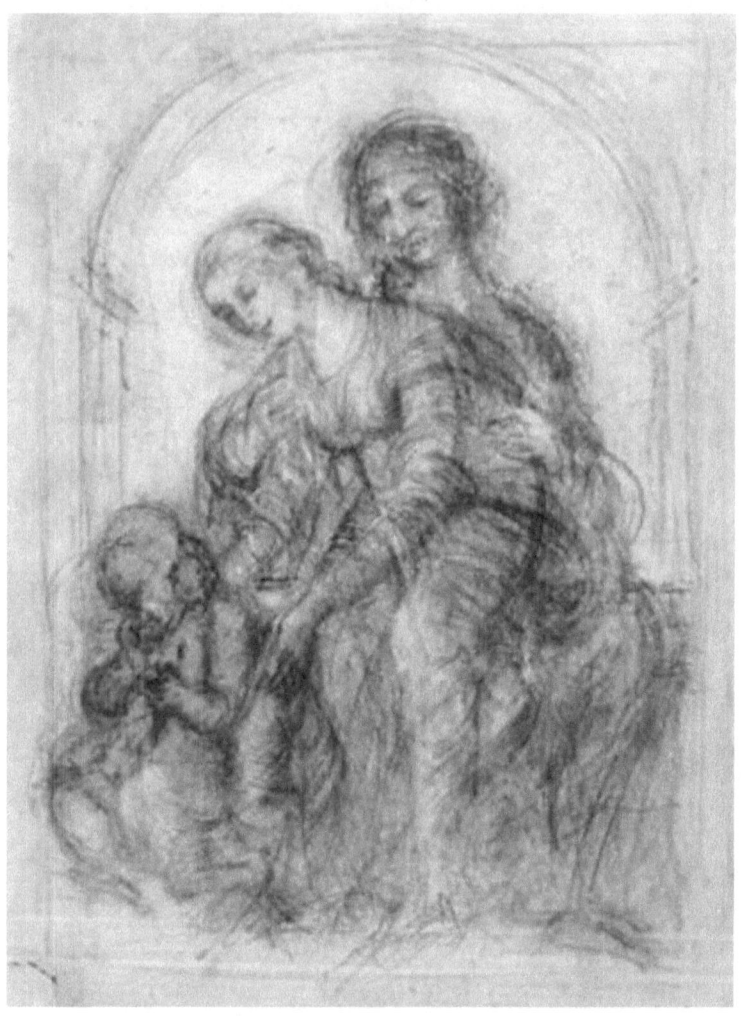

Design for St Anne, c. 1501, Slate pencil on prepared paper, 21.8 x 16.4 cm, Private collection

The composition of the three figures is fairly tight, with the Virgin Mary clearly interacting actively with the infant Jesus.

However, upon closer examination of the positioning of the Virgin and St. Anne one realizes that the Virgin Mother is sitting on St. Anne's lap. It is unclear what meaning this could have and what meaning Leonardo intended to project with that pose. There is no clear parallel in other works of art and women sitting in each other's lap are not a clear cultural or traditional reference that the viewer can relate to. Additionally, although the exact sizes of neither the Mother Virgin nor St. Anne are known, it can be easily extrapolated from the painting that St. Anne is a significantly larger person than Mary. This subtle yet perceptible distortion in size was utilized by Leonardo to emphasize the mother daughter relationship between the two women despite the apparent lack of visual cues to the greater age of St.Anne that would otherwise identify her as the mother.

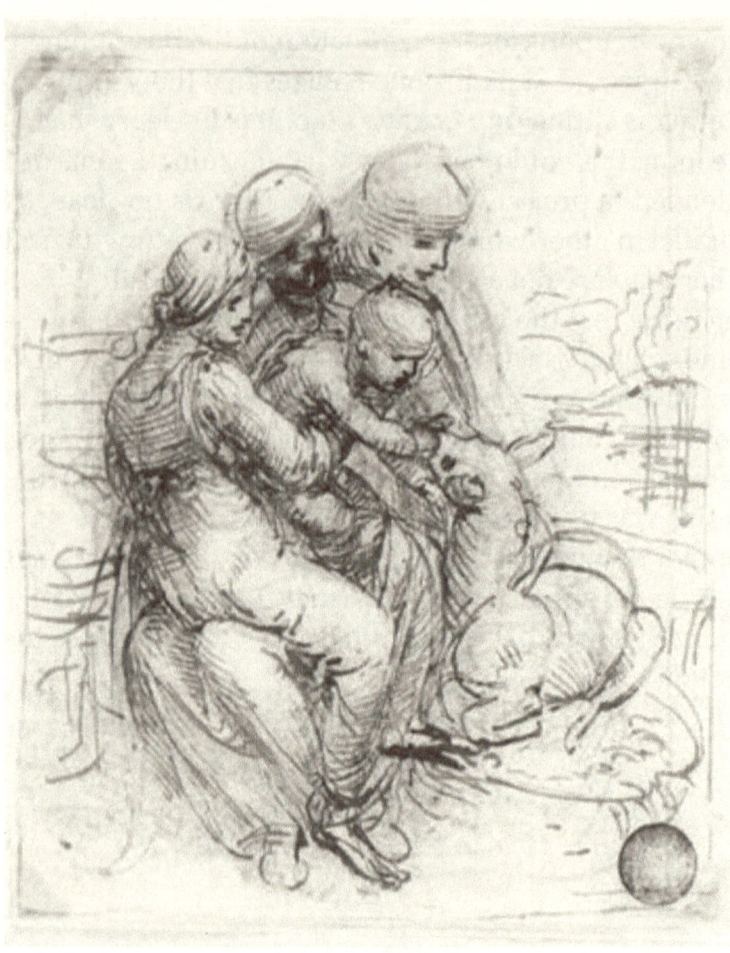

Study of St Anne, Mary, the Christ Child and the young St John, 1501-06, Pencil, pen and ink on paper, Gallerie dell'Accademia, Venice

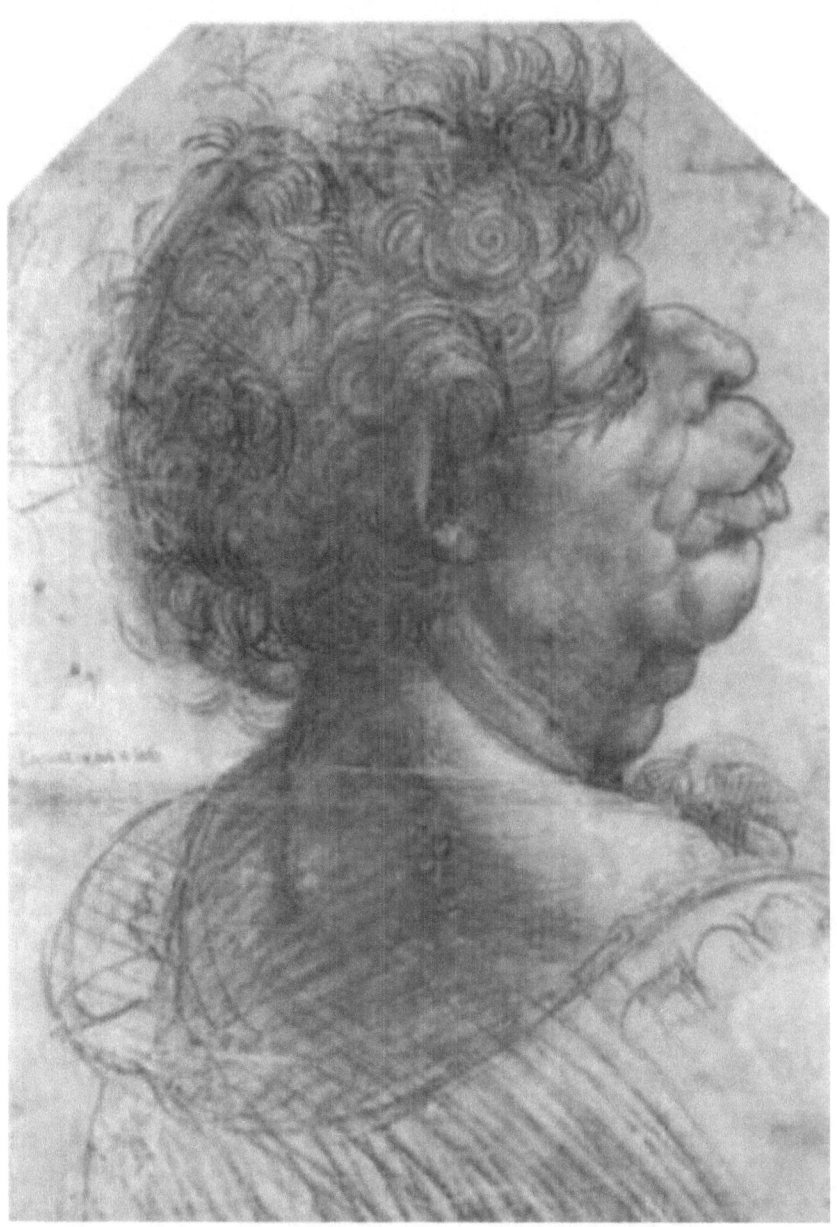

A Grotesque Head Grotesque head, c.1502chalk, 39 x 28 cm, Christ Church, Oxford

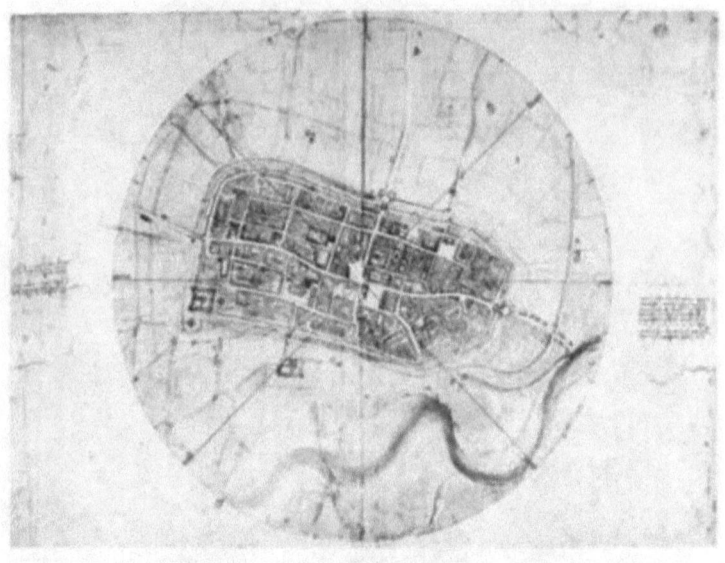

**A plan of Imola, 1502, chalk, wash, ink, 60.2 x 44 cm,
Royal Collection, Windsor Castle, London**

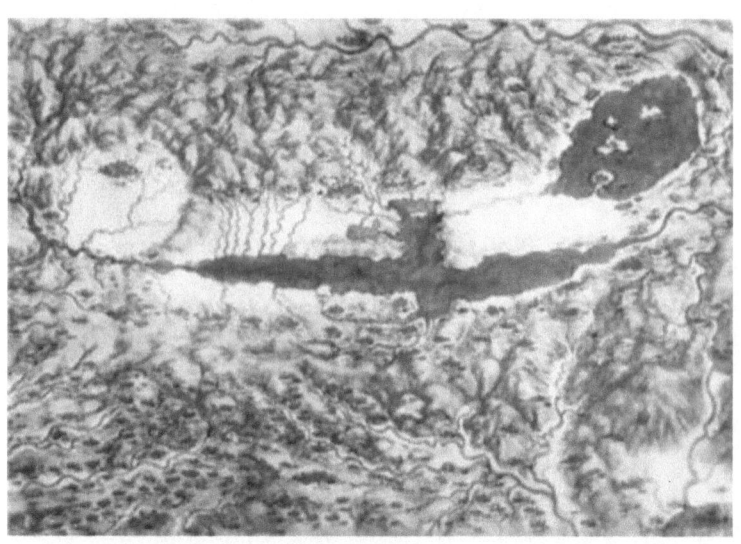

Bird's Eye View of a Landscape, c.1502, chalk, wash, ink, 60.2 x 44 cm, Royal Collection, Windsor Castle

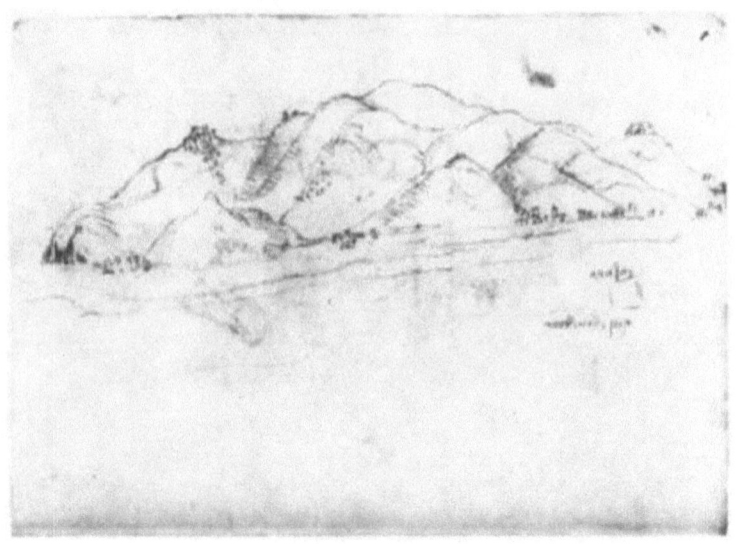

Landscape near Pisa, c.1502, chalk, 21.1 x 15 cm, Biblioteca Nacional, Madrid, Spain

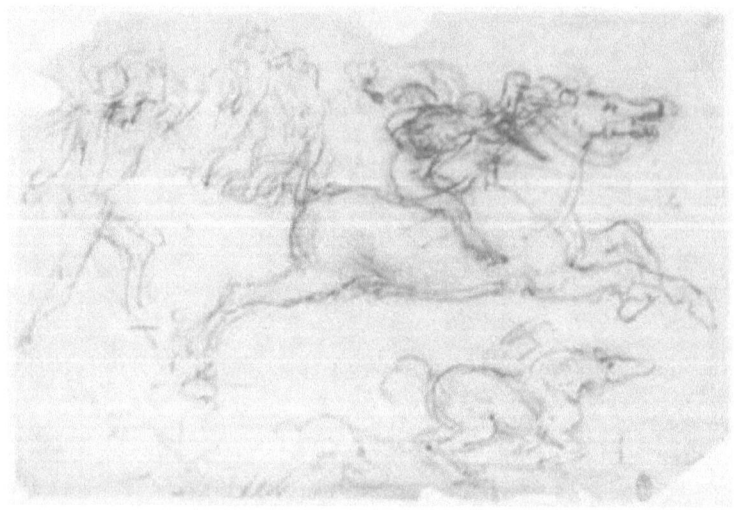

Galloping Rider and other figures, c.1503, chalk, 16.8 x 24 cm, Royal Collection, Windsor Castle, London

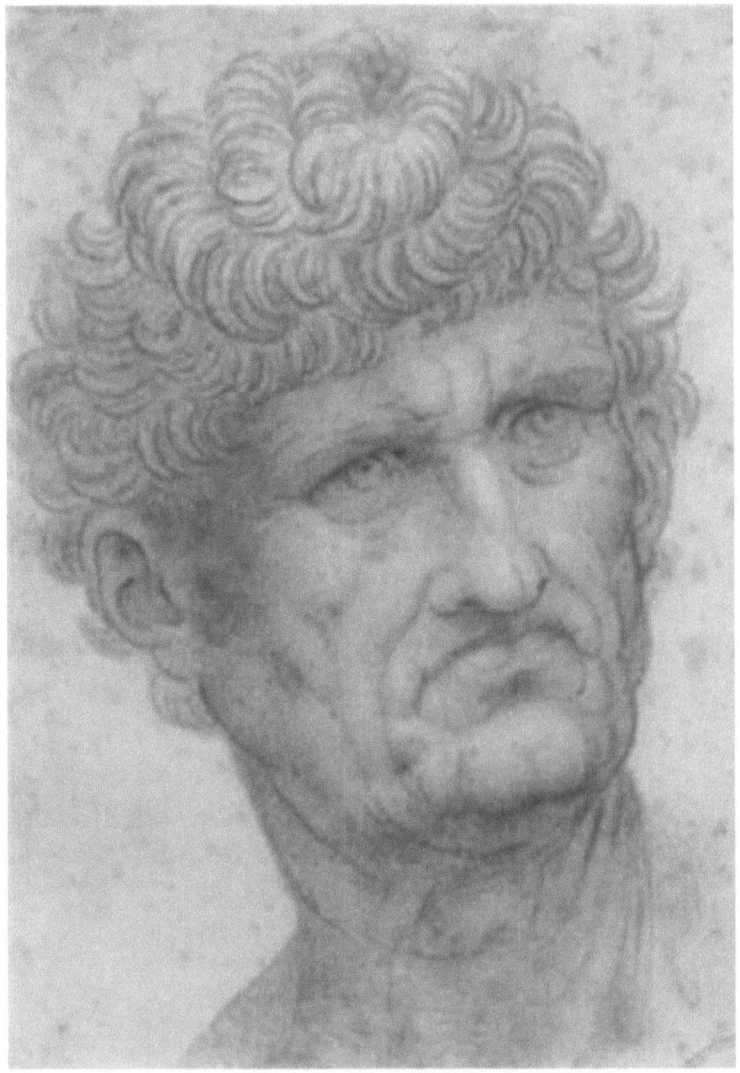

Head of a Man, 1503, chalk, Gallerie dell'Accademia,
Venice, Italy

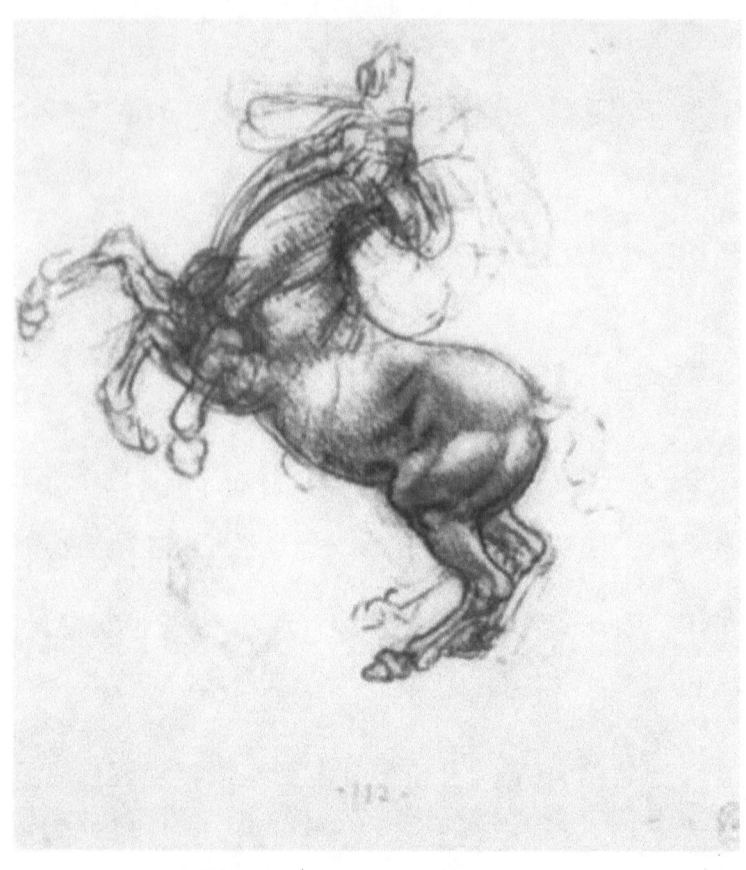

Rearing horse, c.1503, chalk, 15.3 x 14.2 cm, Royal Collection, Windsor Castle, London

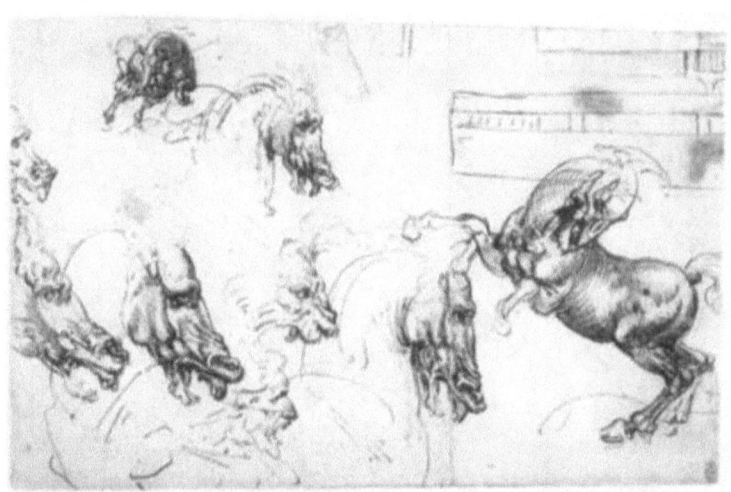

Study of horses for the Battle of Anghiari, c.1503, wash, chalk, ink, 19.6 x 30.8 cm, Royal Collection, Windsor Castle, London

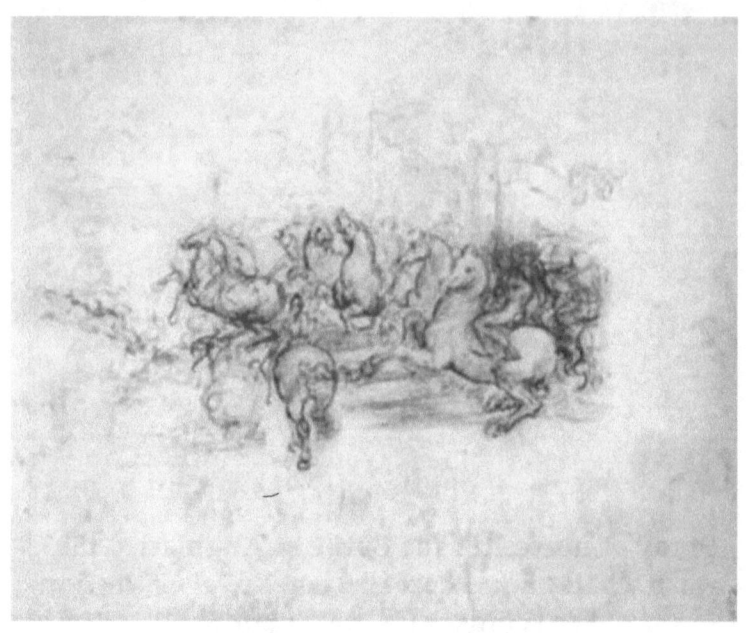

Group of riders in the Battle of Anghiari, c.1504, chalk, 16 x 19.7 cm, Royal Collection, Windsor Castle, London

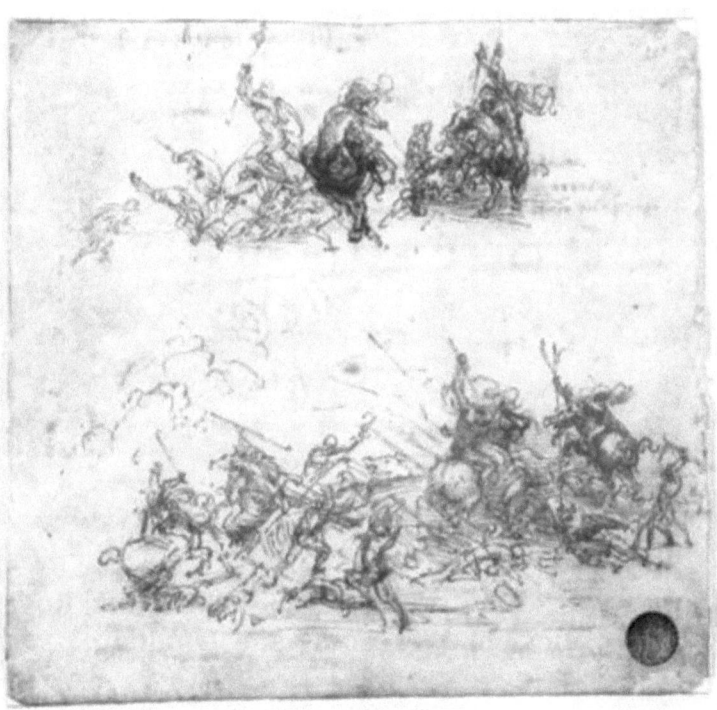

Page from a notebook showing figures fighting on
horseback and on foot, c.1504, ink, Gallerie
dell'Accademia, Venice, Italy

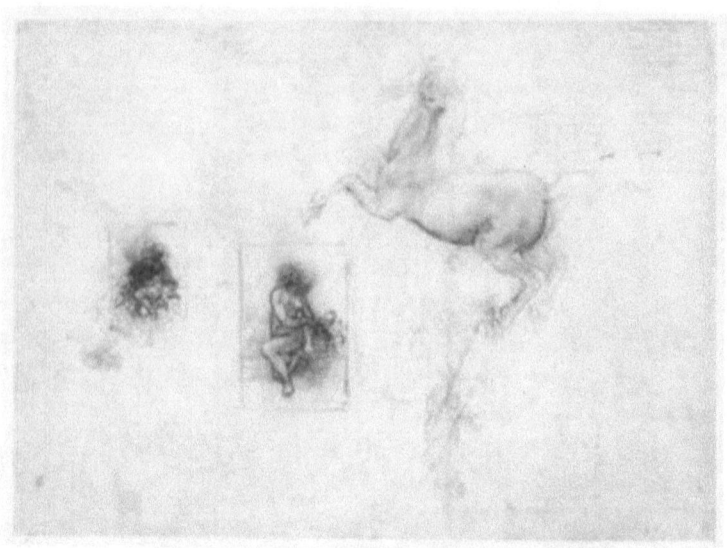

Studies of Leda and a horse, c.1504, chalk, ink, Royal Collection, Windsor Castle, London

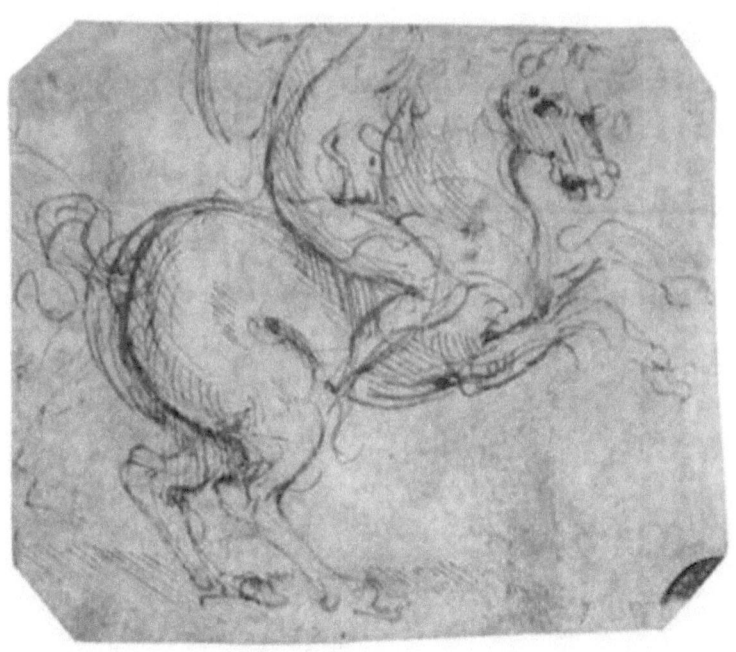

Study of a rider, c.1504, chalk, Gallerie
dell'Accademia, Venice, Italy

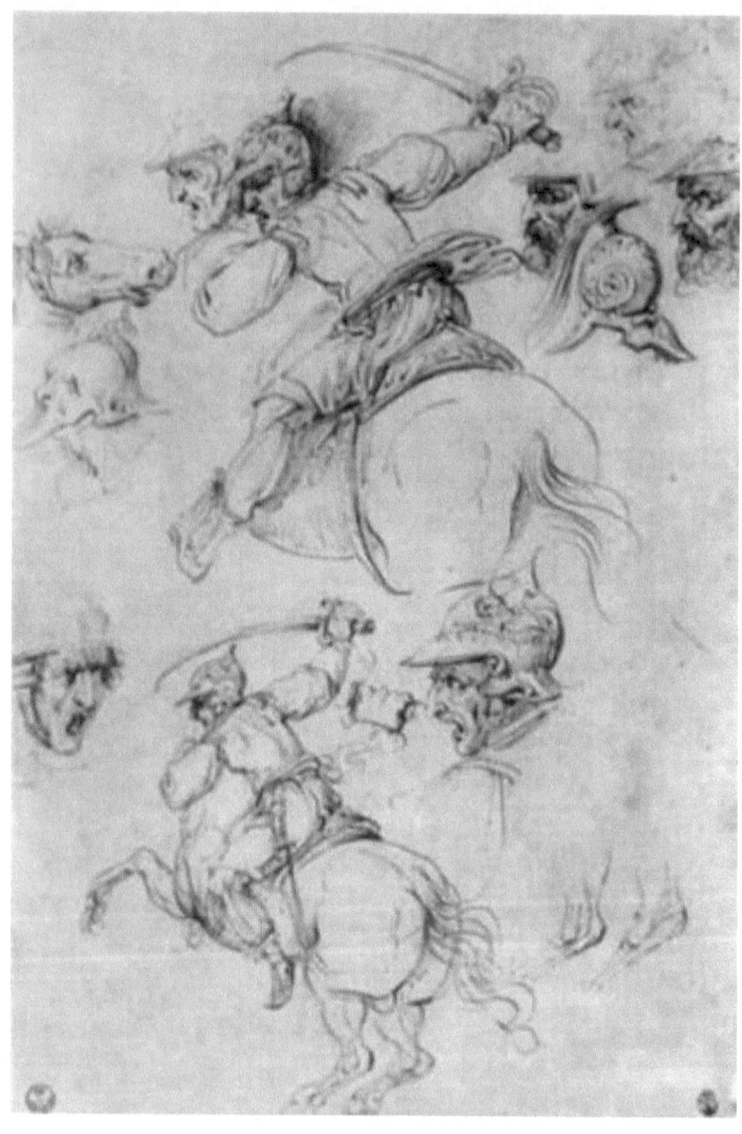

Study of battles on horseback, c.1504, ink, Galleria degli Uffizi, Florence, Italy

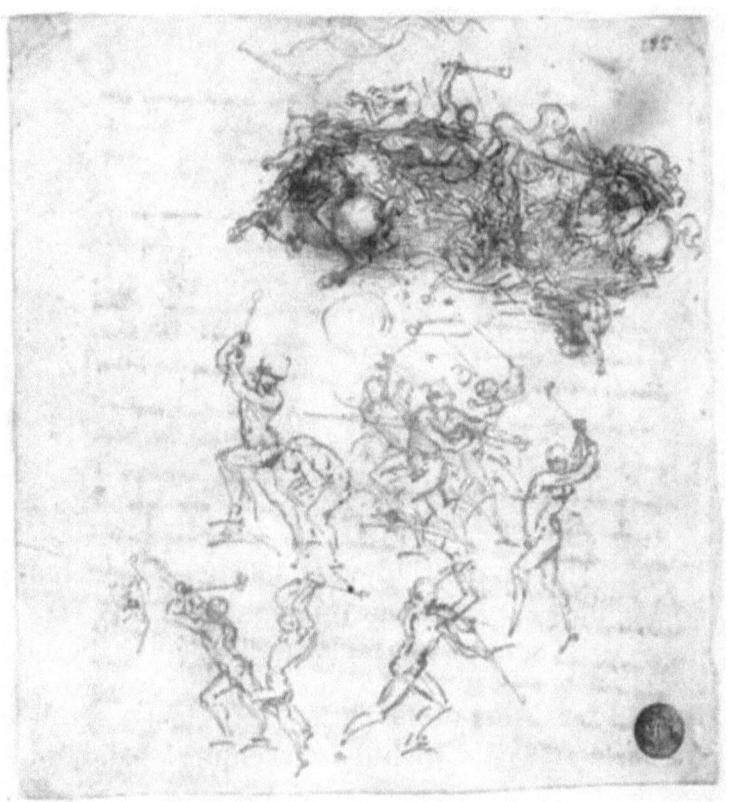

Study of battles on horseback and on foot, c.1504, ink, Gallerie dell'Accademia, Venice, Italy

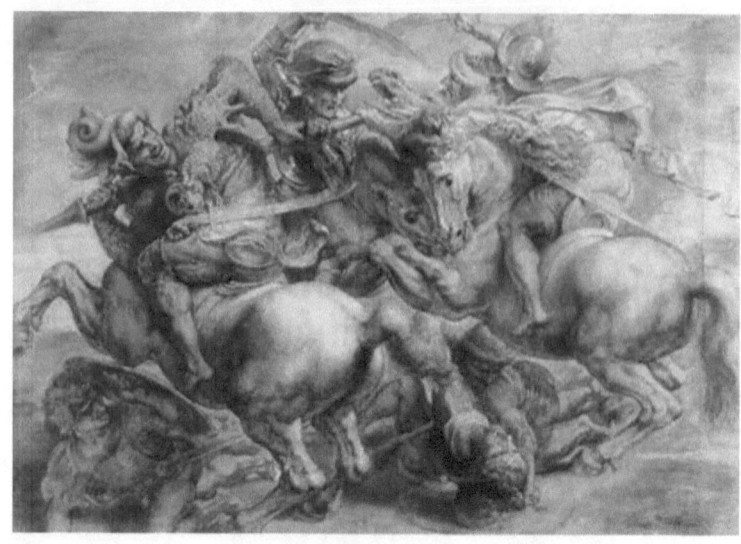

**The Battle of Anghiari (detail), 1503-05, Black chalk,
pen and ink, watercolour on paper, 45.2 x 63.7 cm,
Louvre, Paris**

This is the best copy of the Battle of Anghiari executed
by an unknown artist in mid-16th century. At the sides
it was made up by Rubens.

The Republic of Florence, which came into being in
1494, decided to create an assembly hall for their most
important political committee, the "High Council",
which was suited to the requirements and pretensions
of the new republic. The majority of the construction
work on the Sala del Gran Consiglio in the Florentine
Palazzo Vecchio had been completed shortly before
1500. The pictorial program was to include two large
wall paintings intended to express the self confidence
of the new republic. It was planned that two important
victories from recent Florentine history should be
depicted: the Battle of Anghiari and the Battle of

Cascina. The choice of artist had to measure up to the importance of the commission, and the decision was made in favour of two of the most highly esteemed Florentine artists of the age, Leonardo da Vinci and the young Michelangelo.

Neither of the two artists completed his works and we only know of their projects indirectly by their being mentioned in documents, or in the form of copies or sketches that have been associated with the project.

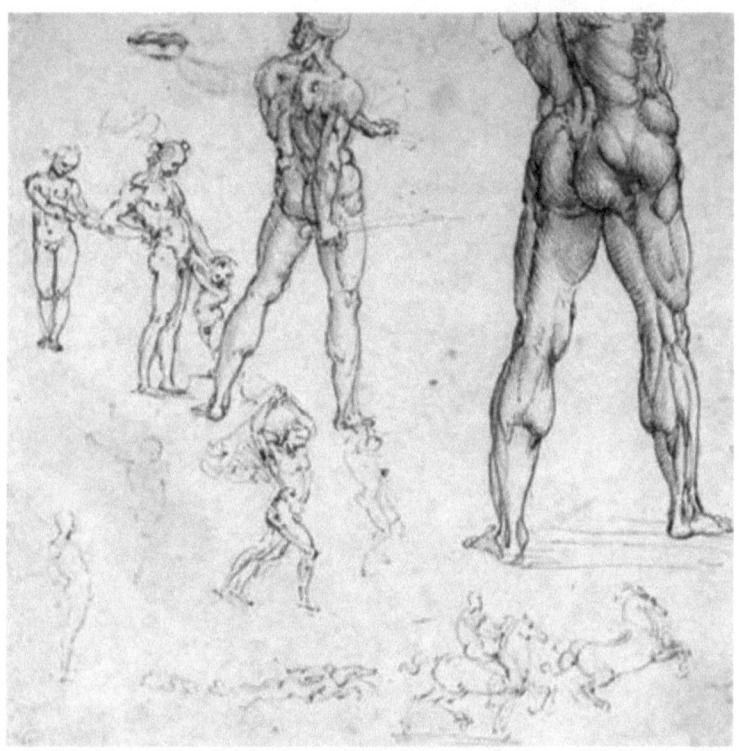

Anatomical studies, c.1505, ink, Biblioteca Reale, Turin, Italy

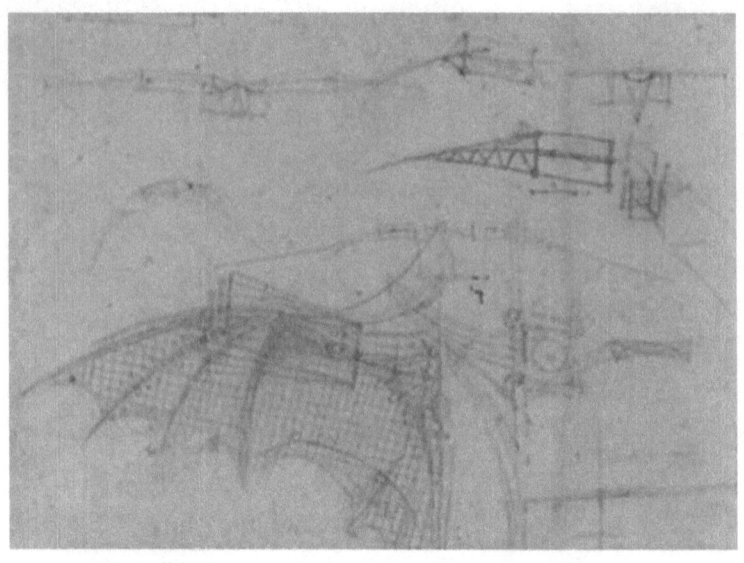

Design for a Flying Machine, c.1505, chalk

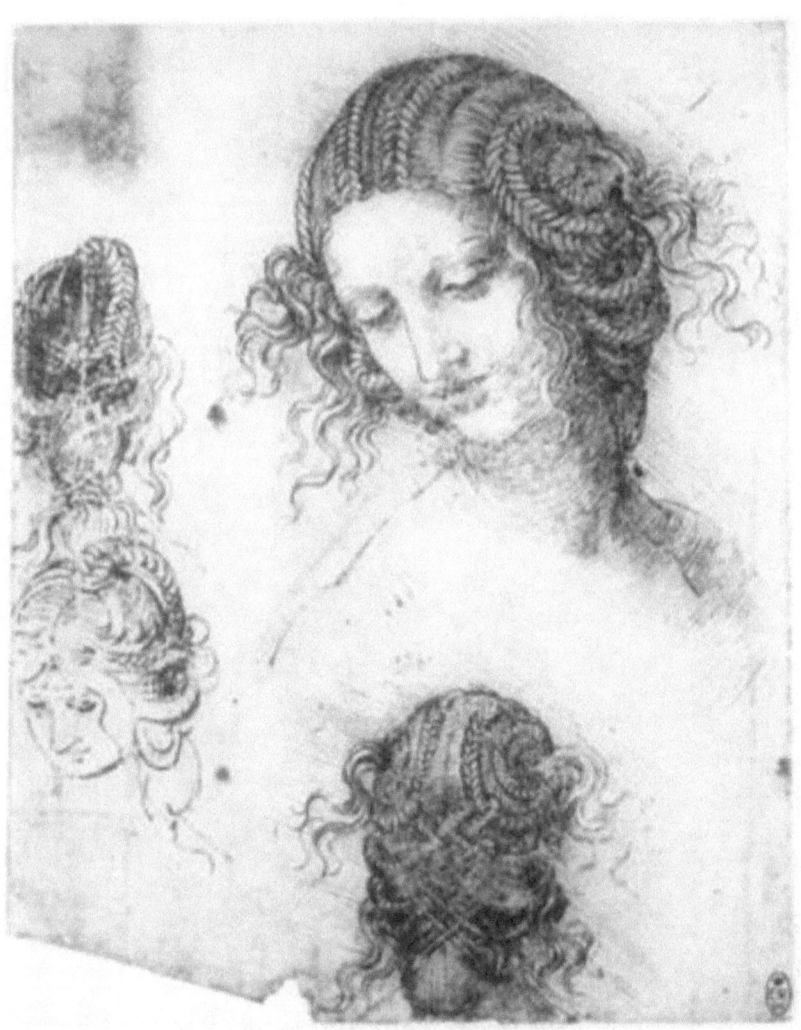

Head of Leda, c.1505, chalk, ink, Royal Collection,
Windsor Castle, London, UK

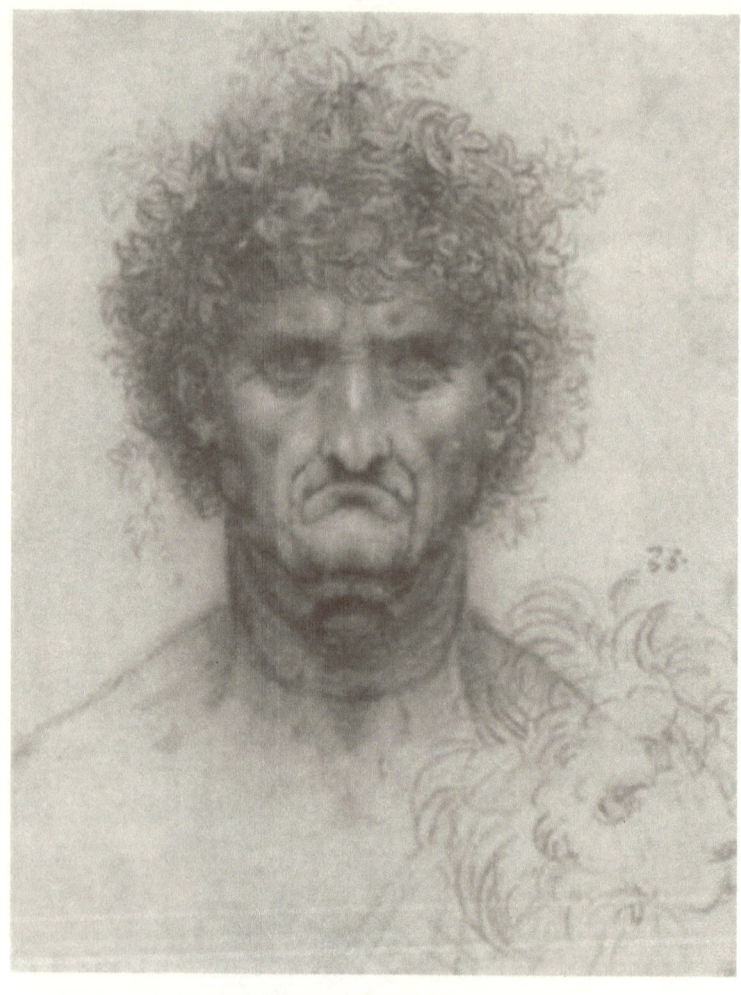

Old man with ivy wreath and lion's head, c.1505, chalk, Royal Collection, Windsor Castle, London

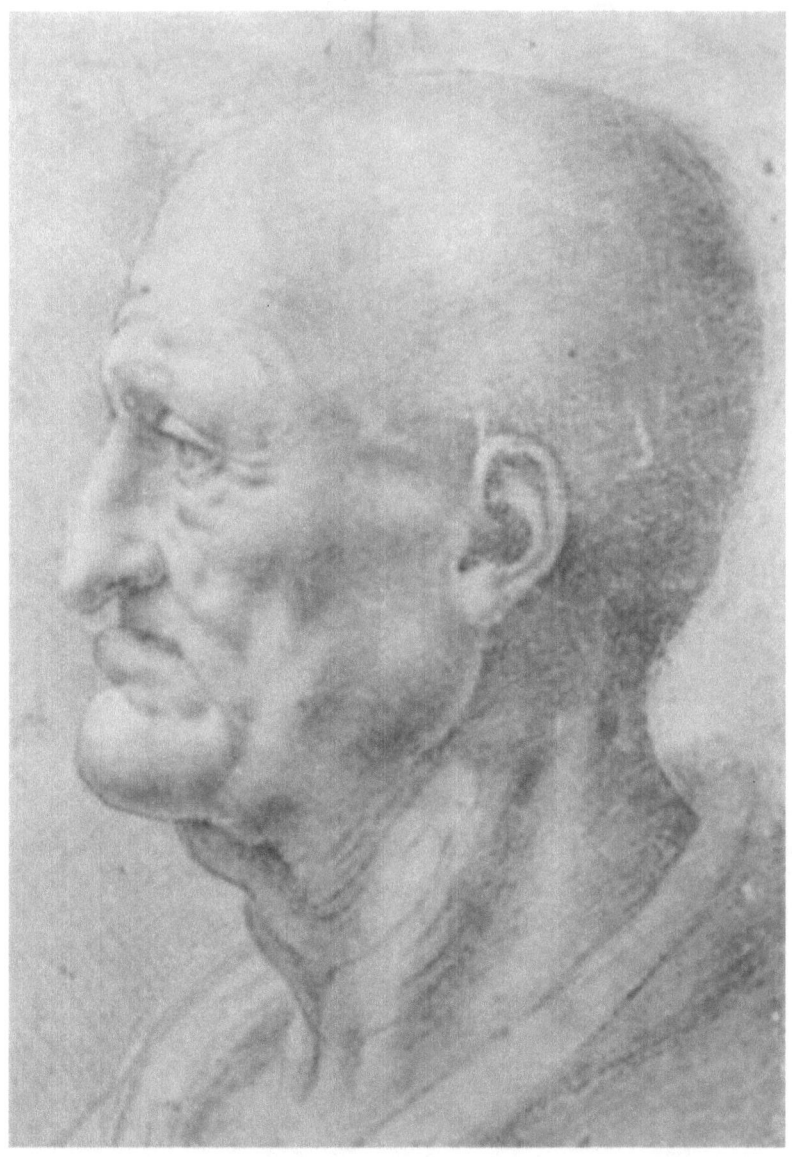

Profile of an old man, c.1505, ink, Galleria degli
Uffizi, Florence, Italy

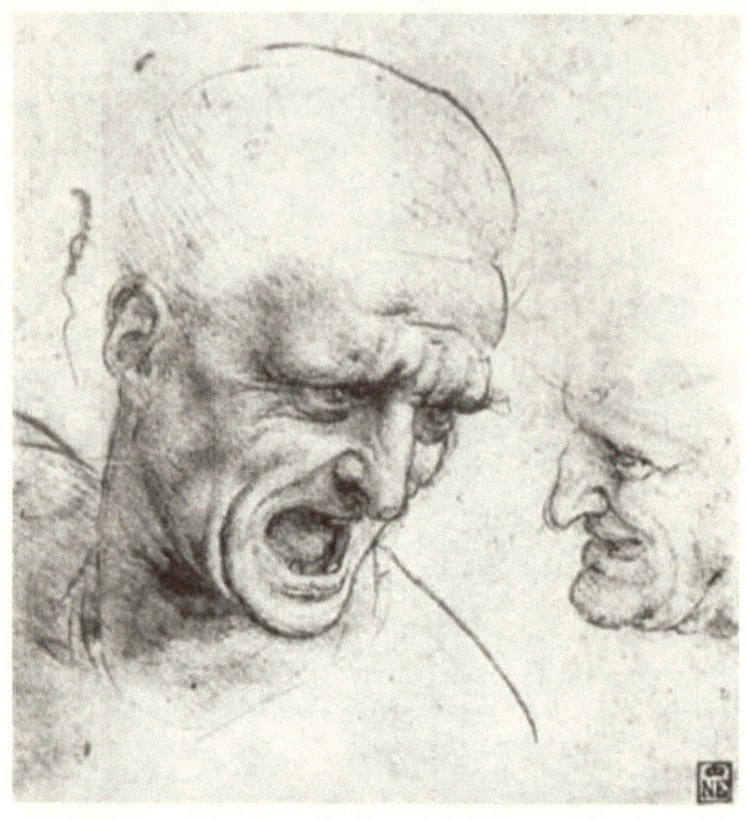

Studies for the heads of two soldiers in 'The Battle of Anghiari', c.1505, chalk, Museum of Fine Arts, Budapest, Hungary

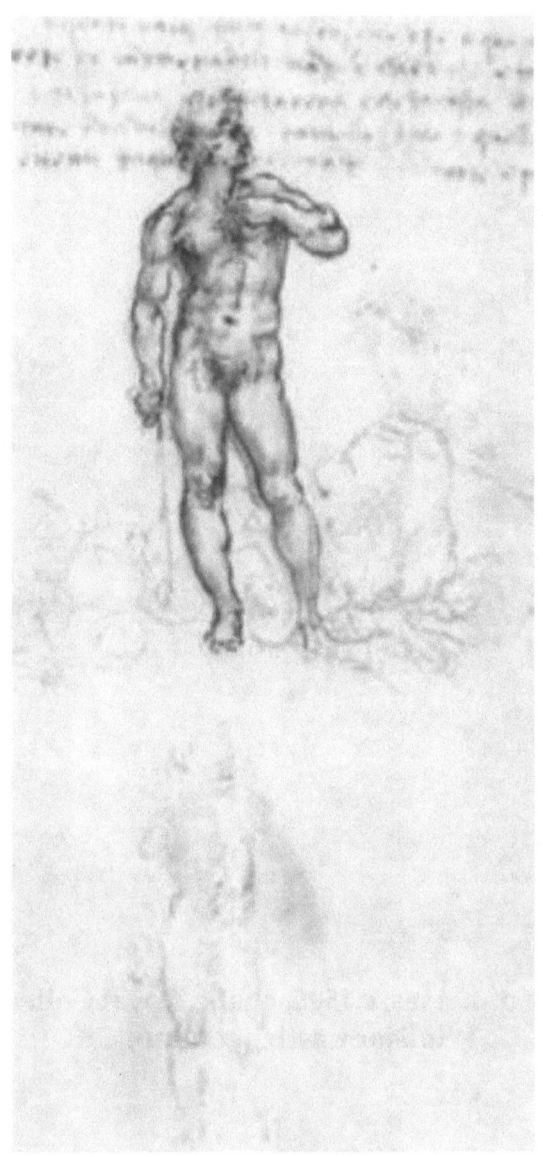

**Study of David by Michelangelo, 1505, ink, Royal
Collection, Windsor Castle, London, UK**

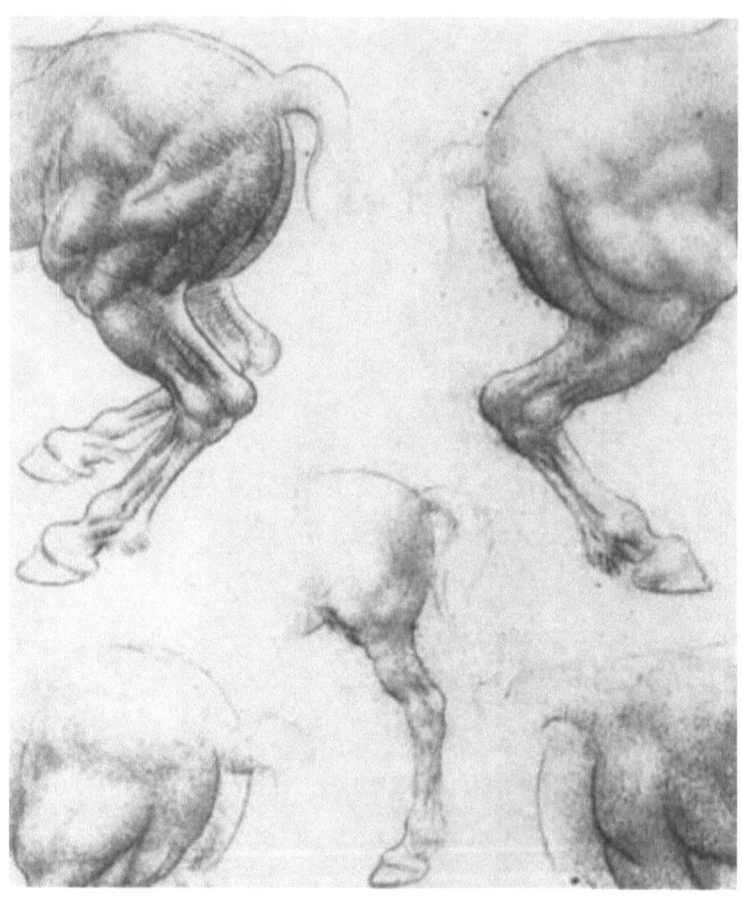

Study of horses, c.1505, chalk, Royal Collection, Windsor Castle, London, UK

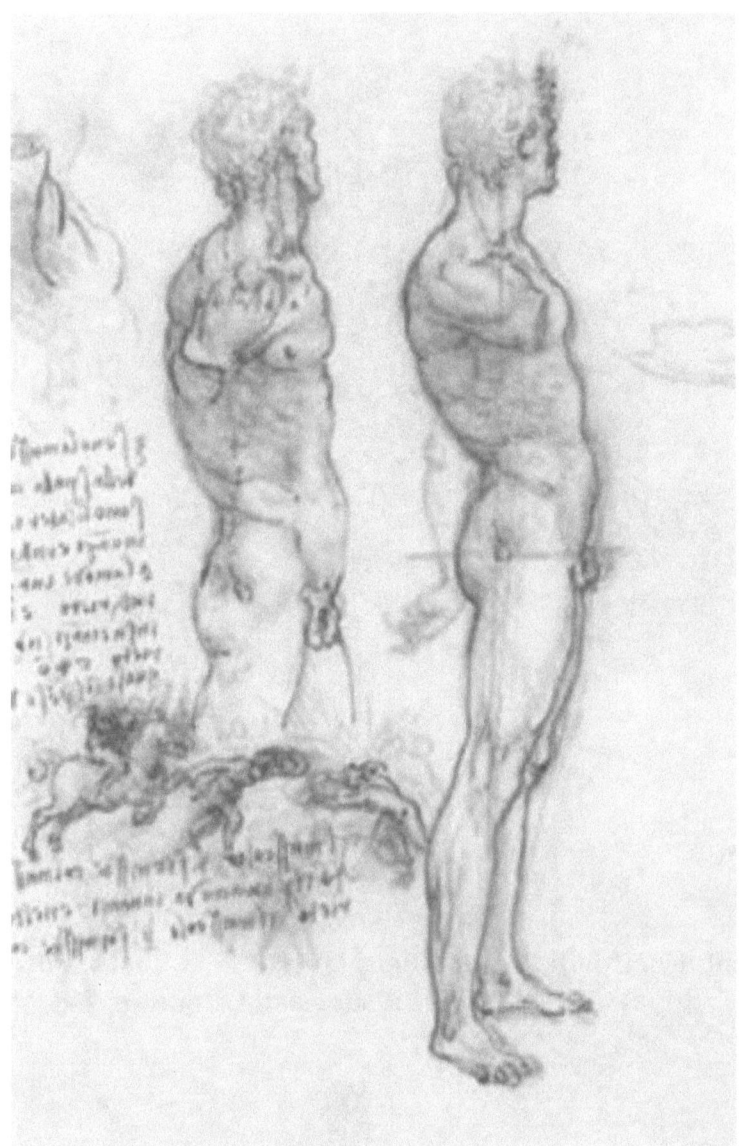

The anatomy of a male nude and a battle scene,
c.1505, chalk, Royal Collection, Windsor Castle,
London, UK

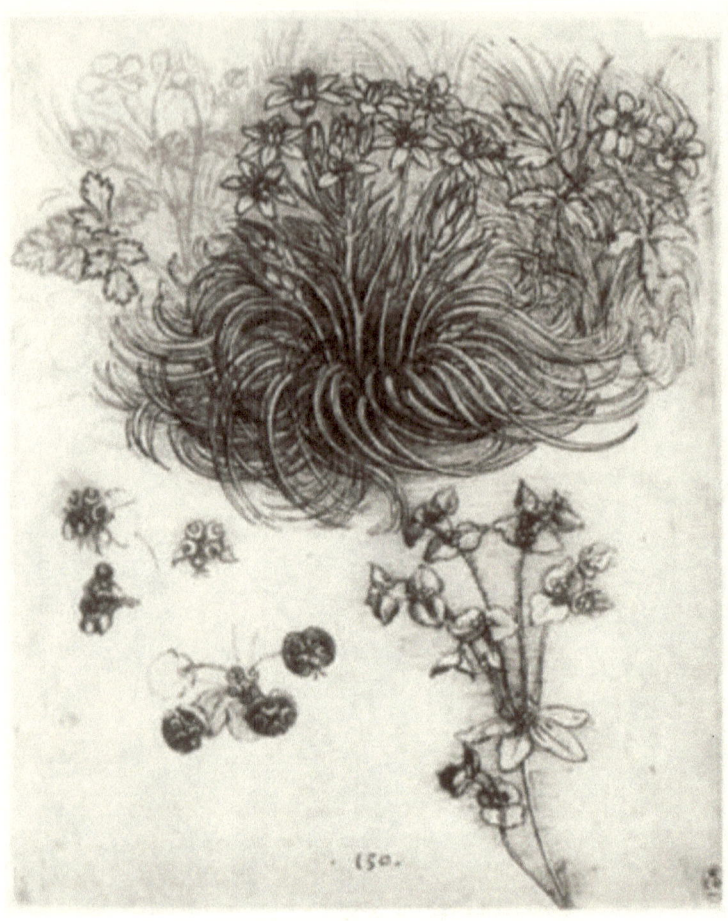

Stof Bethlehem and other plants, c.1506, chalk, ink, Royal Collection, Windsor Castle, London, UK

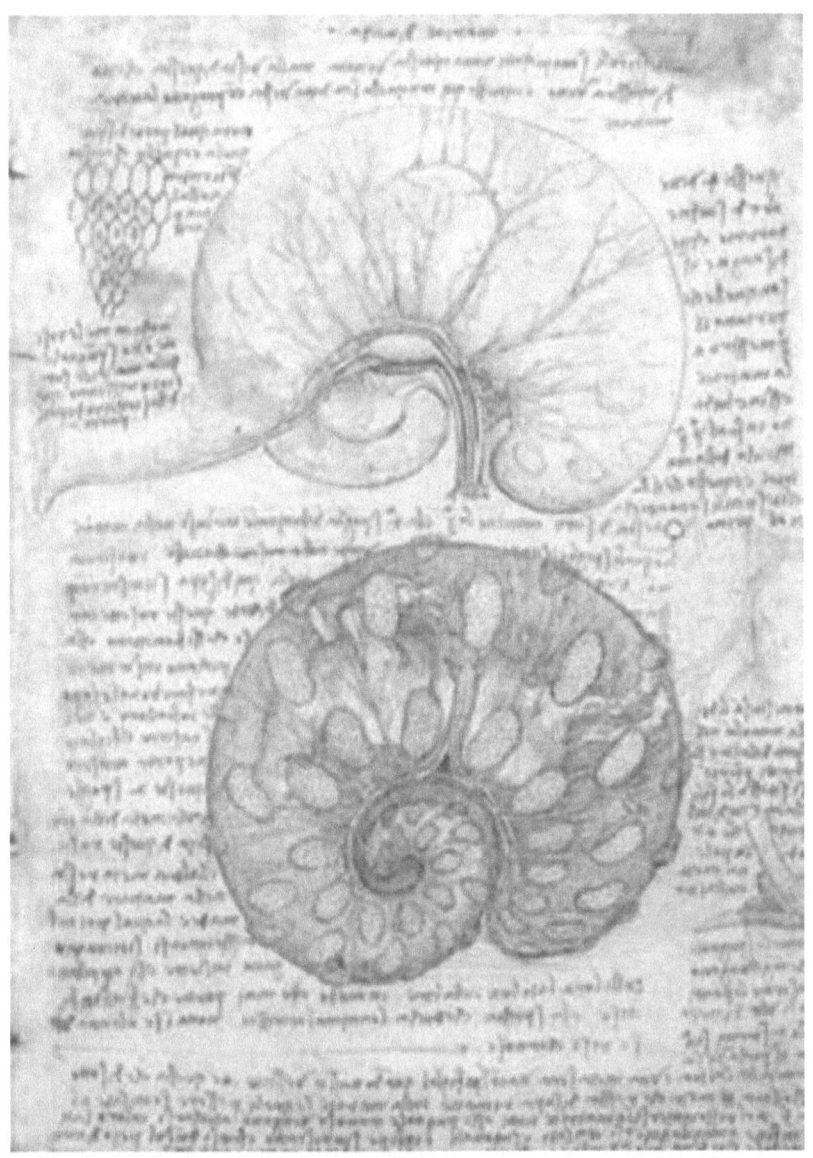

Drawing of the uterus of a pregnant cow, 1508, ink

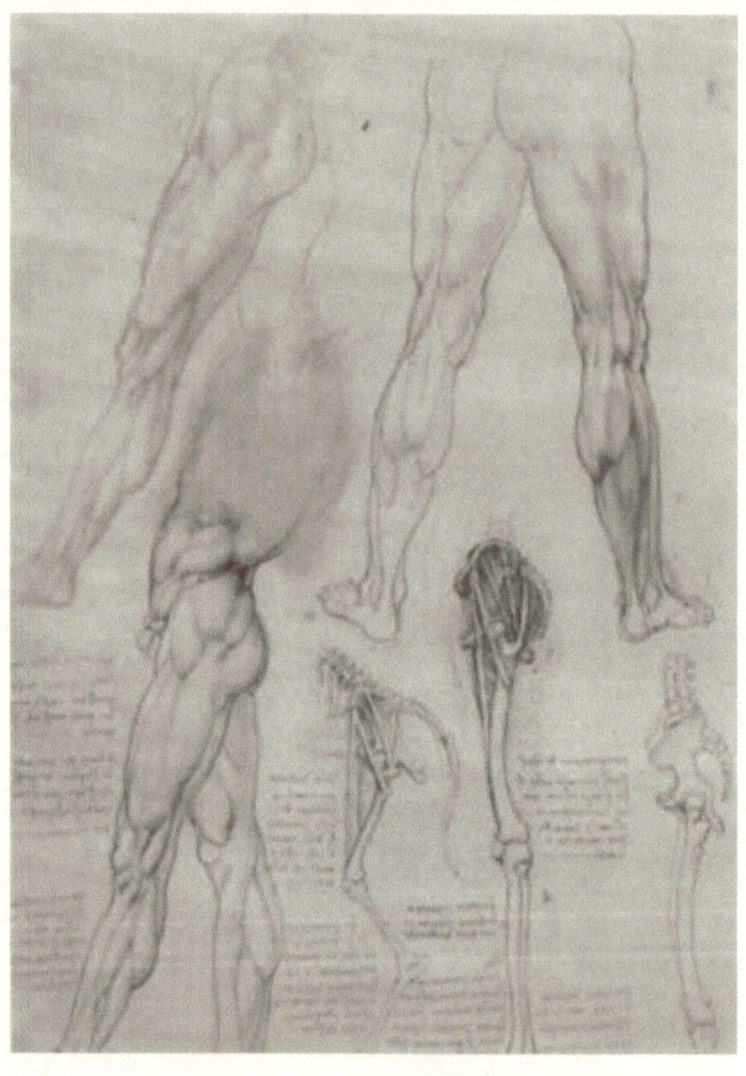

Studies of legs of man and the leg of a horse, c.1506, chalk, ink, Royal Collection, Windsor Castle, London, UK

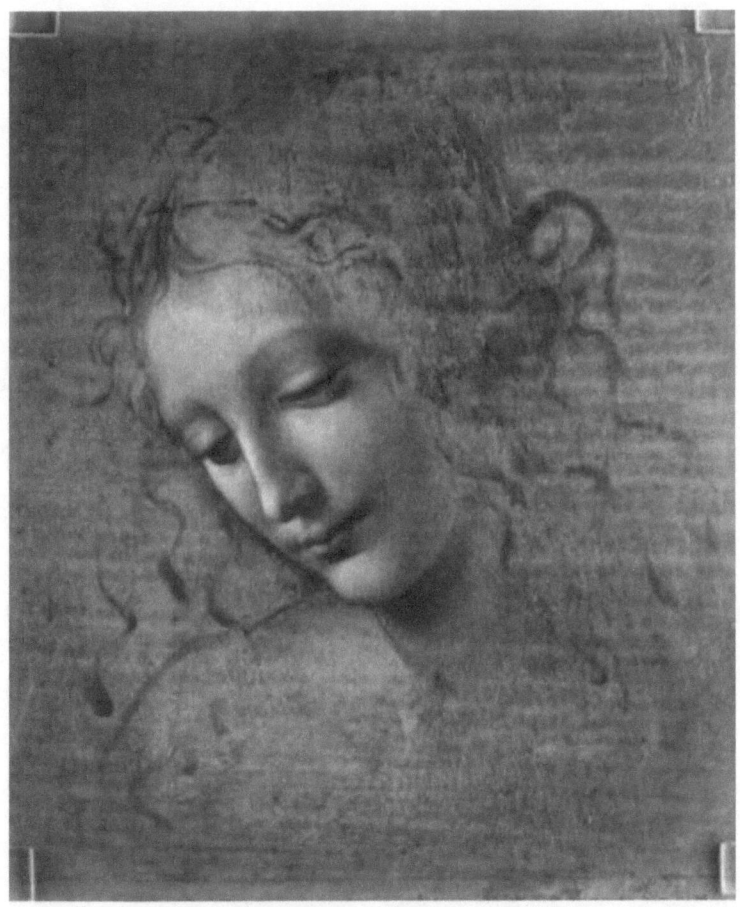

Head of a Young Woman with Tousled Hair (Leda),
c.1508, Galleria Nazionale, Parma, Italy

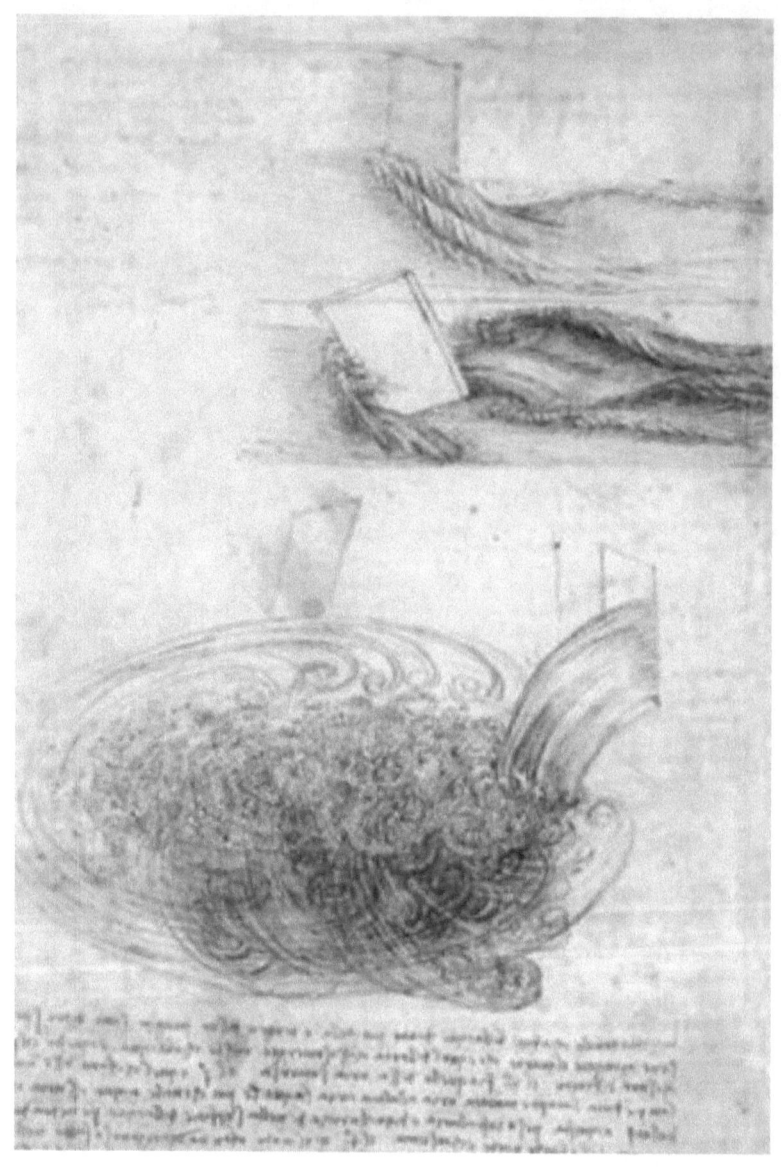

**Studies of Water passing Obstacles and falling,
c.1508, private Collection**

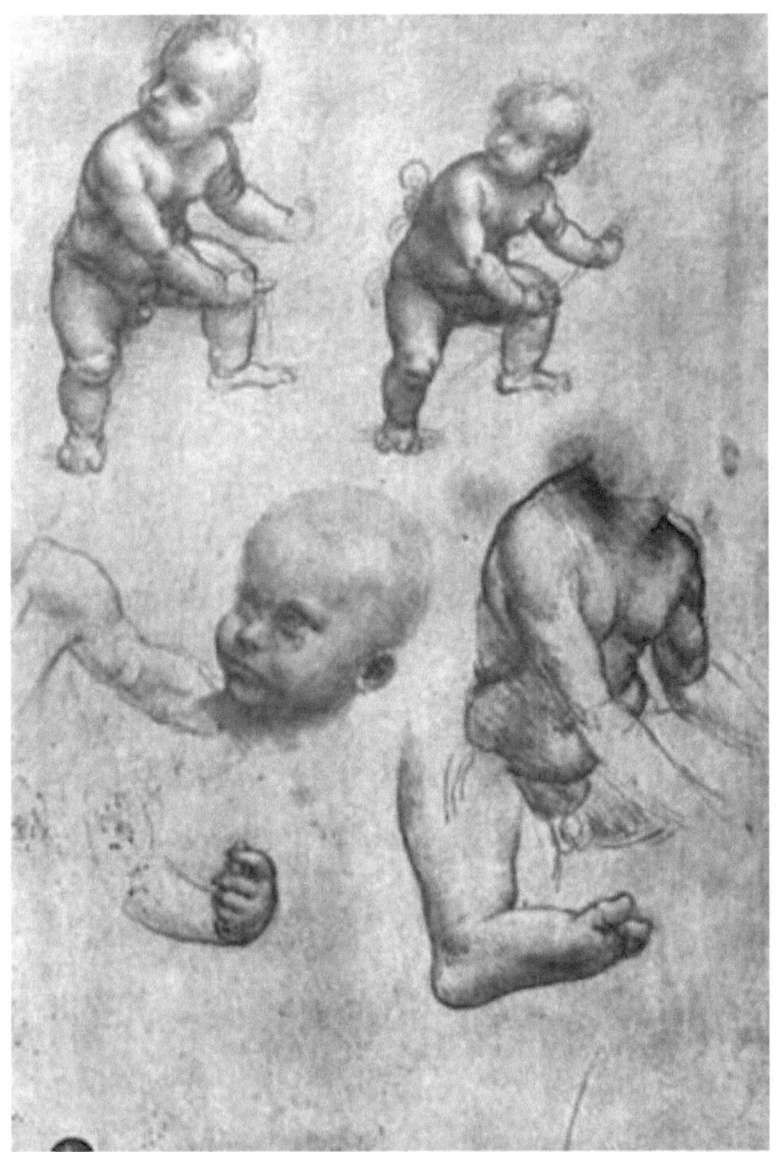

Study of a child, c.1508, chalk, Galleria degli Uffizi, Florence, Italy

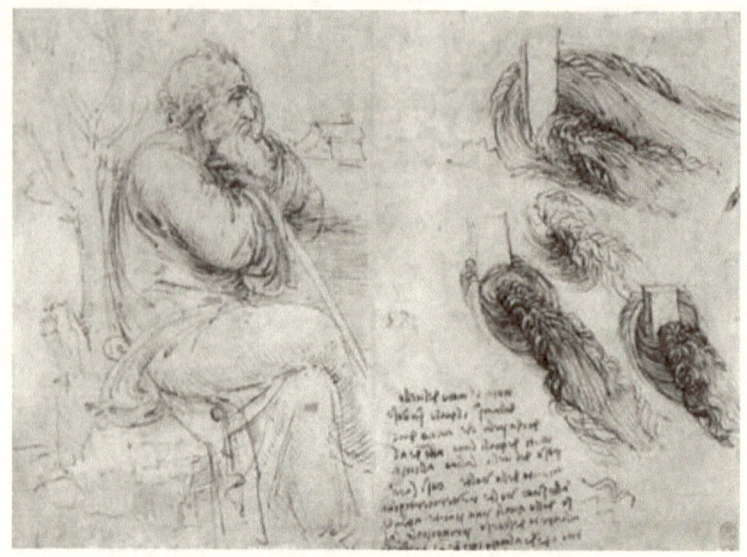

A seated man, and studies and notes on the movement of water, c.1510, ink, Royal Collection, Windsor Castle, London, UK

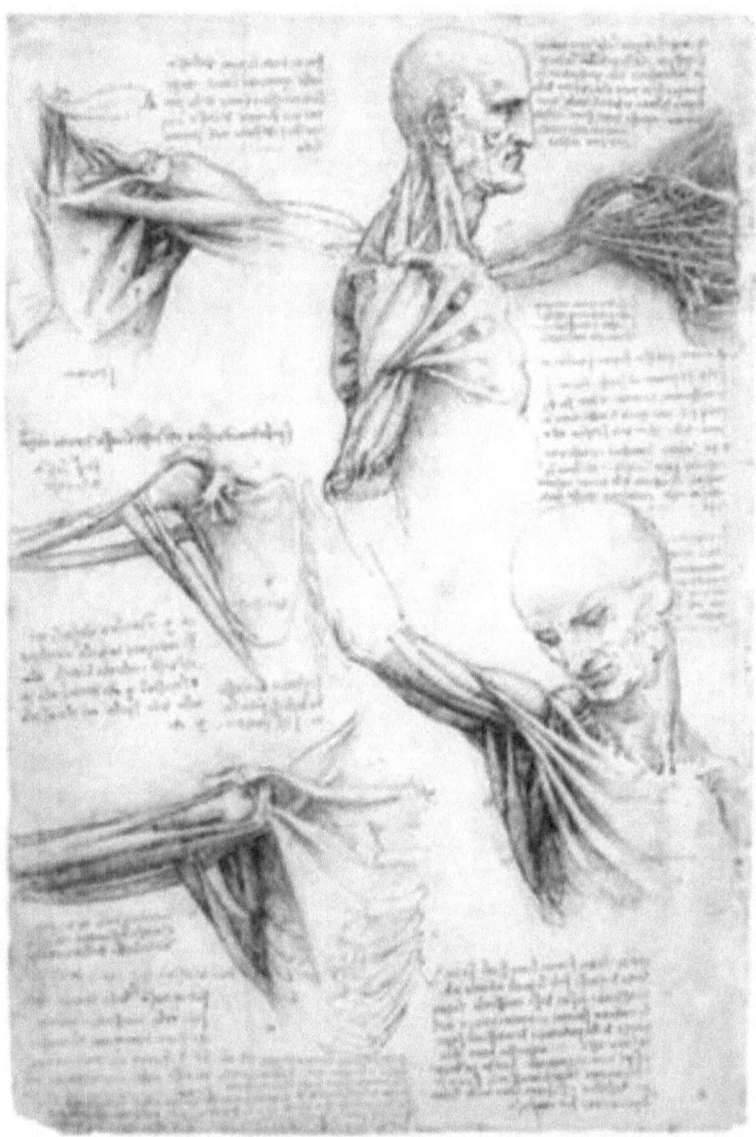

Anatomical studies of the shoulder, 1510, chalk, ink, Royal Collection, Windsor Castle, London, UK

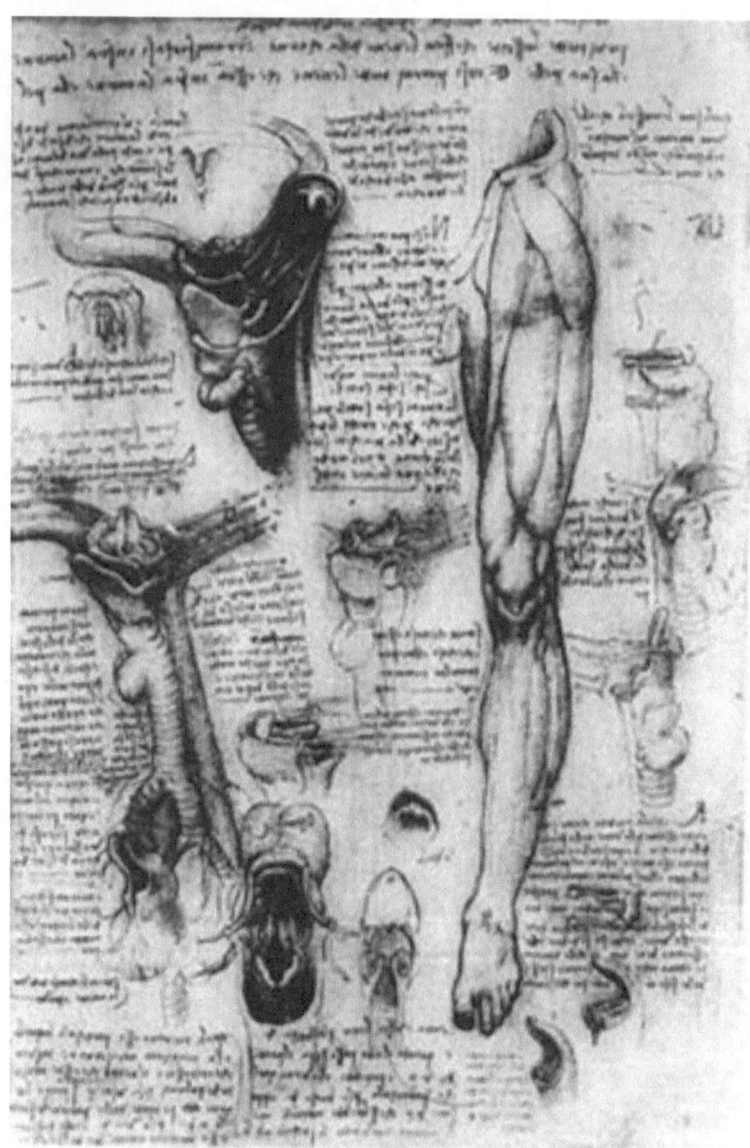

Anatomical studies (larynx and leg), 1510, ink, Royal Collection, Windsor Castle, London, UK

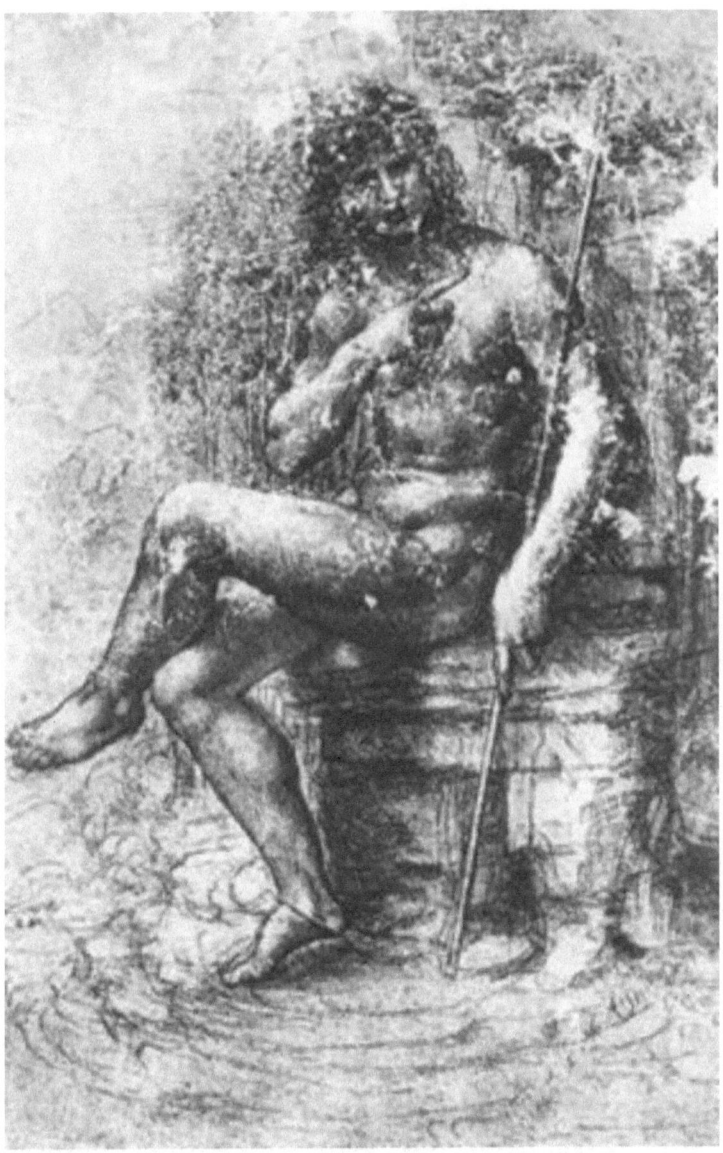

**Study for St. John in the Wilderness, 1510, chalk,
Museo del Sacromonte, Varese, Italy**

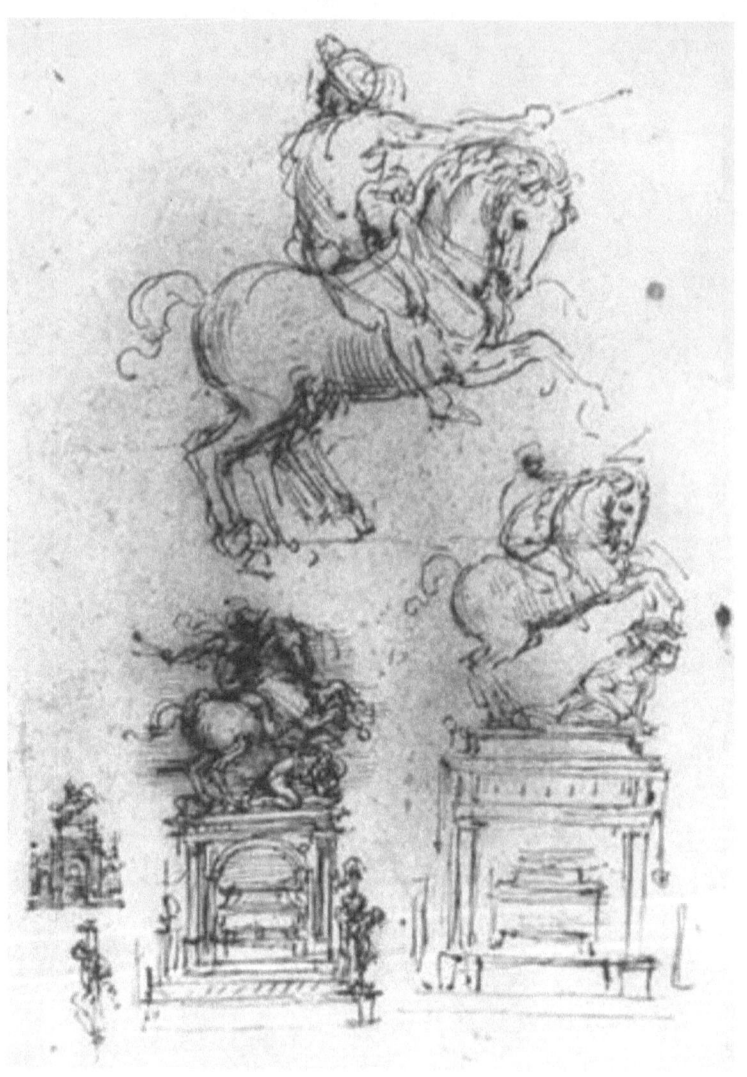

**Study for the Trivulzio Equestrian Monument, c.1510,
ink, Royal Collection, Windsor Castle, London**

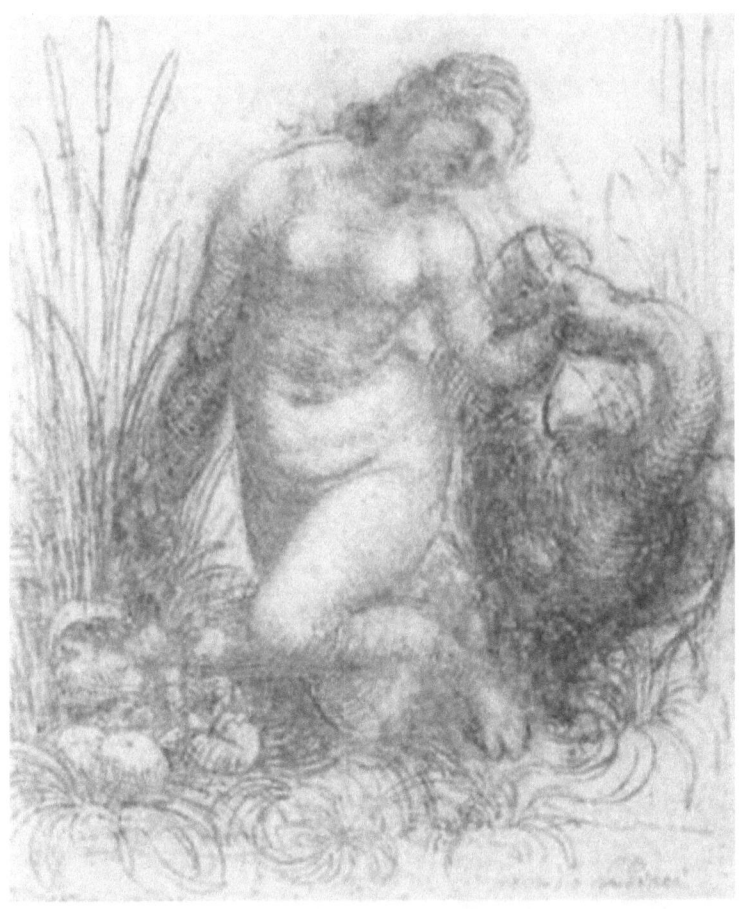

**Leda and the Swan, 1503-07, Pen and ink and wash
over black chalk on paper, 16 x 13.9 cm, Devonshire
Collection, Chatsworth**

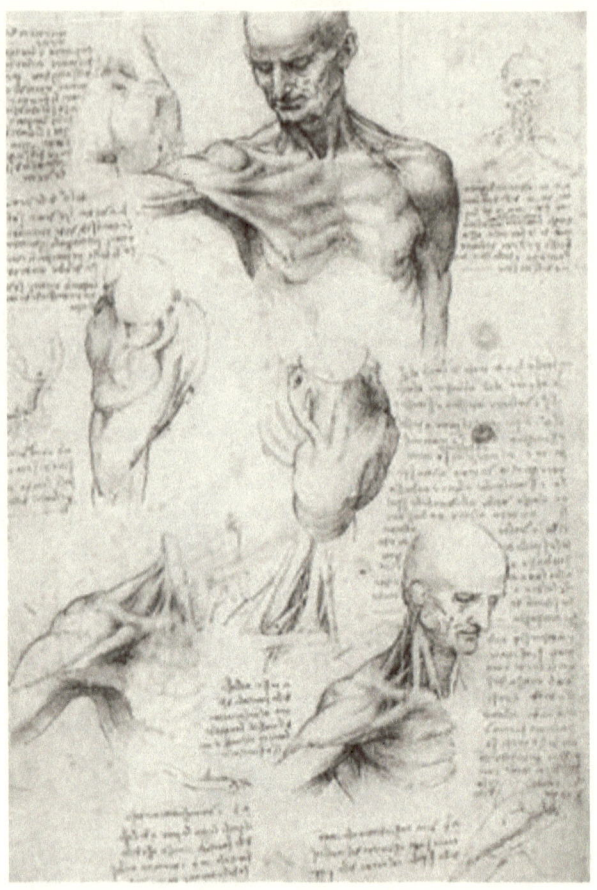

Anatomical studies of a male shoulder, 1509-10, Pen and ink on paper, 29.2 x 19.8 cm, Royal Library, Windsor

Leonardo left hundreds of notebooks filled with drawings in which he explored ideas, compositions, or inventions. His curiosity led him to sketch and puzzle out diverse subjects, such as running water, growing plants, and human anatomy.

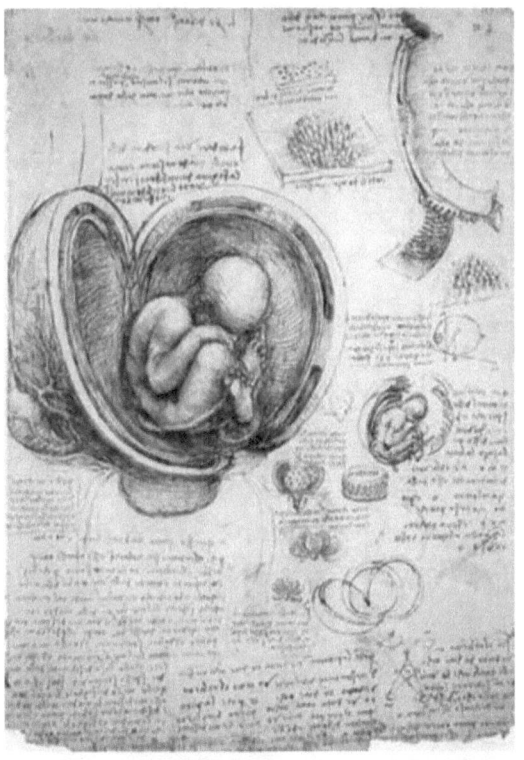

Studies of embryos, 1509-14, Black and red chalk, pen and ink wash on paper, 30.5 x 22 cm, Royal Library, Windsor

The sheet includes studies from a number of years. The note "book on water to Mr. Marcho Ant" refers to the anatomical expert Marcantonio della Torre, who died in Pisa in 1511 and with whom Leonardo carried out dissections of human bodies. This drawing of the fetus was the result of knowledge rather than direct observation of nature. Leonardo had examined the fetus of a cow and allowed his observations of the placenta to influence this drawing.

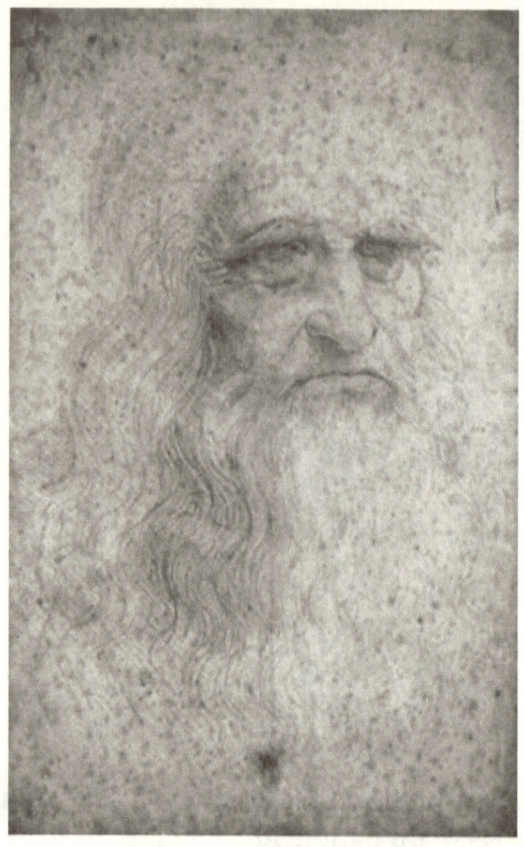

Self-Portrait, c. 1512, Red chalk on paper, 33.3 x 21.3 cm, Biblioteca Reale, Turin

A hand-written note from the 16th century titles the drawing "Leonardus Vincius (in red chalk) self-portrait at an advanced age (in charcoal)," so that its interpretation as Leonardo's self-portrait during the last years of his life is generally accepted nowadays. It is reminiscent of Gianpaolo Lomazzo's words from the late 16th century: *"Leonardo's hair and beard were so long, and his eyebrows were so bushy, that he appeared to be the sheer idea of noble wisdom."*

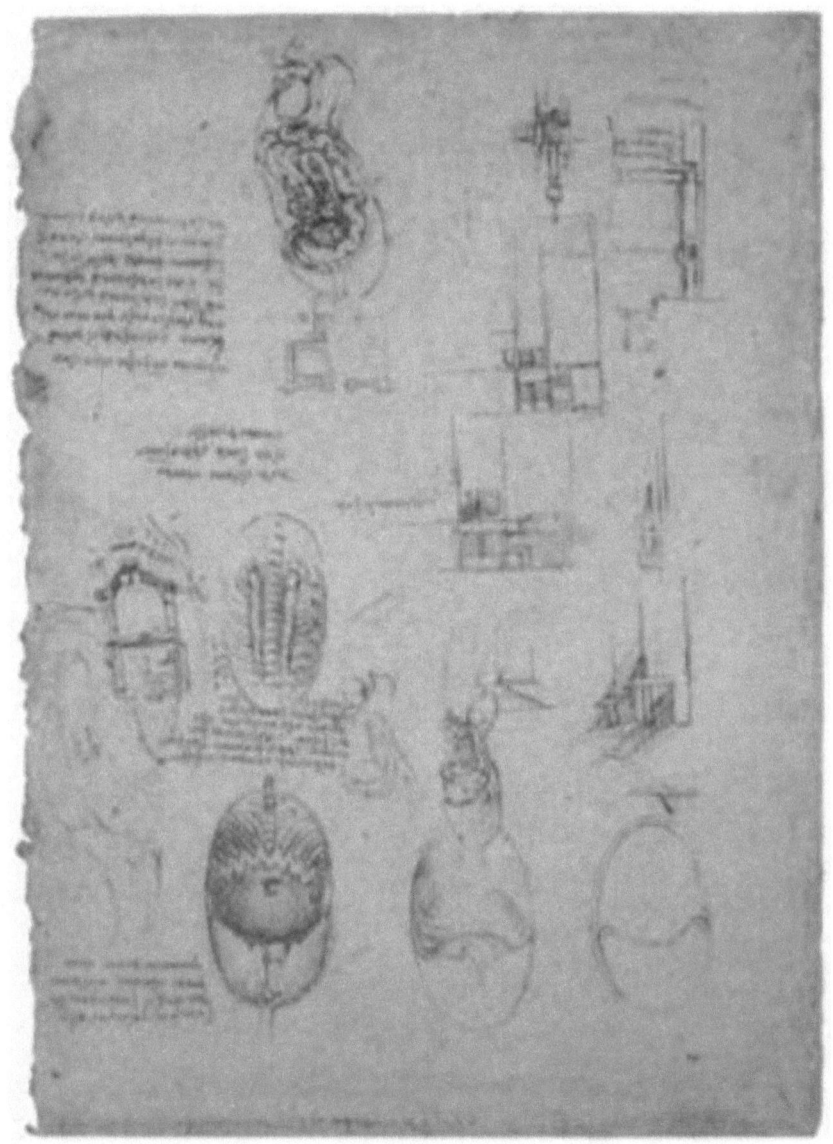

**Studies of the Villa Melzi and anatomical study, 1513,
ink, Royal Collection, Windsor Castle, London, UK**

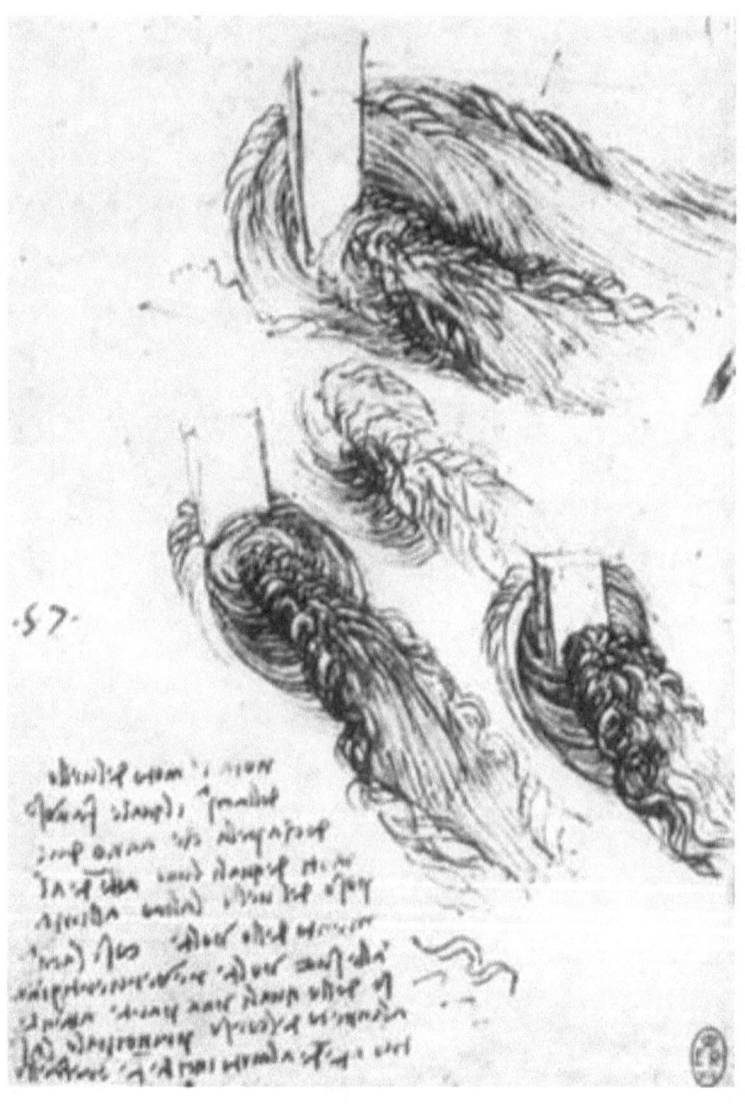

Study of water, c.1513, ink, Royal Collection, Windsor Castle, London, UK

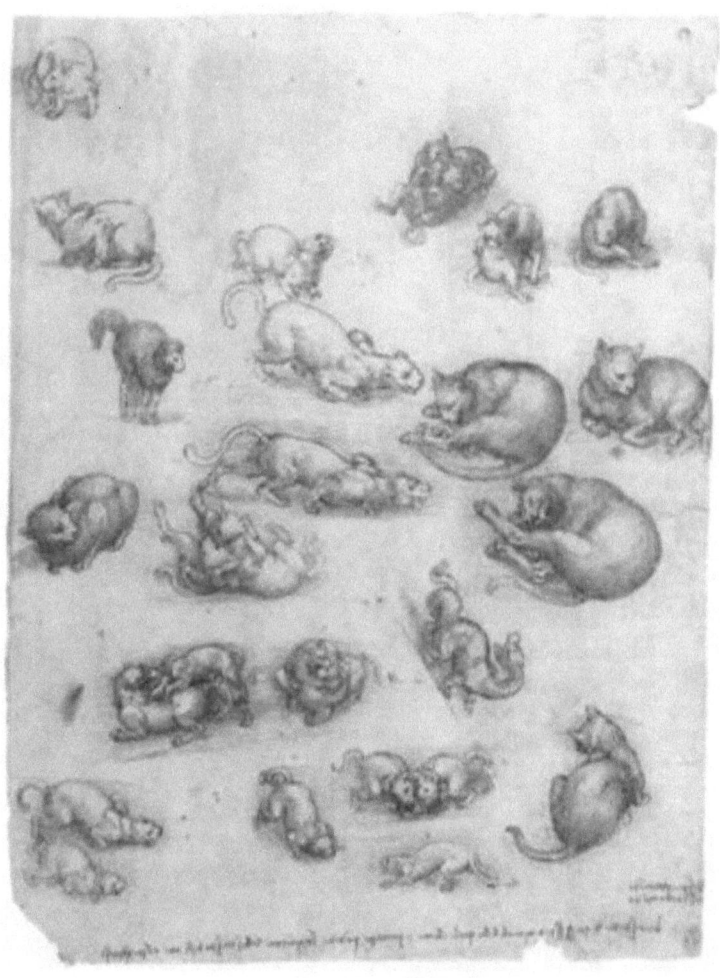

**Study sheet with cats, dragon and other animals,
c.1513, chalk, ink, Royal Collection, Windsor Castle,
London, UK**

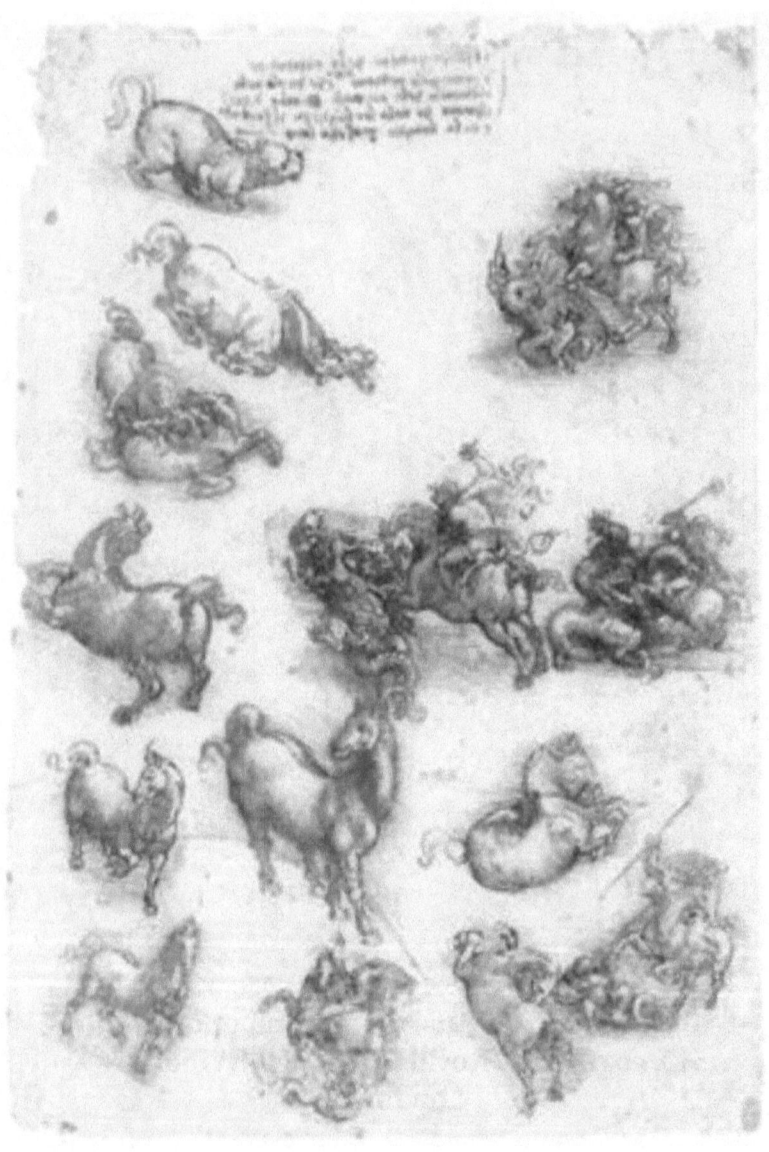

**Study sheet with horses, c.1513, chalk, ink, Royal
Collection, Windsor Castle, London, UK**

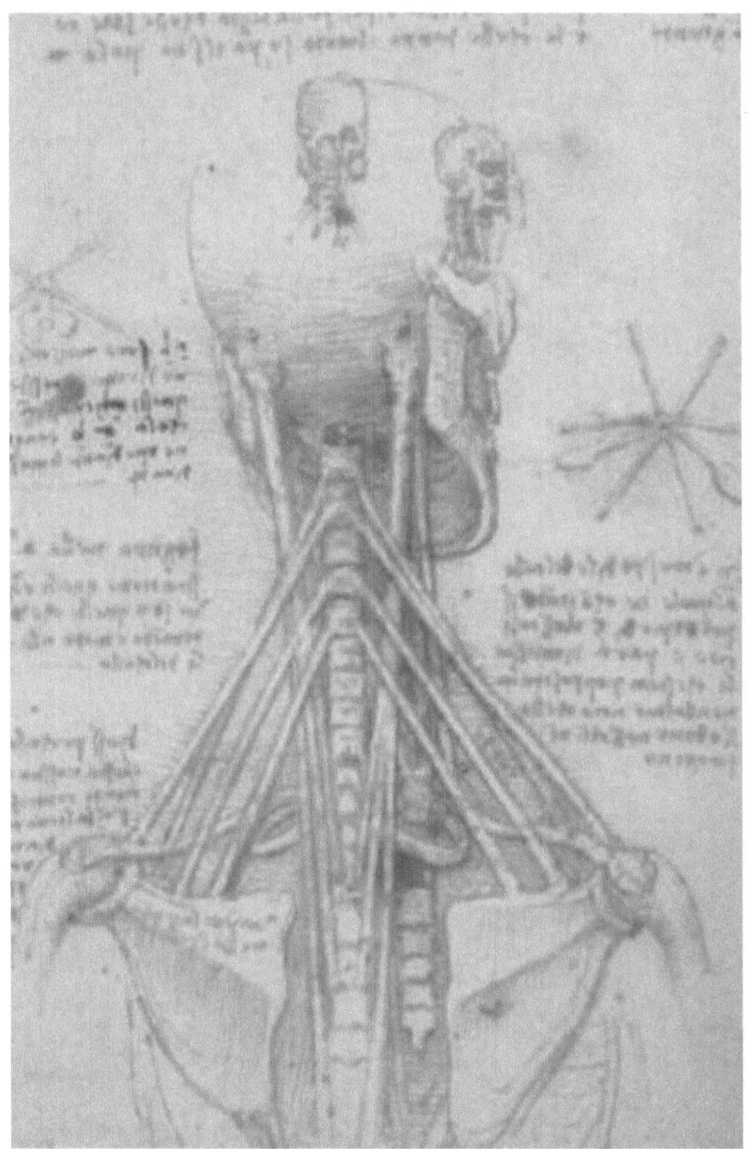

Anatomy of the Neck, 1515, chalk

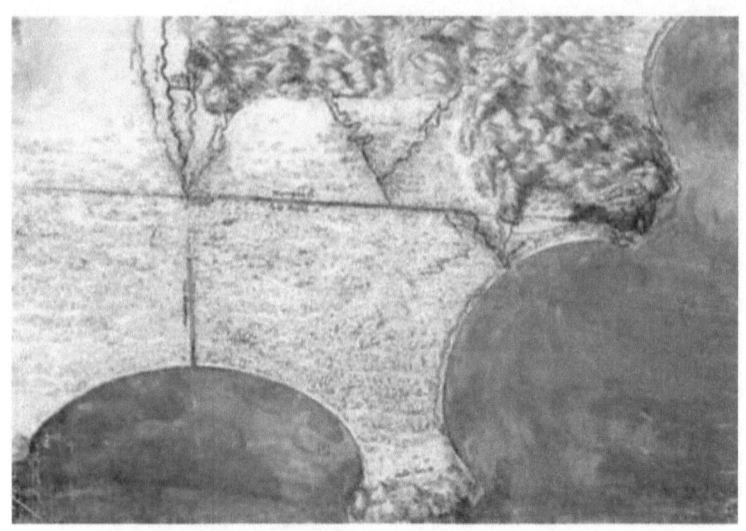

**Bird's eye view of sea coast, c.1515, ink, Royal
Collection, Windsor Castle, London**

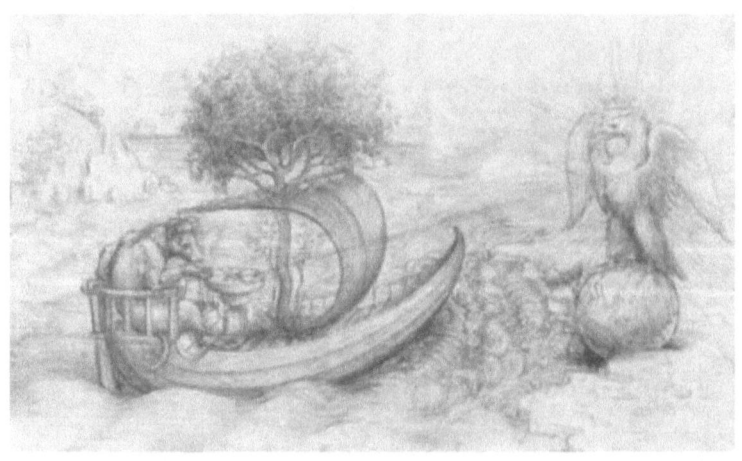

**Allegory, c.1516, chalk, Royal Collection, Windsor
Castle, London**

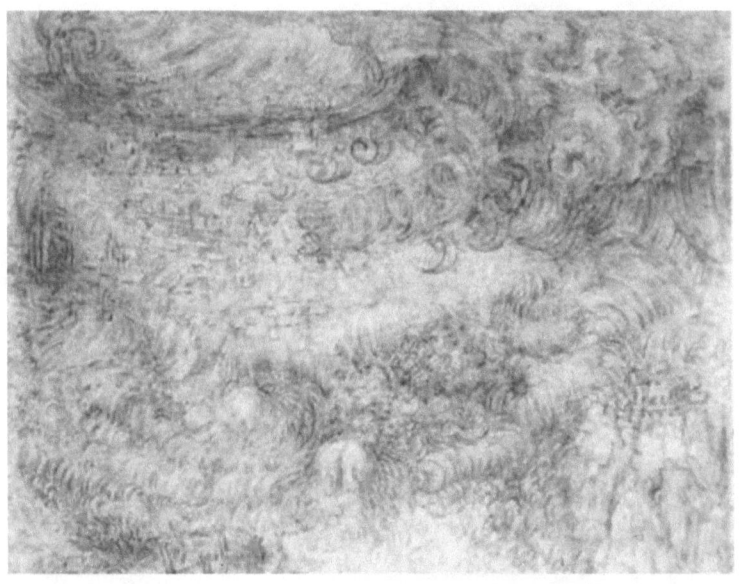

Deluge over a city, c.1517, chalk, Royal Collection,
Windsor Castle, London

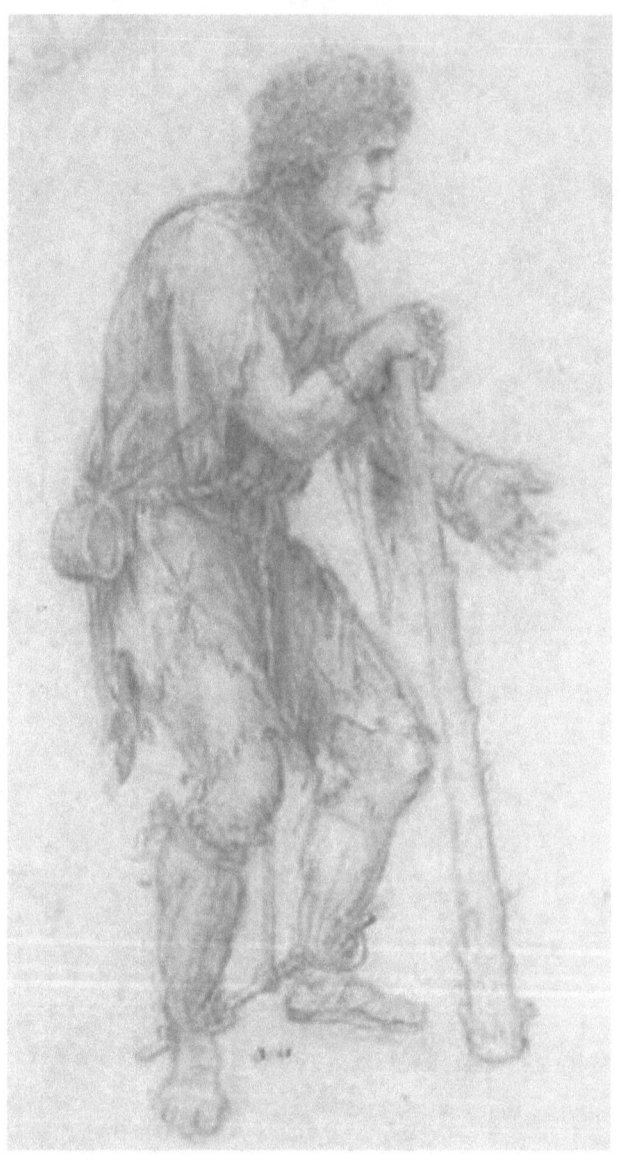

**Masquerader in the guise of a Prisoner, c.1517, chalk,
Royal Collection, Windsor Castle, London**

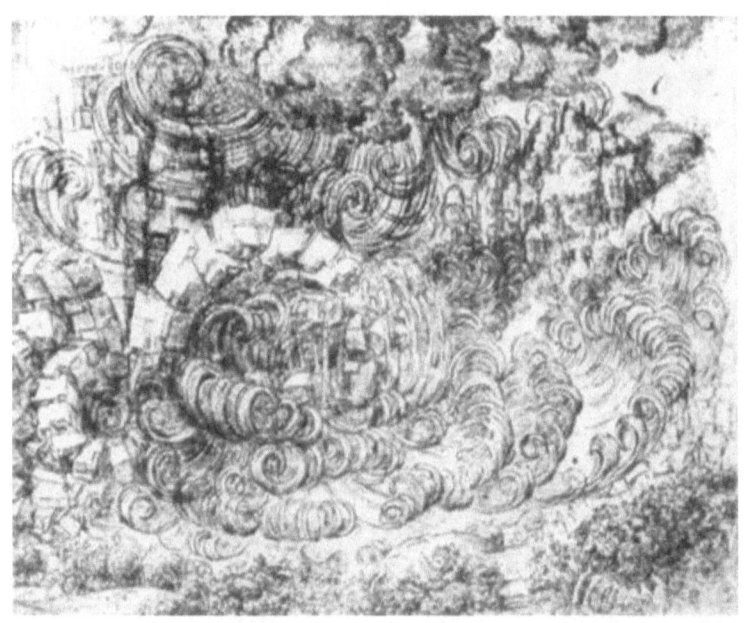

Natural disaster, c.1517, chalk, ink, Royal Collection,
Windsor Castle, London

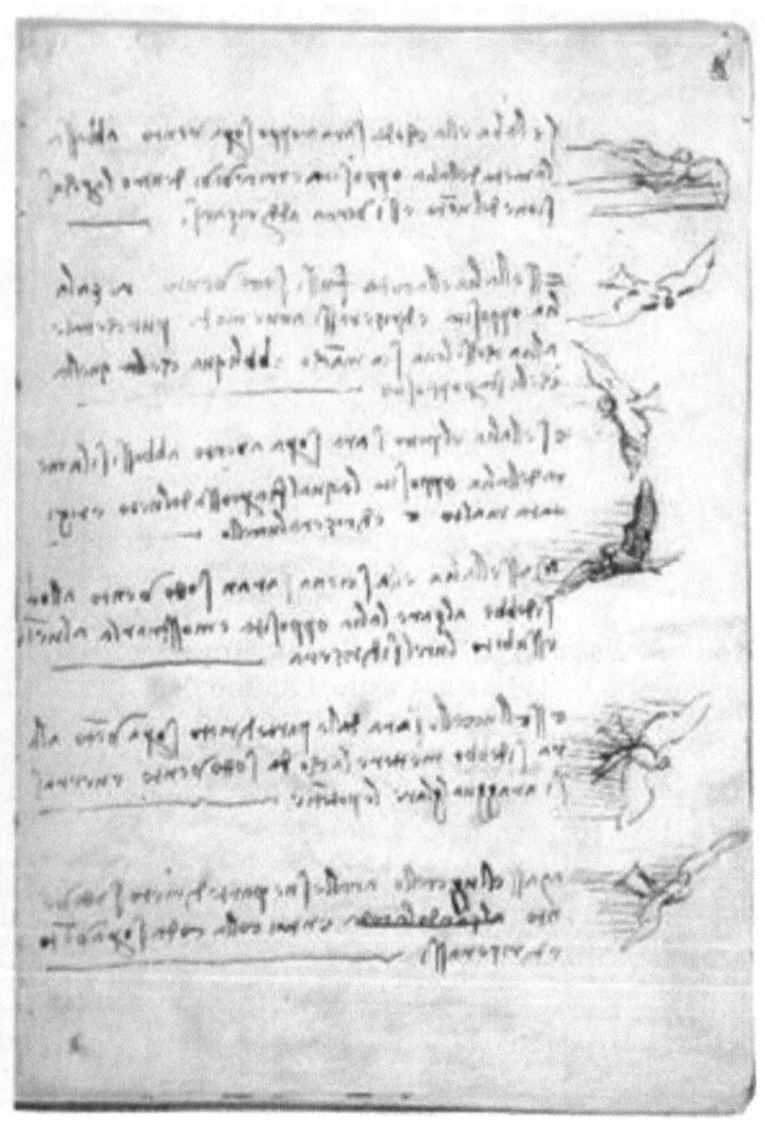

Codex on the flight of birds, n.d., Biblioteca Reale, Turin, Italy

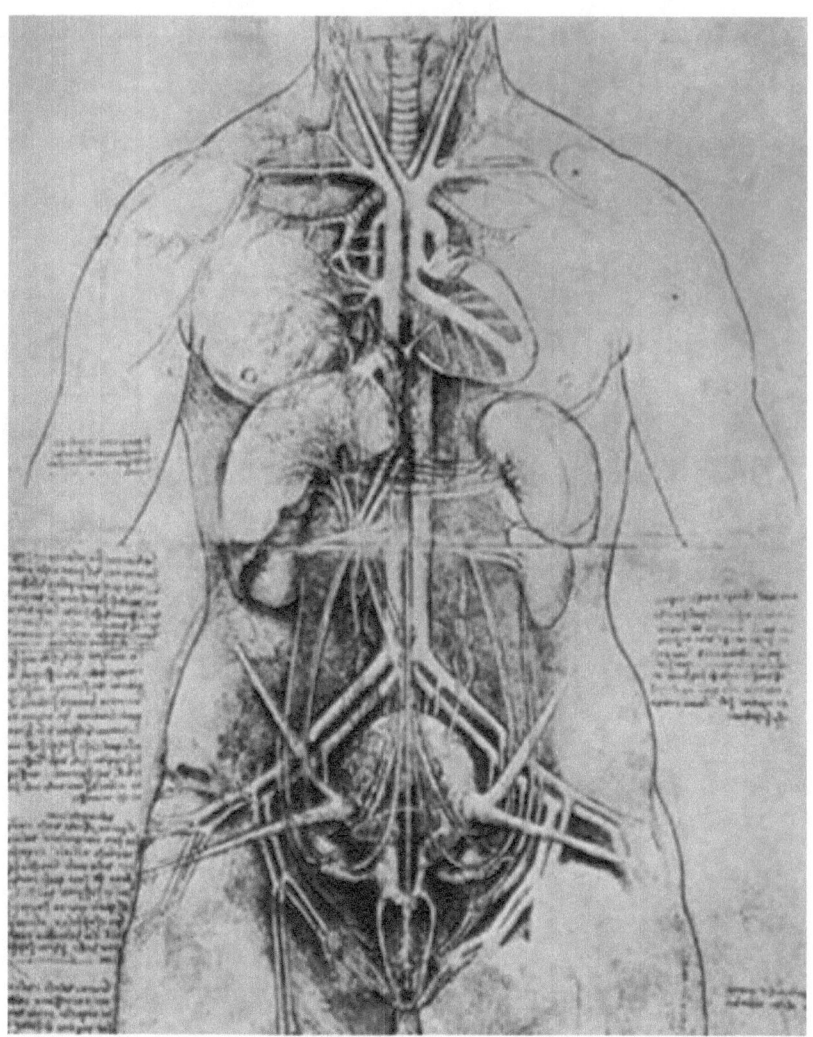

Drawing of a Woman's Torso, n.d., ink, Biblioteca
Ambrosiana, Milan, Italy

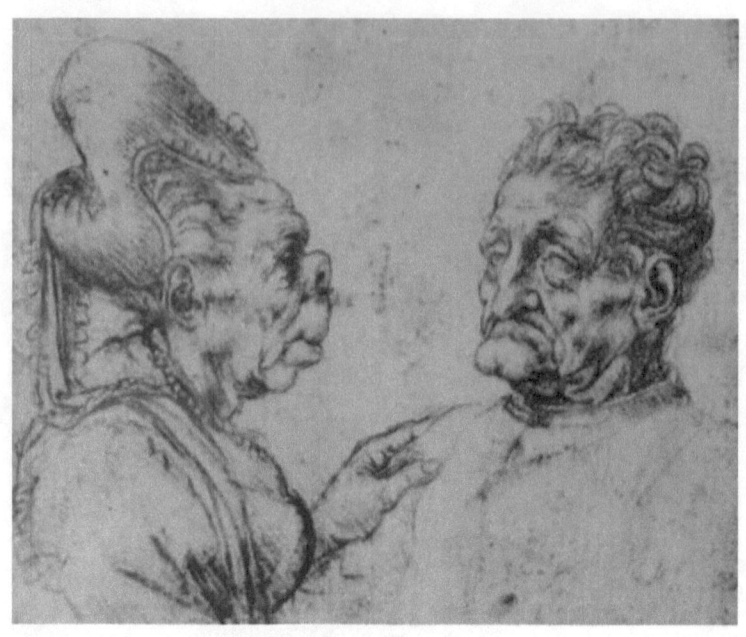

Caricature, n.d., ink, Galleria degli Uffizi, Florence, Italy

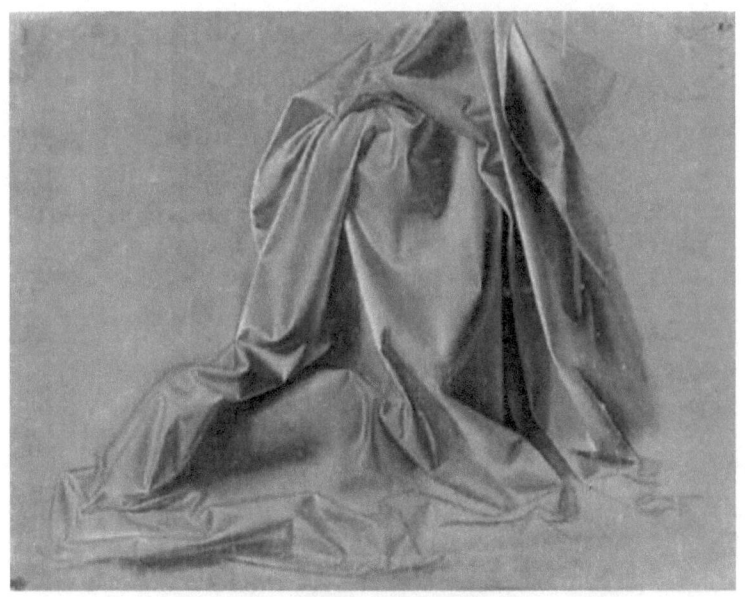

Drapery for a seated figure, n.d., tempera, Musée du
Louvre, Paris, France

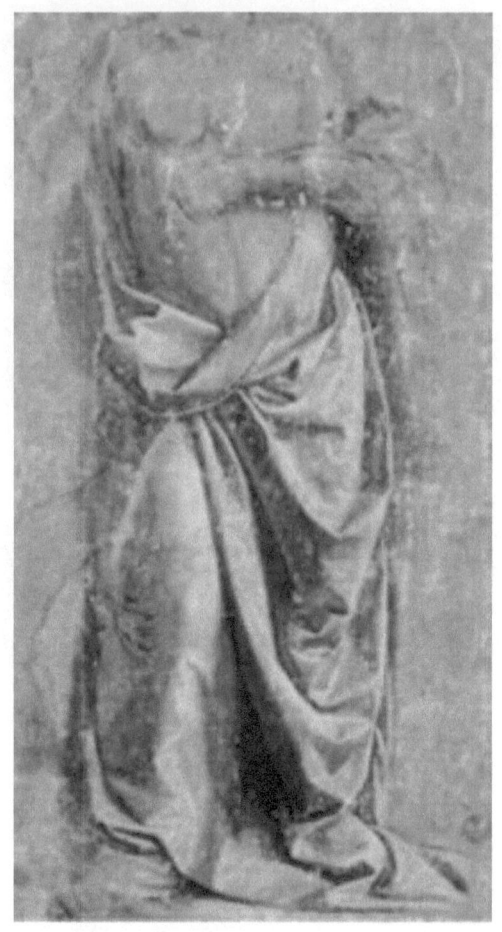

Drapery Study for a Standing Figure Seen from the Front

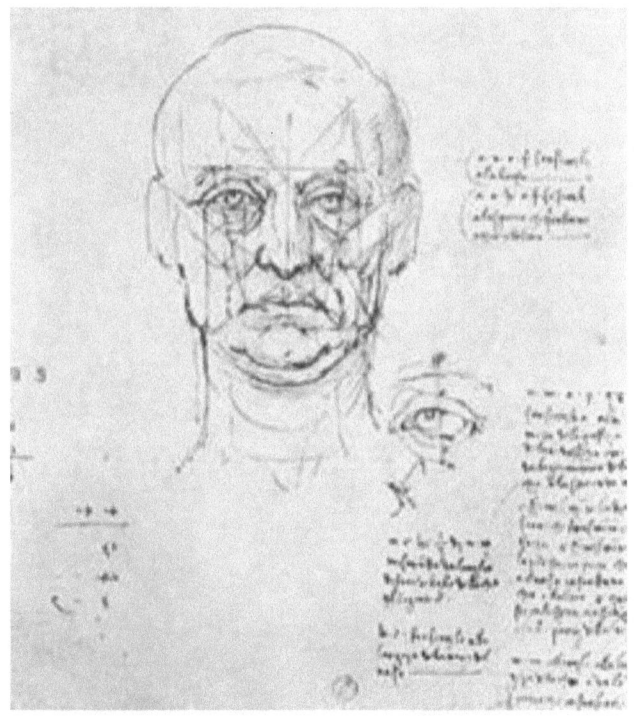

Studies of the Proportions of the Face and Eye

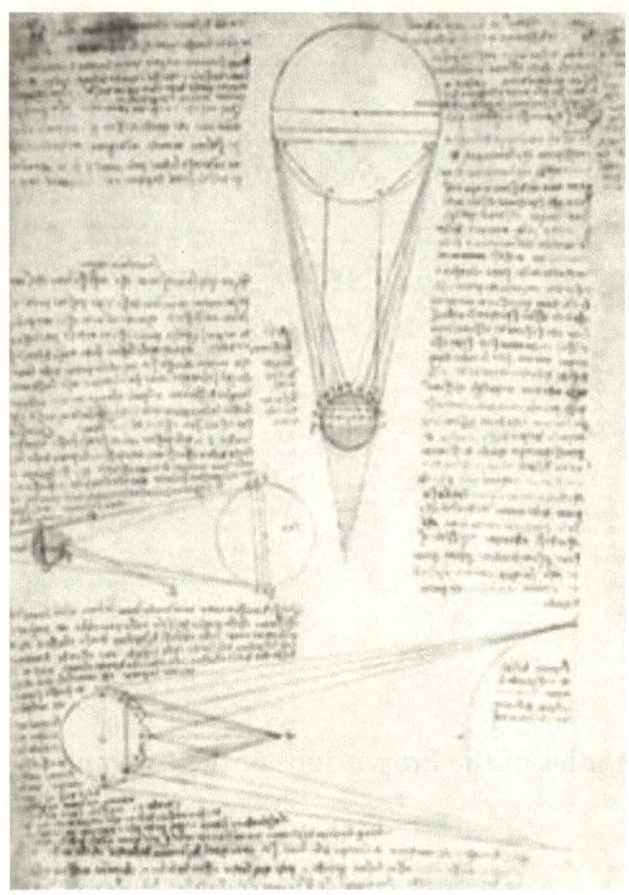

Studies of the Illumination of the Moon 1r from Codex Leicester

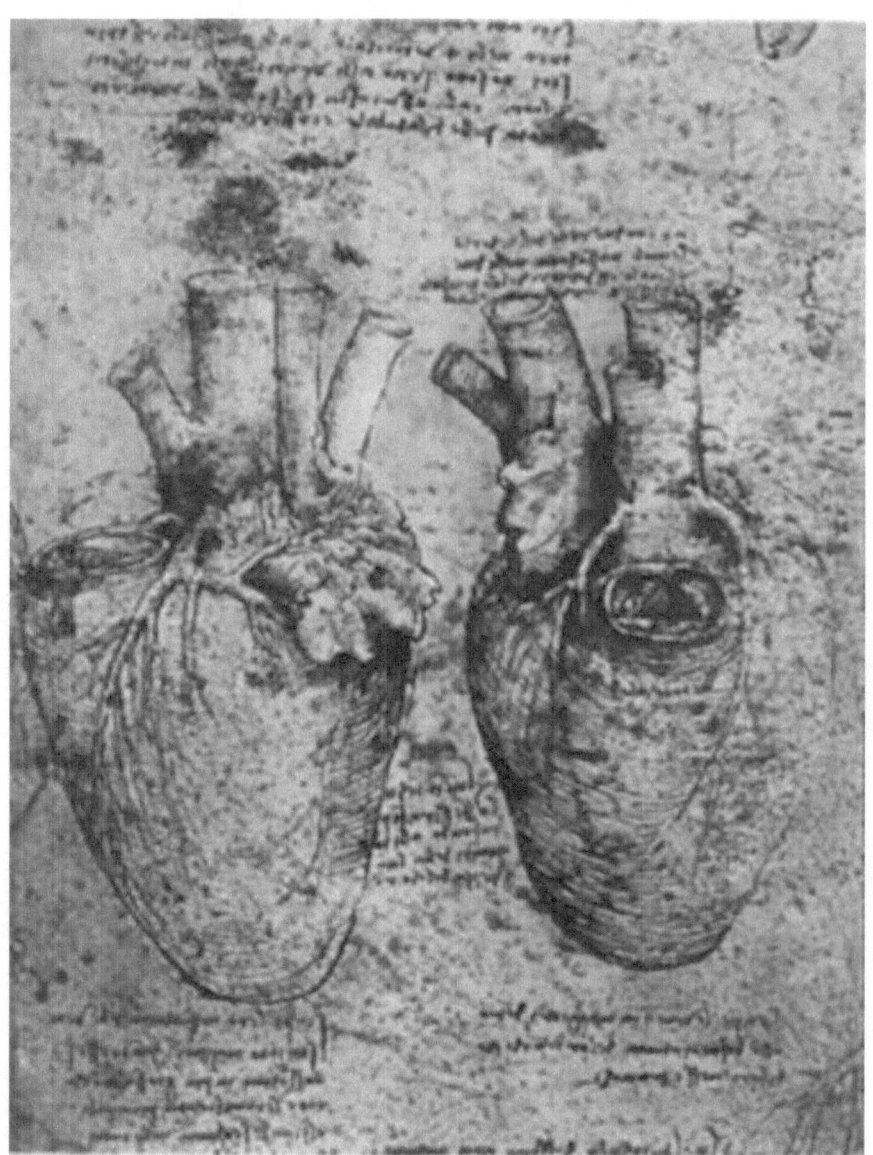

Heart and its Blood Vessels, n.d., Biblioteca
Ambrosiana, Milan, Italy

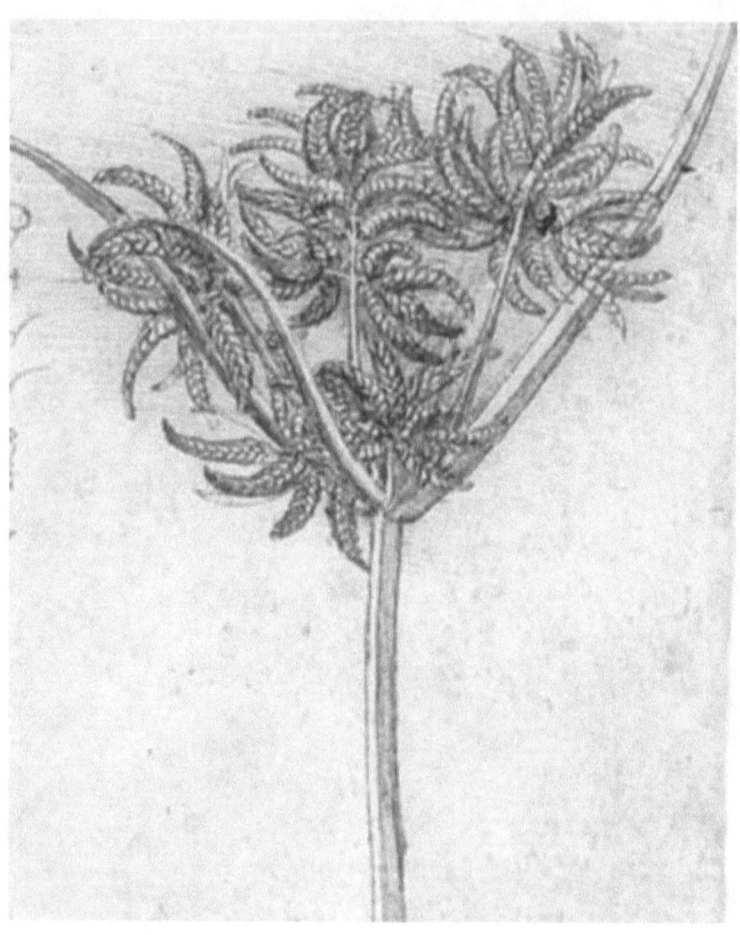

Sedge, n.d., pencil

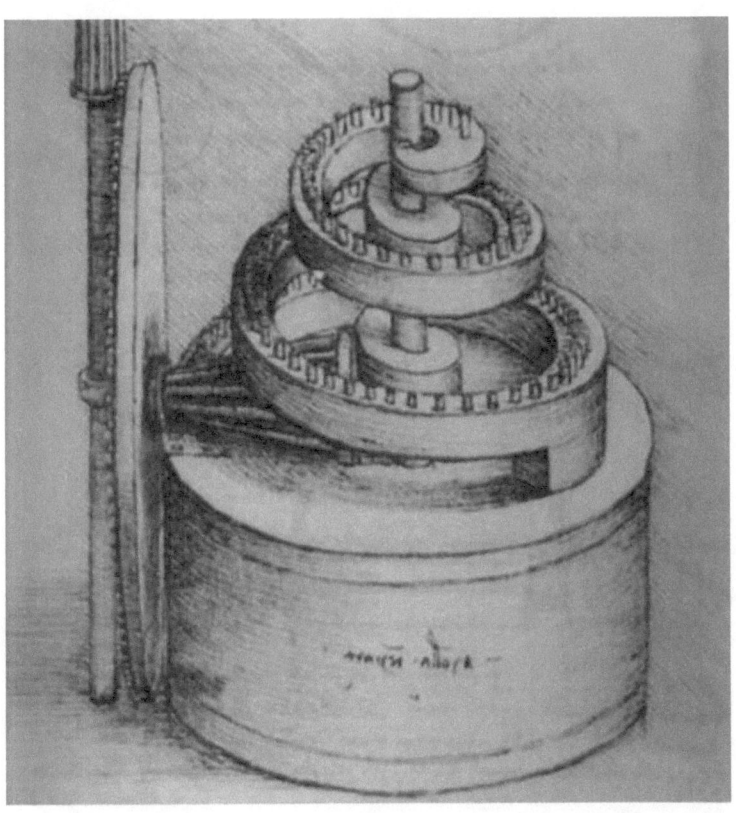

Spring Device, n.d., ink, Museo del Prado, Madrid,
Spain

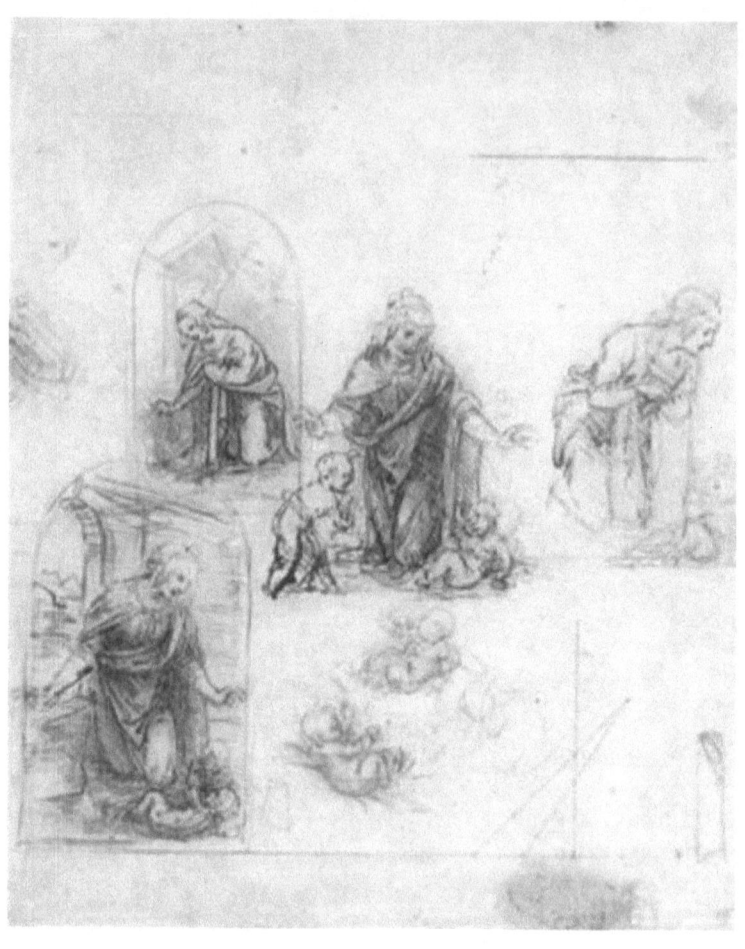

Studies for a Nativity, n.d., Metropolitan Museum of Art, New York City

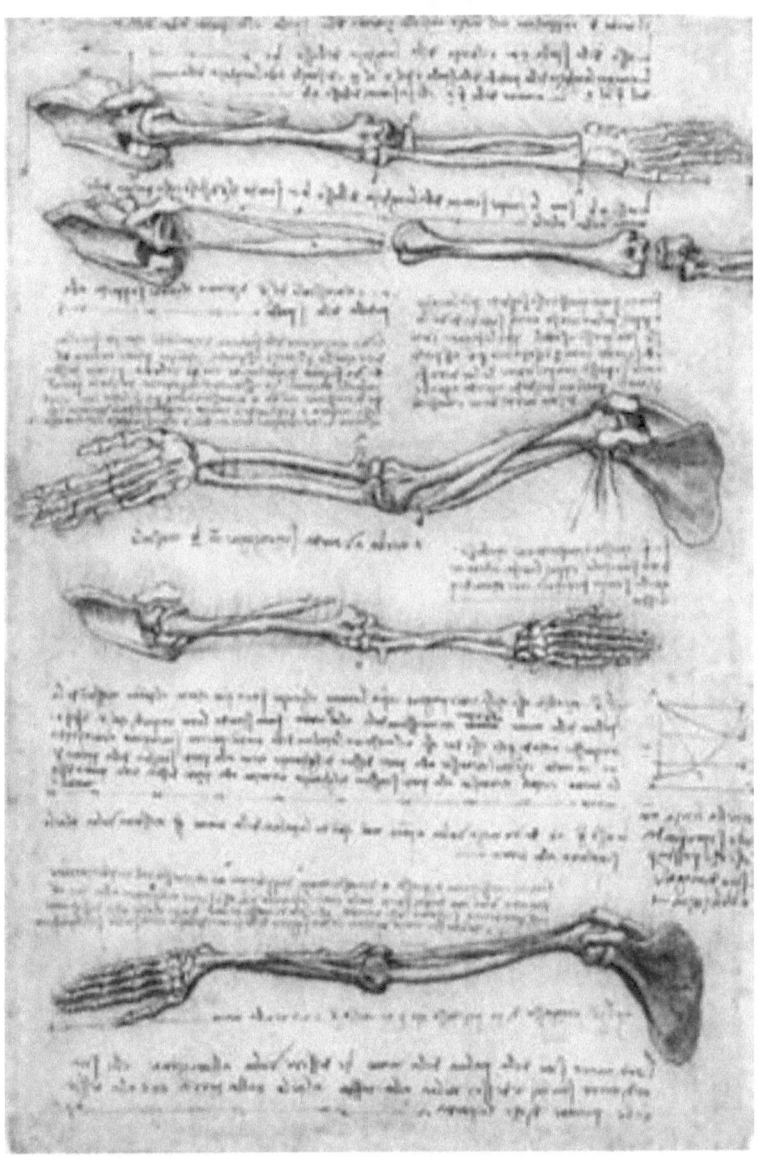

Studies of the Arm showing the Movements made by the Biceps, n.d., ink

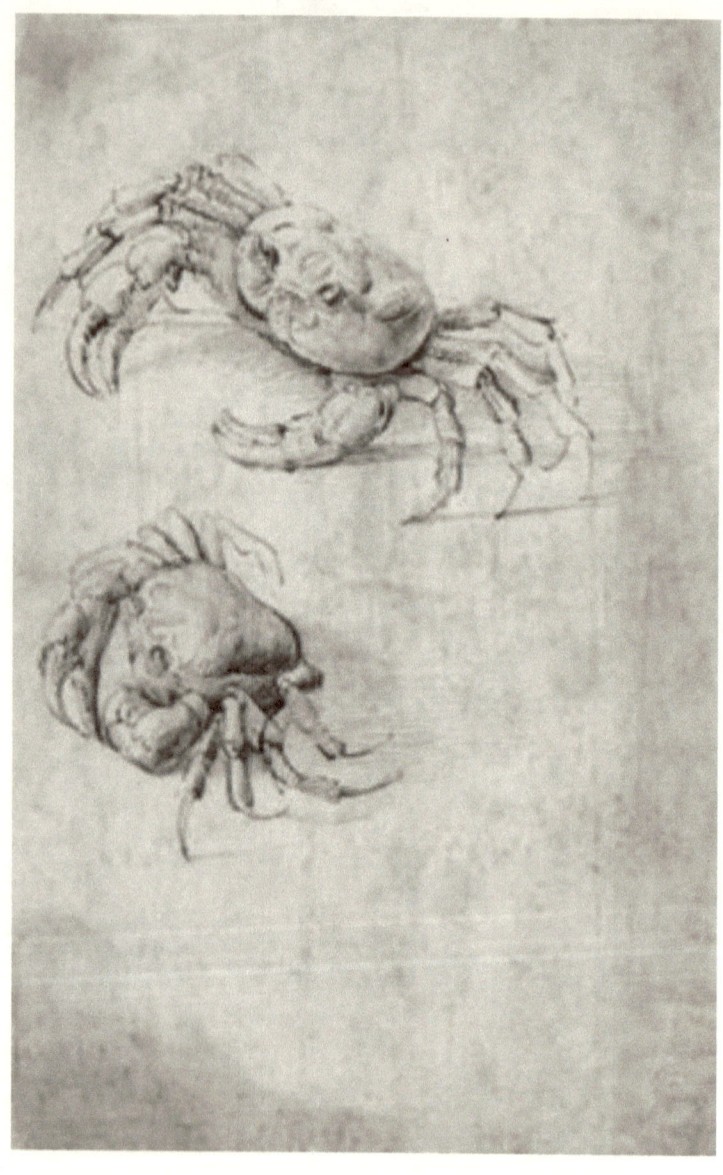

Studies of crabs, ink, Wallraf-Richartz Museum, Cologne, Germany

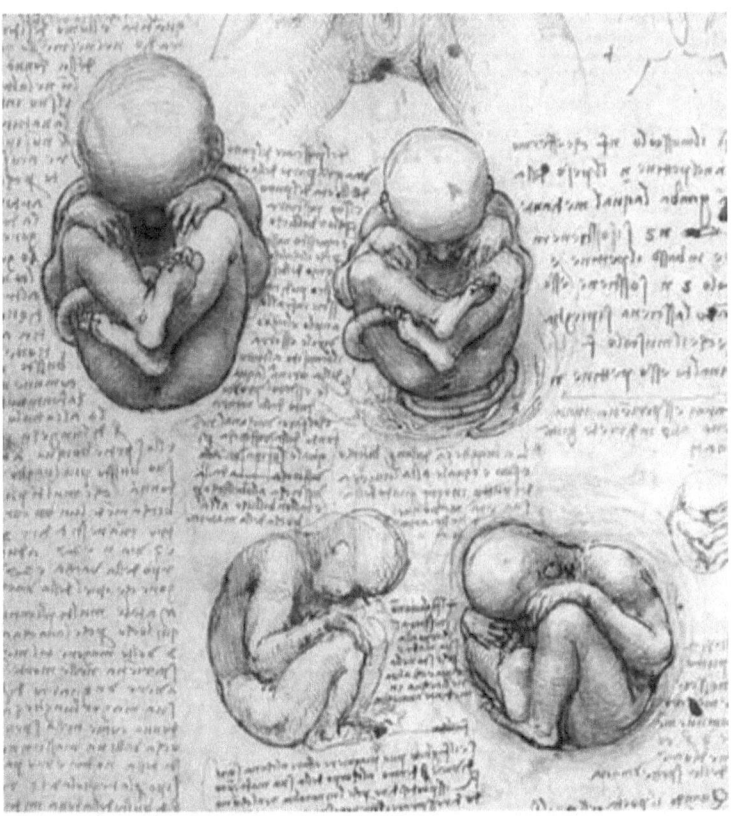

Views of a Foetus in the Womb, n.d., ink, chalk

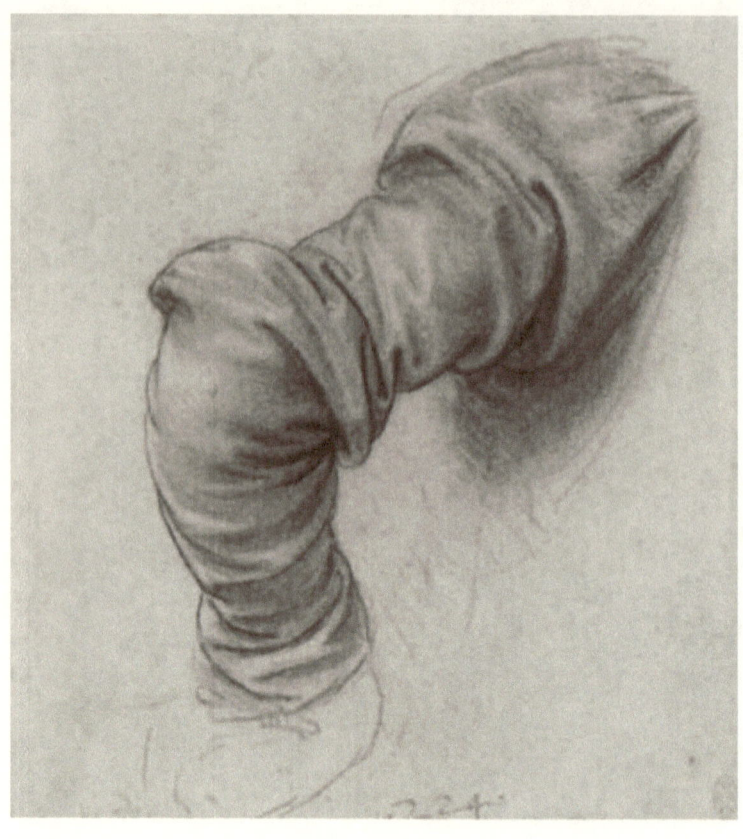

Drapery Study for the Right Sleeve of Saint Peter, n.d., chalk

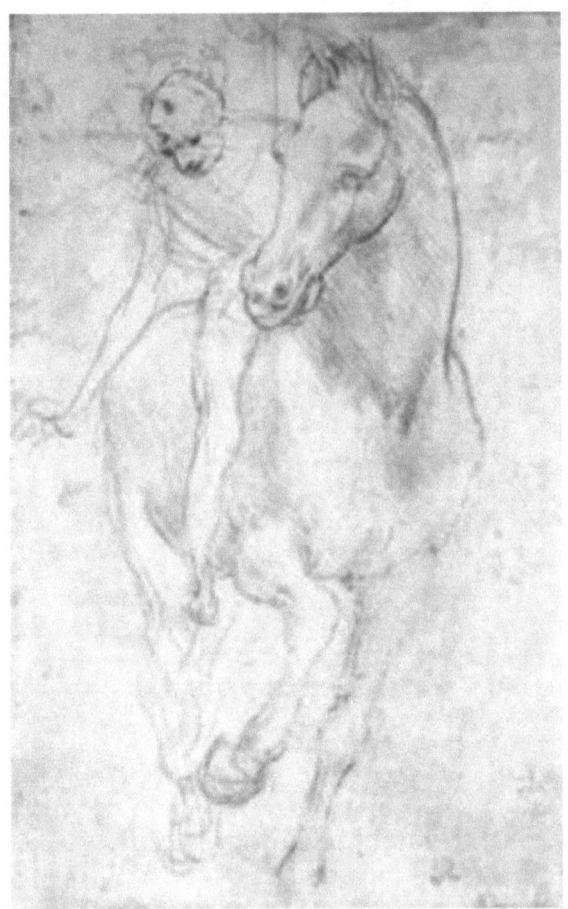

Study of a Horse and Rider, n.d., chalk

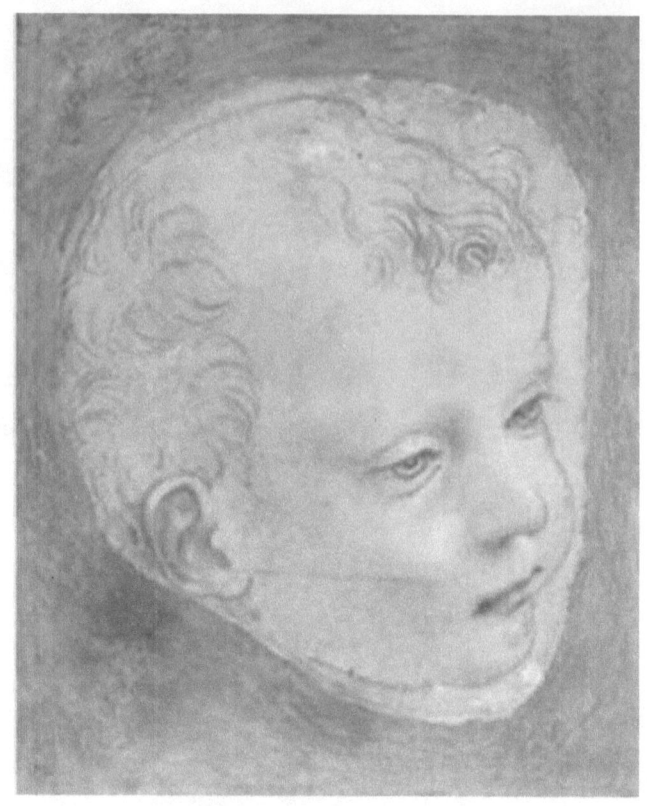

Head of a Child, n.d., ink

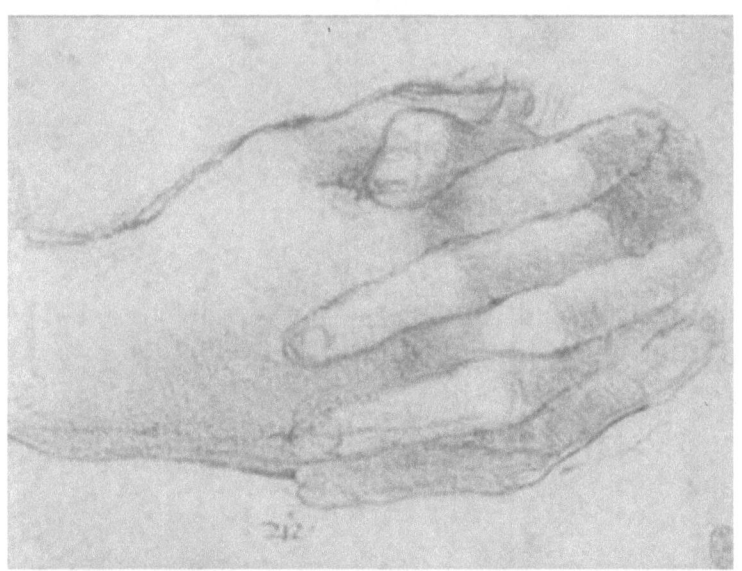

Study for the Hands of Saint John, n.d., chalk

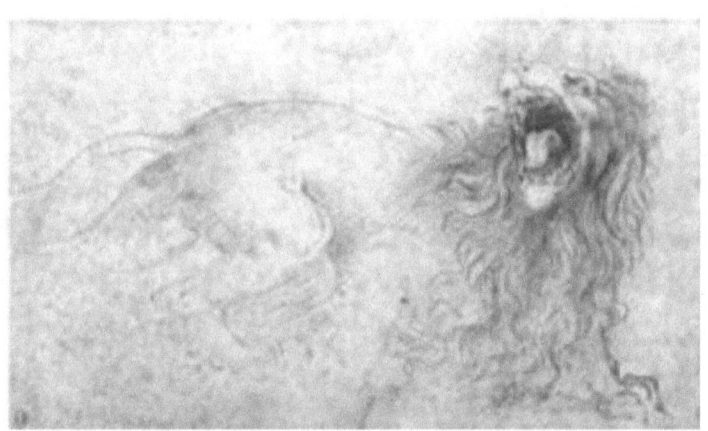

Sketch of a roaring lion, n.d., ink

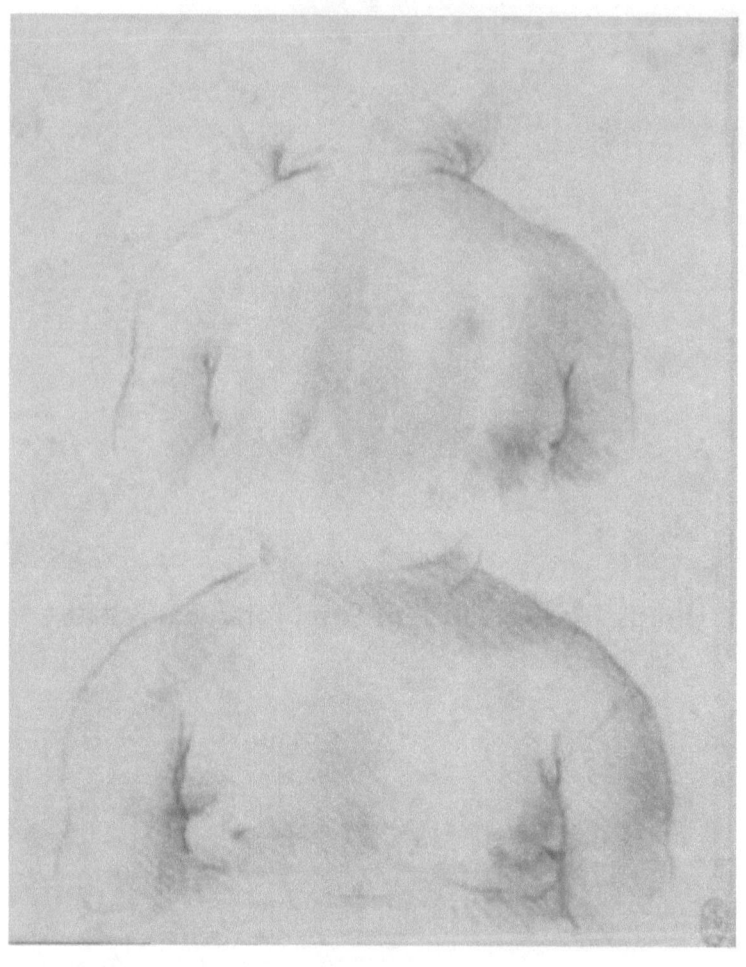

Torso and Shoulders of a Child Seen from Front and Back, n.d., chalk

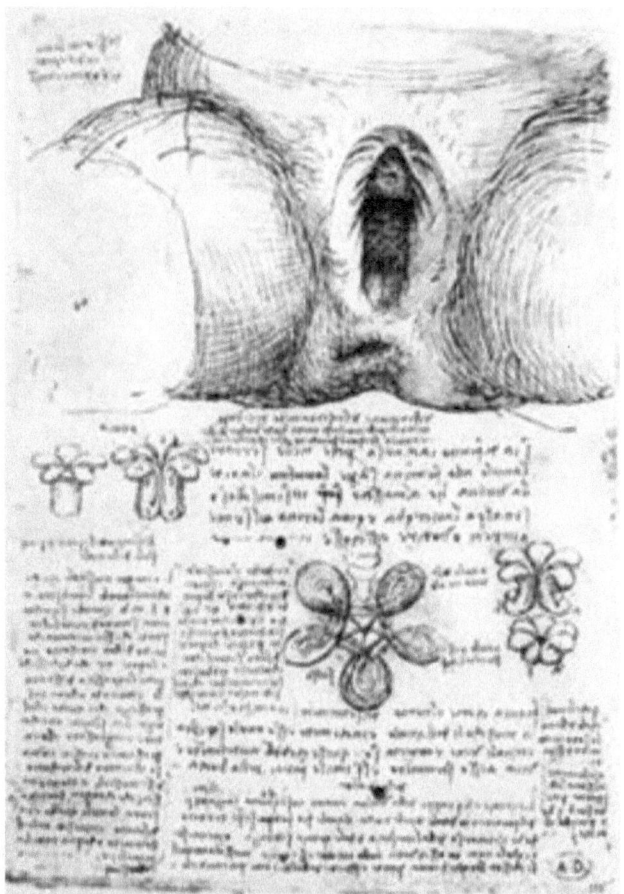

The Female Sexual Organs, n.d., ink

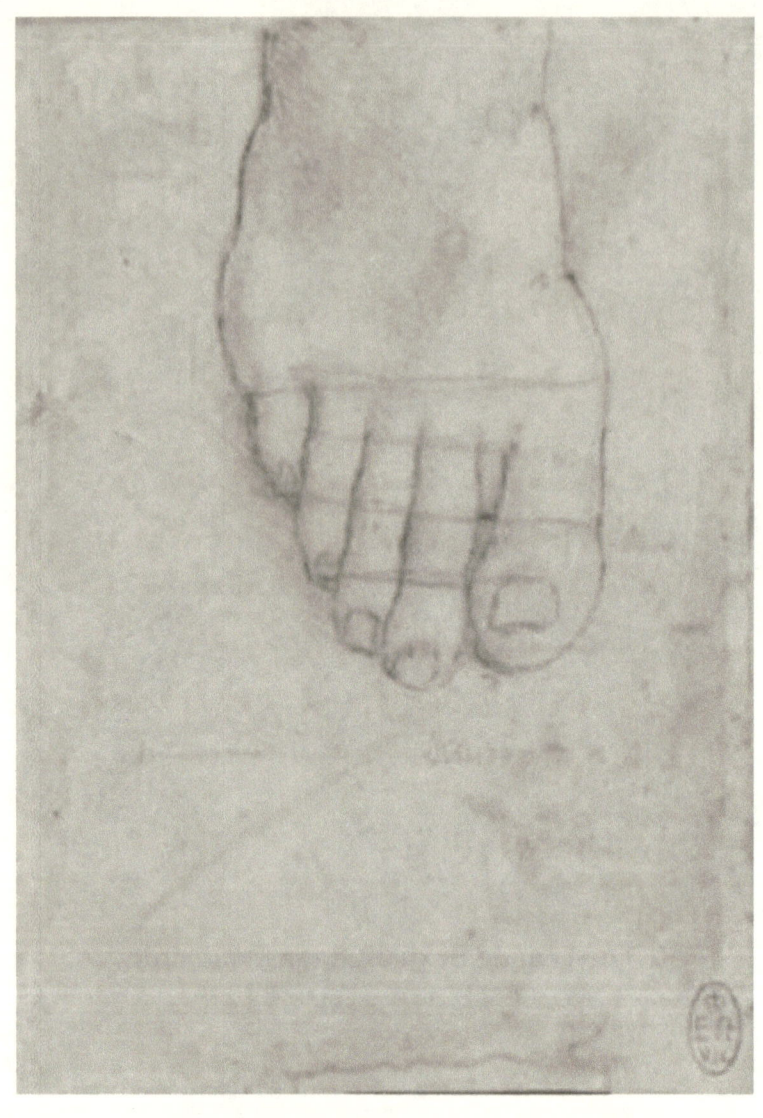

Measured Study of a Foot, n.d., chalk

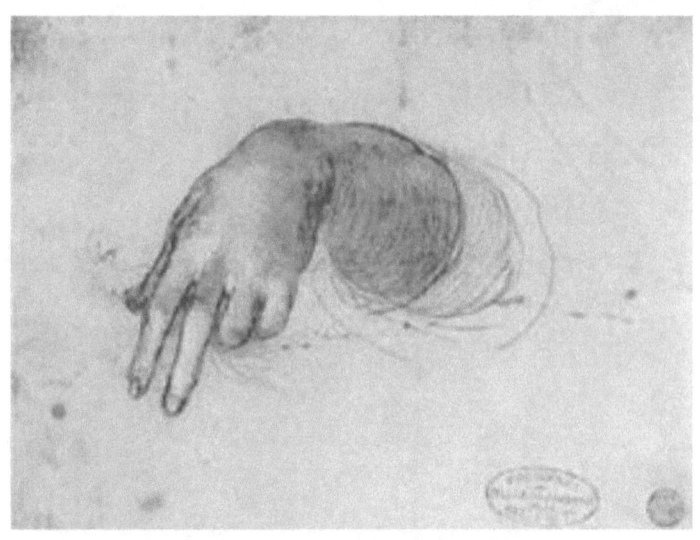

Study of a hand, n.d., ink

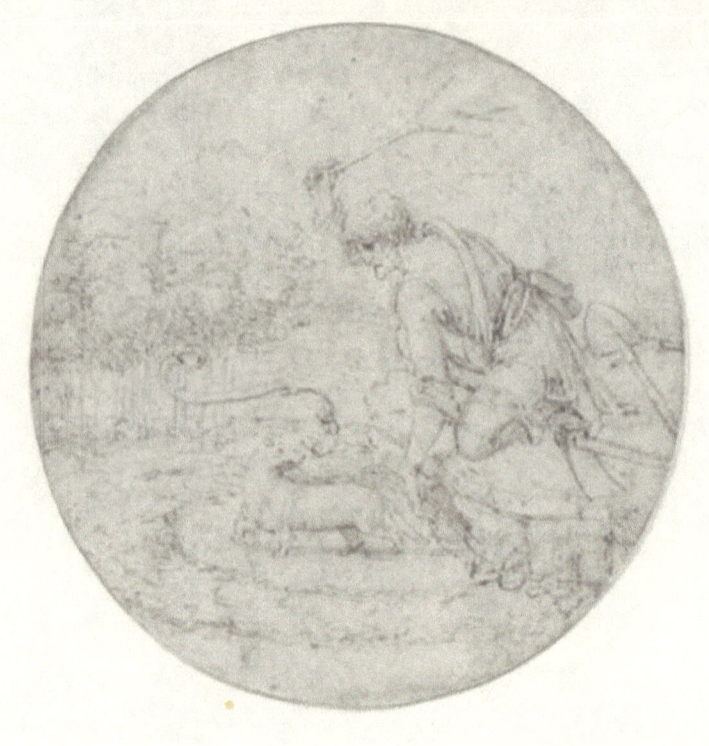

**The Ermine as a Symbol of Purity and Moderation,
n.d., ink**

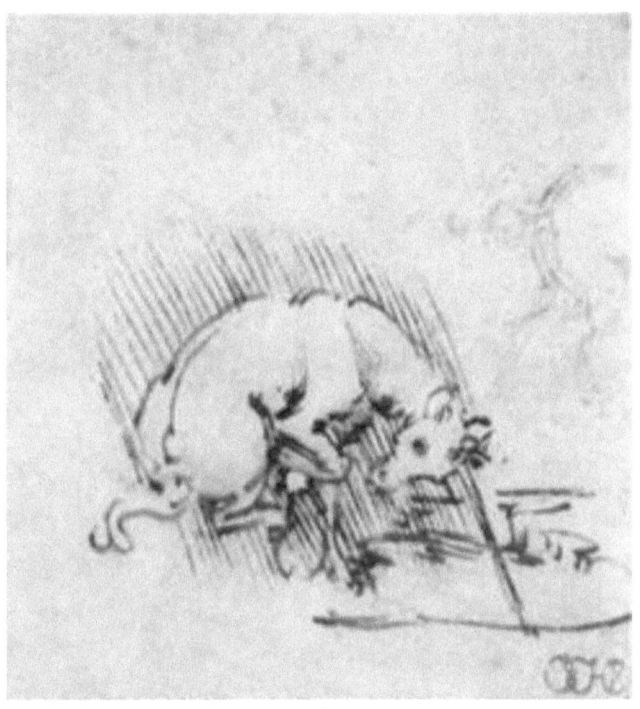

A Unicorn Dipping its Horn into a Pool of Water, n.d.,
ink

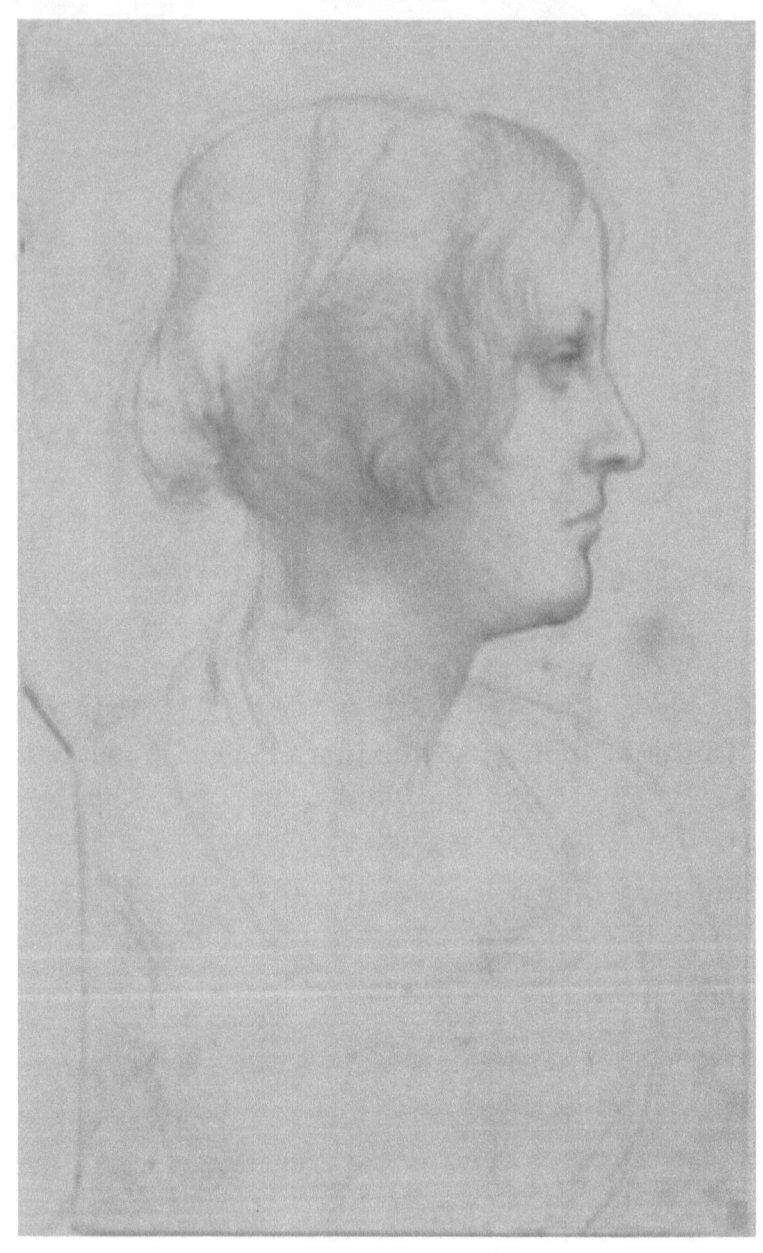

Portrait of a Young Woman in Profil, n.d., chalk

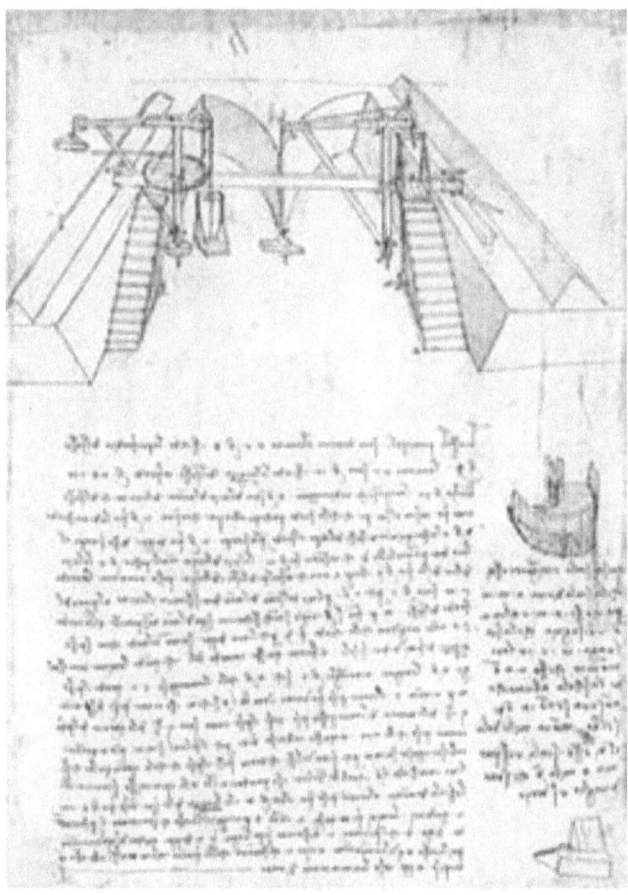

**Pulley System for the Construction of a Staircase, n.d.,
ink**

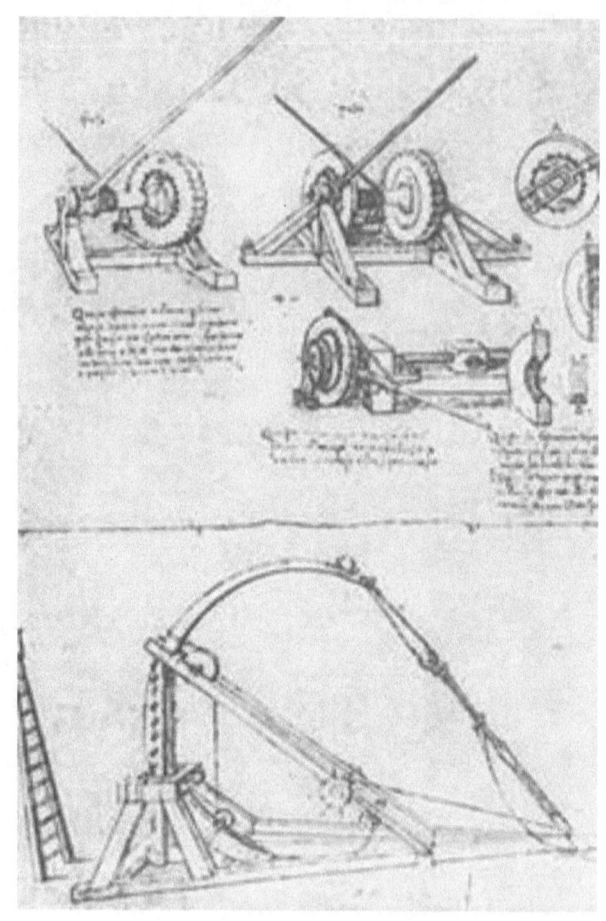

Designs for a Catapult, n.d., ink

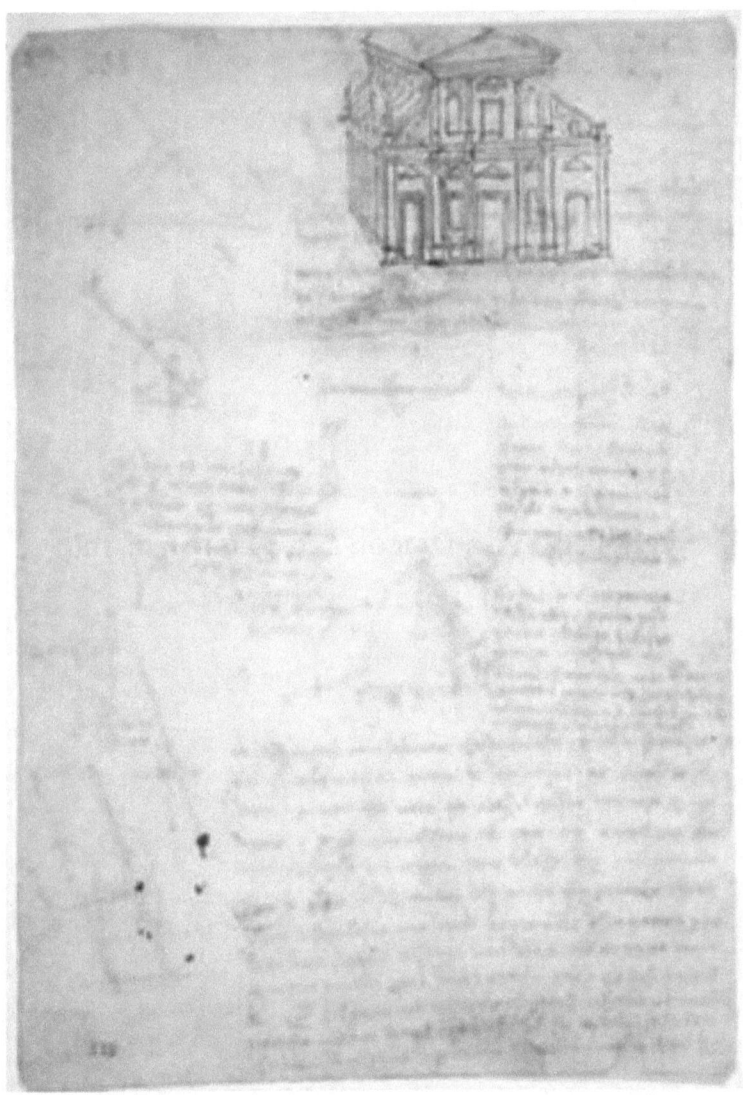

A Church Viewed in Perspective, n.d., ink

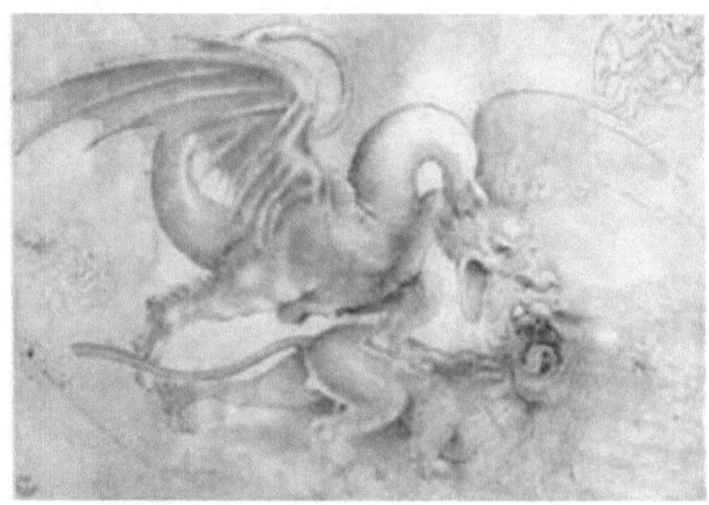

Fight between a Dragon and a Lion, n.d., ink

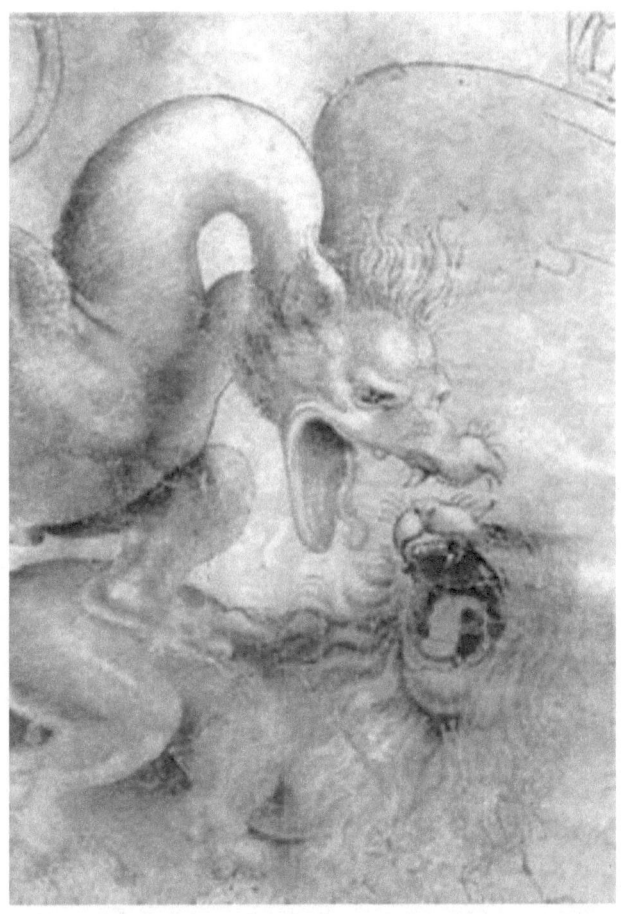

Fight between a Dragon and a Lion (detail)

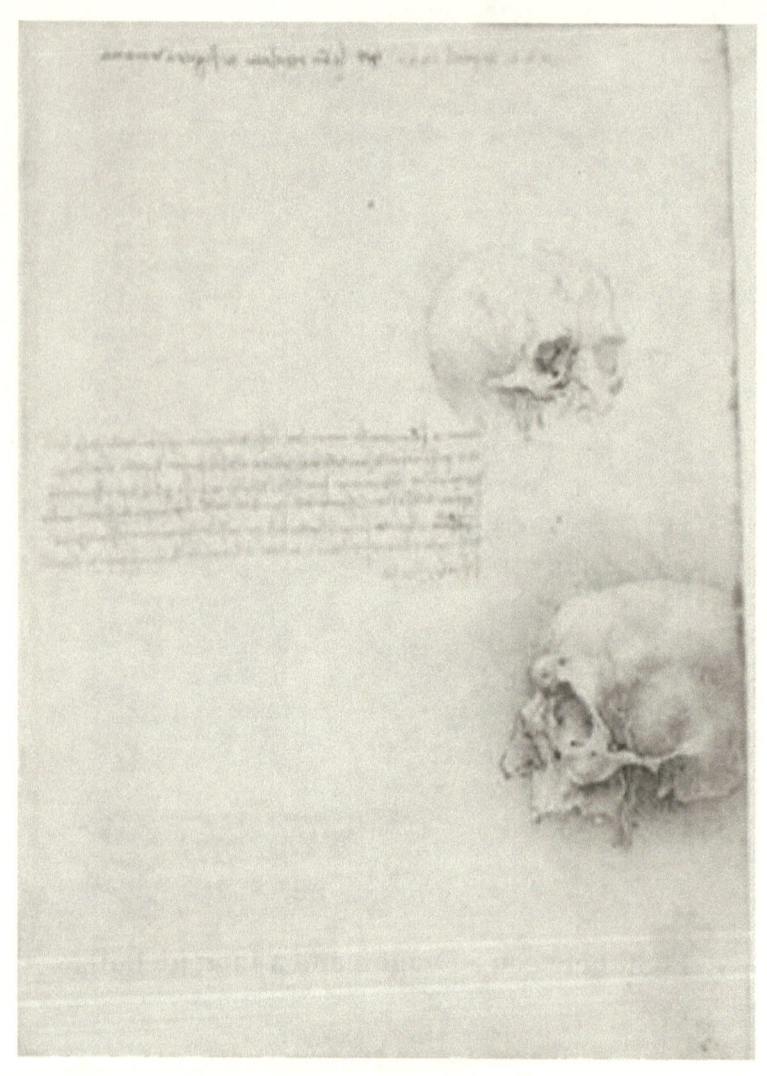

Studies of a Cranium, n.d., ink

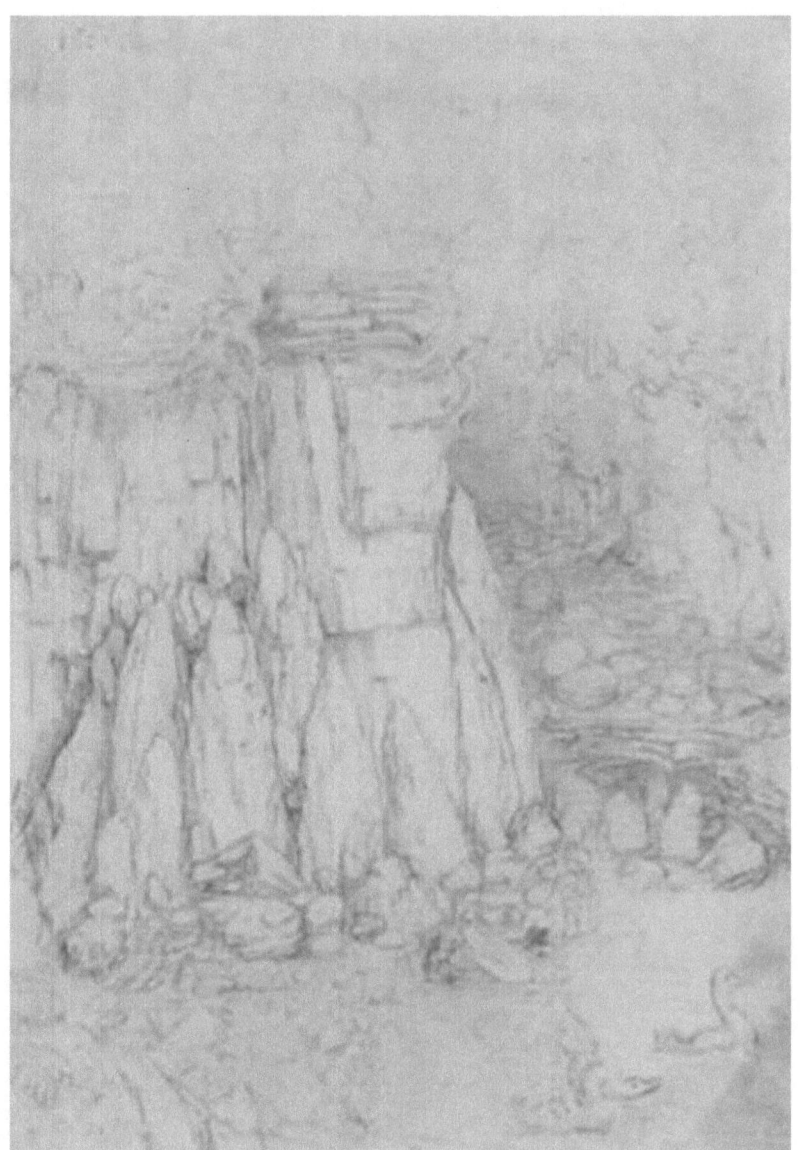

A Rocky Ravine, n.d., ink

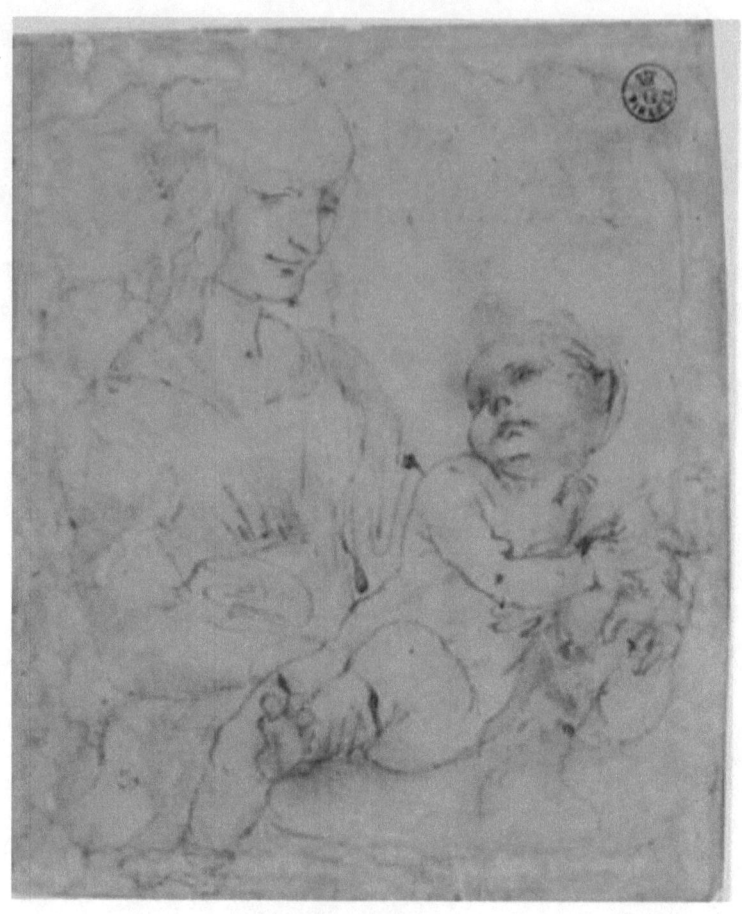

Virgin and Child with a Cat, n.d., ink

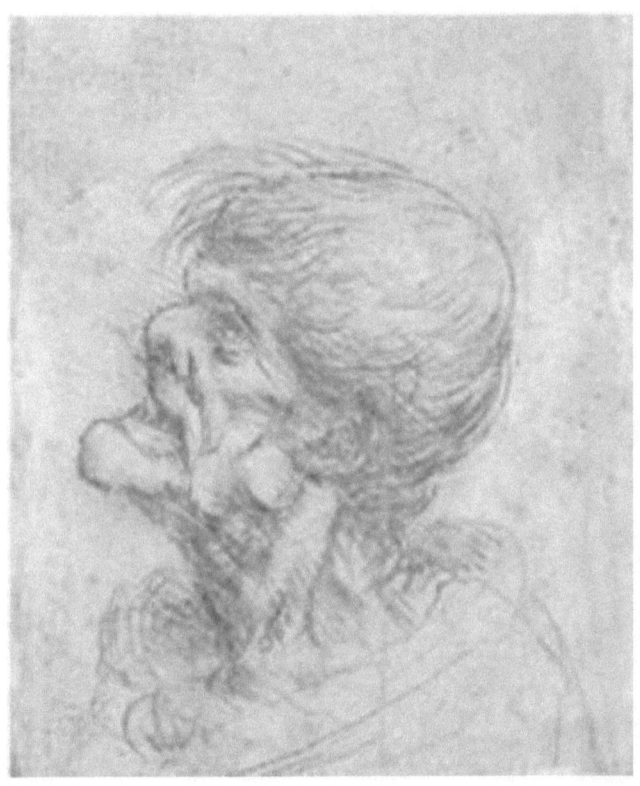

Caricature Head Study of an Old Man, n.d., chalk

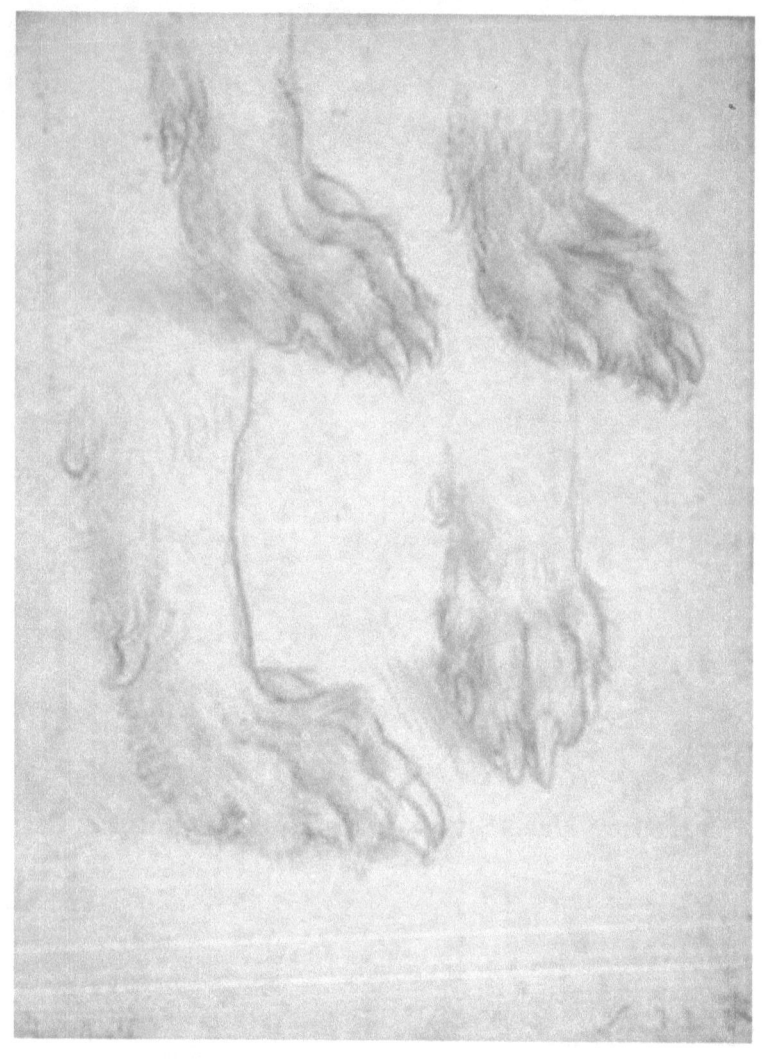

Studies of a Dog's Paw, n.d., chalk

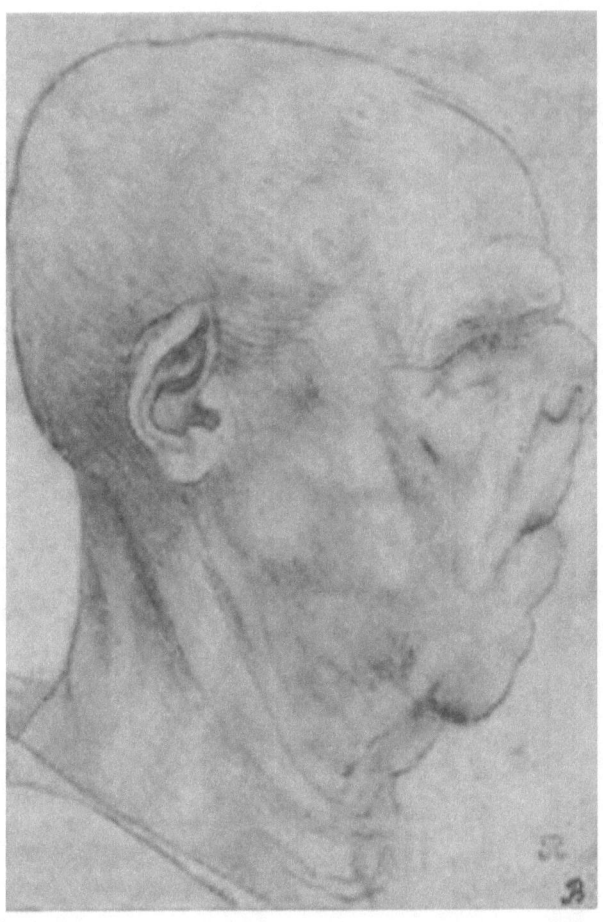

Caricature of the head of an old man, in profile to the
right, n.d., ink

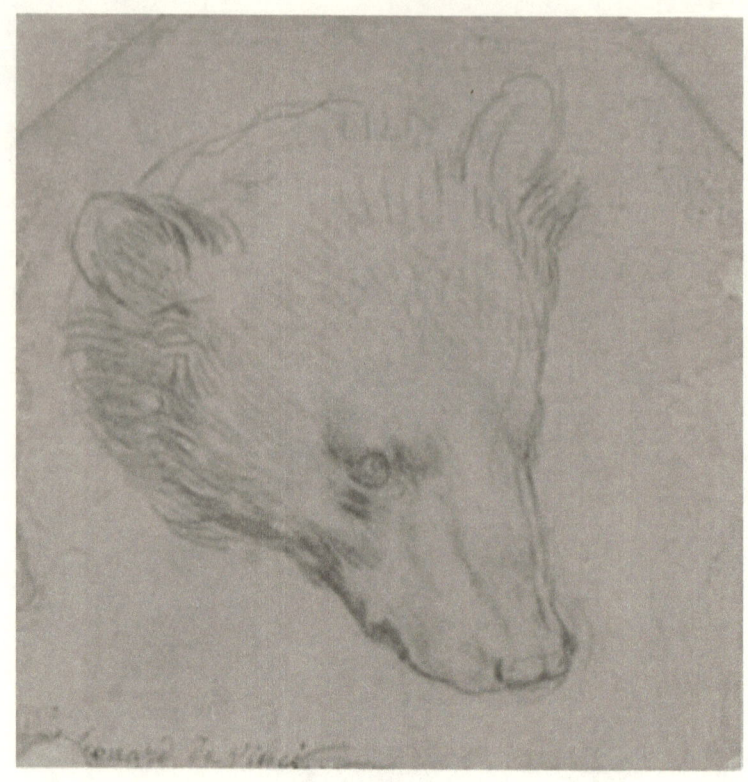

Study of a Bear's Head, n.d., chalk

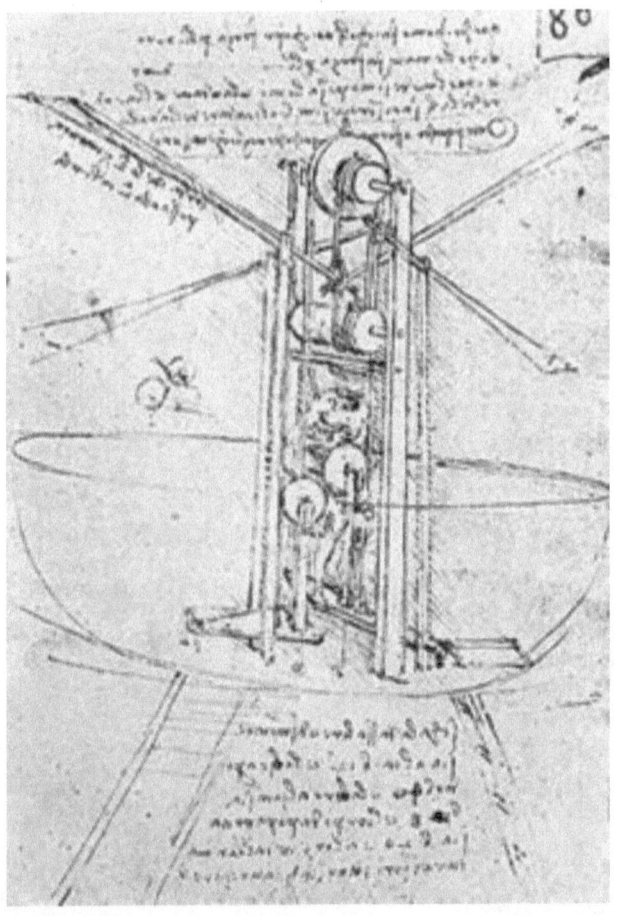

**Vertically Standing Bird's-winged Flying Machine,
n.d., ink**

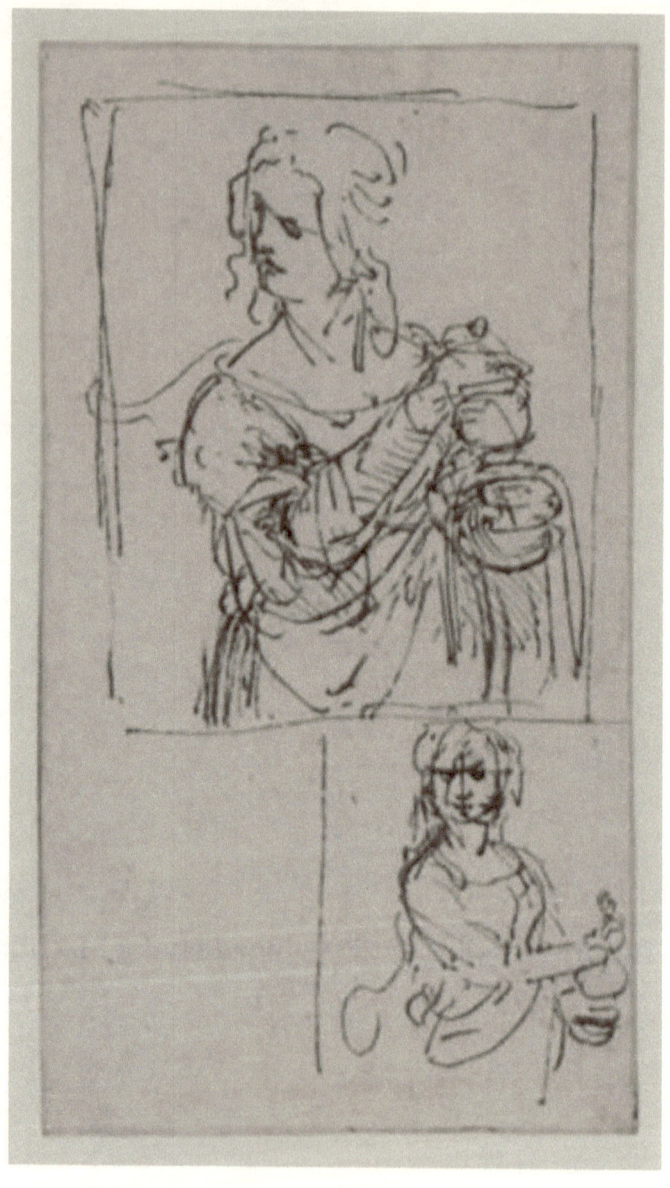

Designs for a Saint Mary Magdalene, n.d., ink

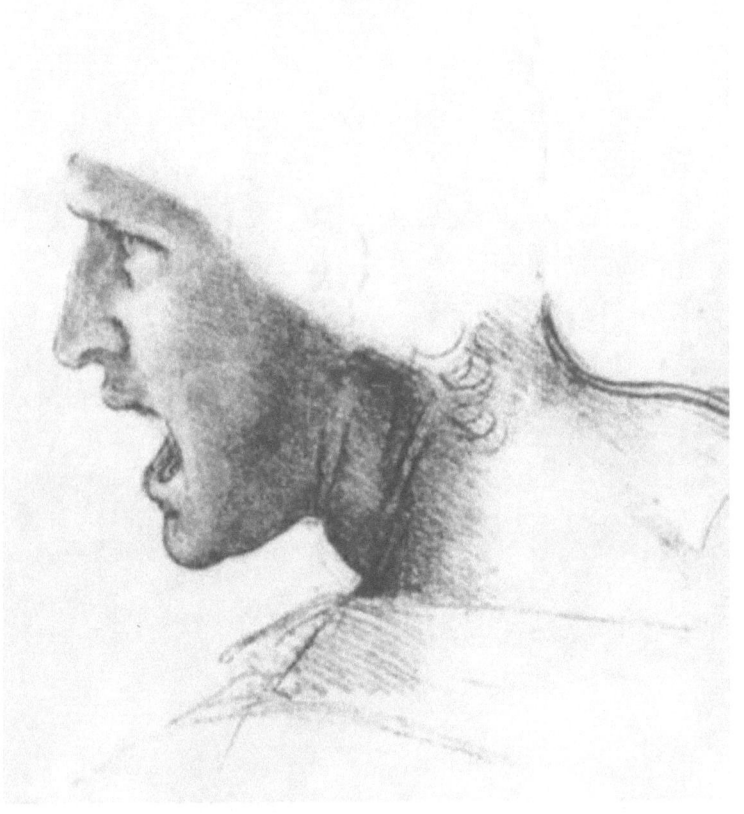

Study of a Figure for the Battle of Anghiari, n.d.,
chalk

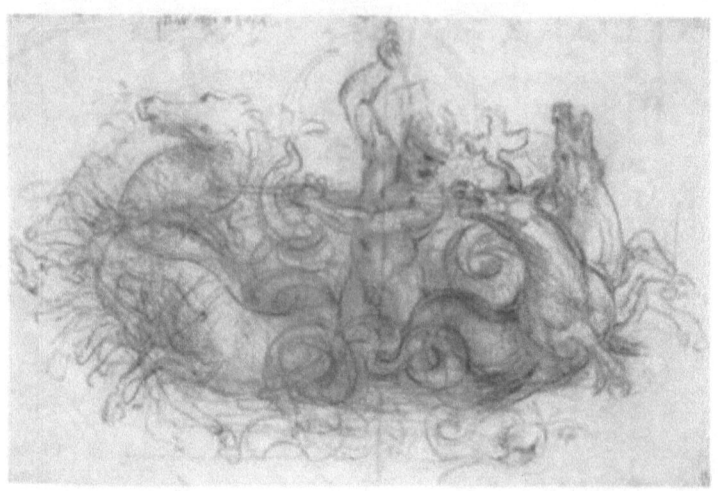

Neptune

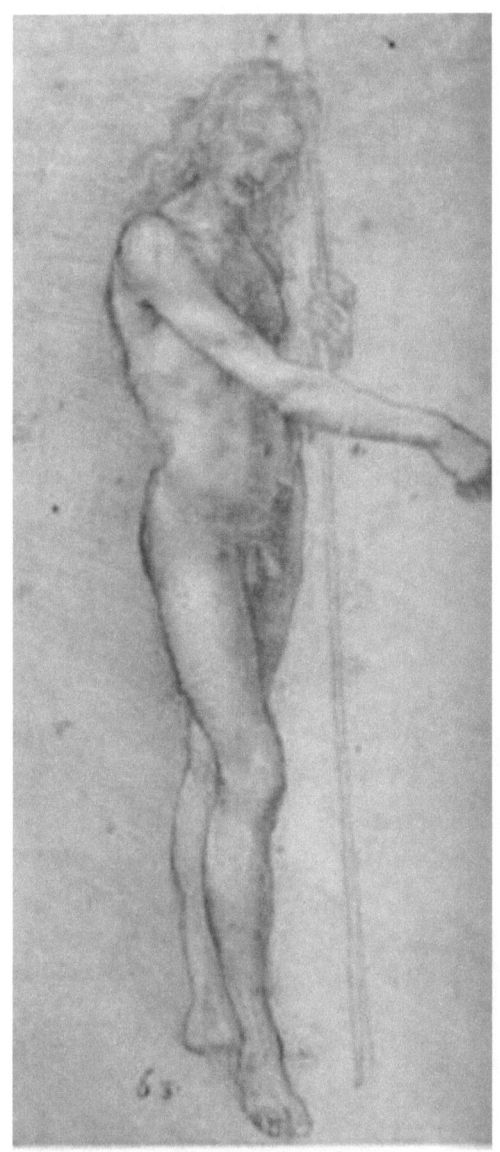

Man with a Staff

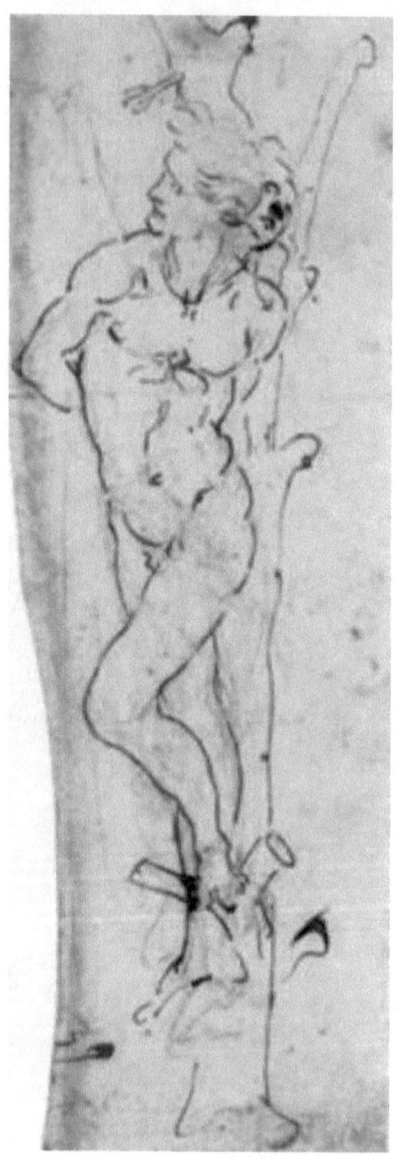

Saint Sebastion

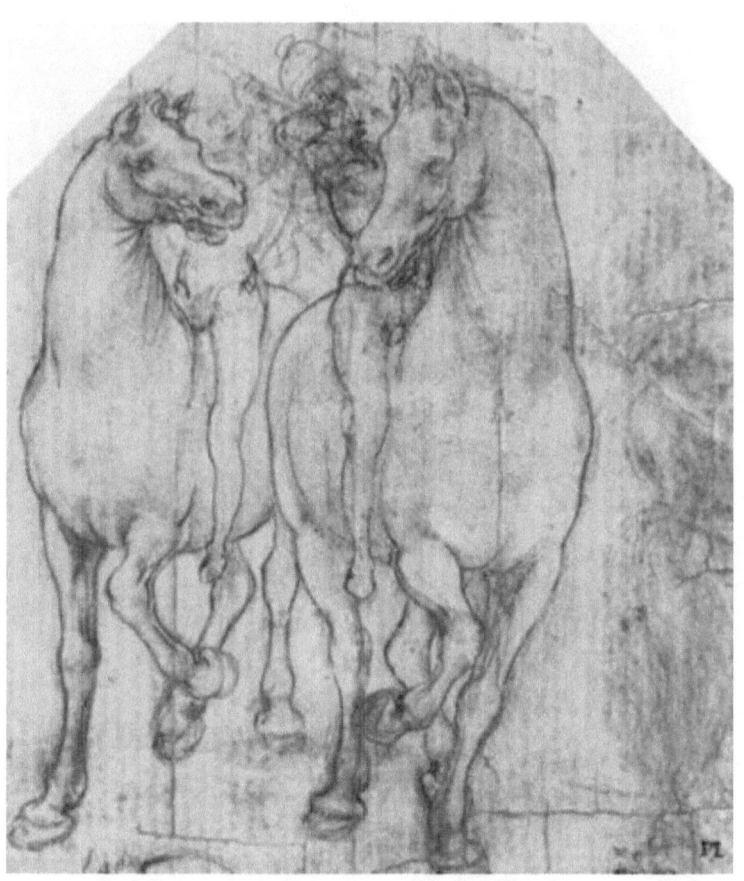

Study of Horse and Rider

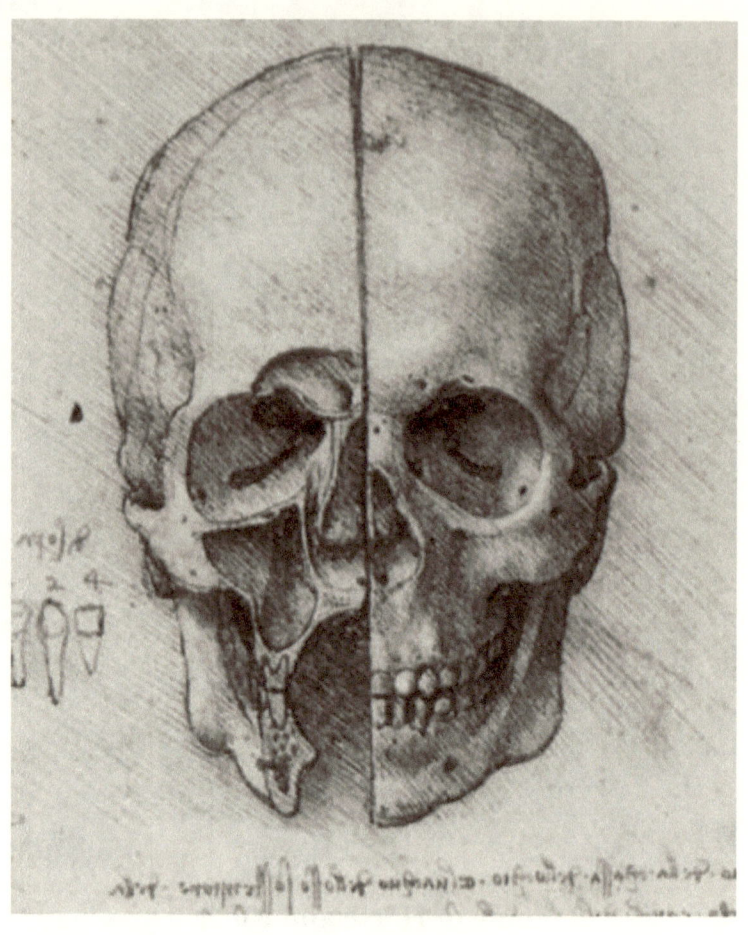

View of a Skull

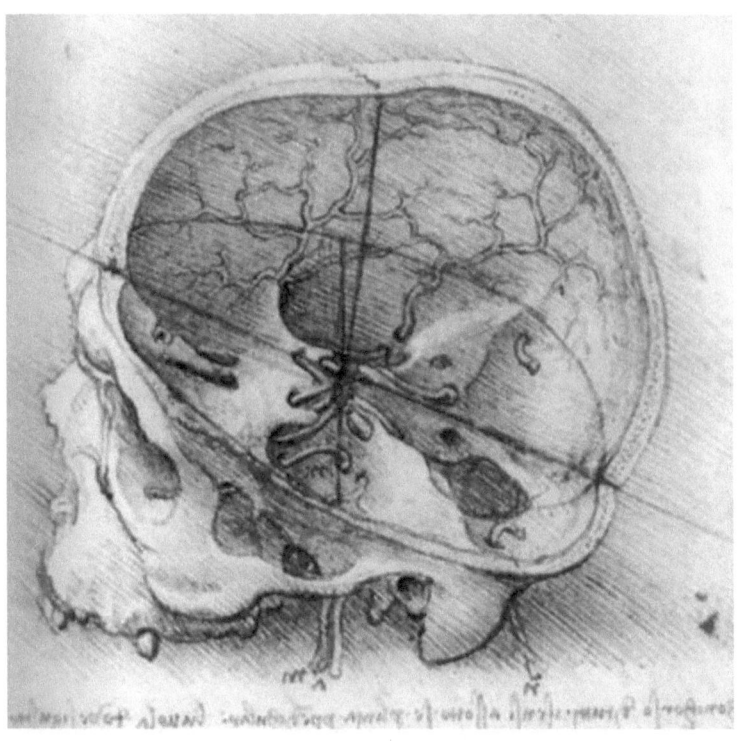

View of a Skull

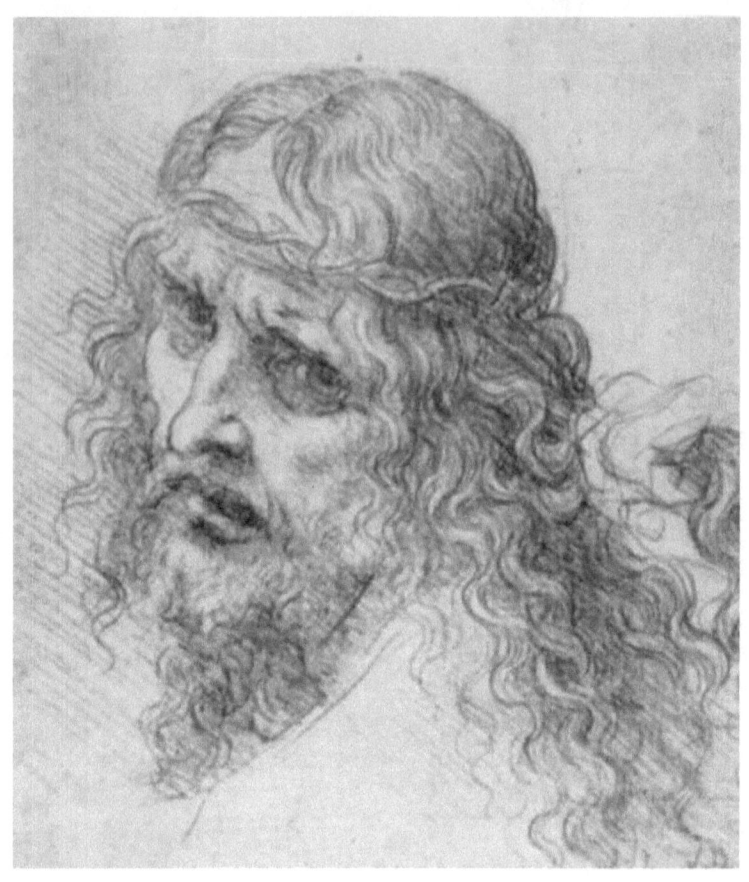

Christ Figure

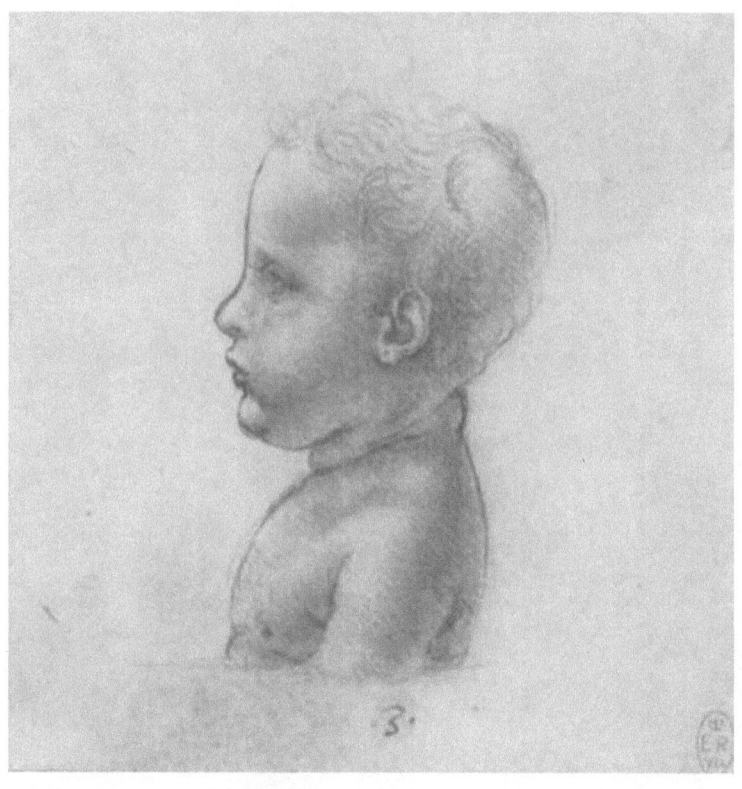

Head and Shoulders of a Child in Profile

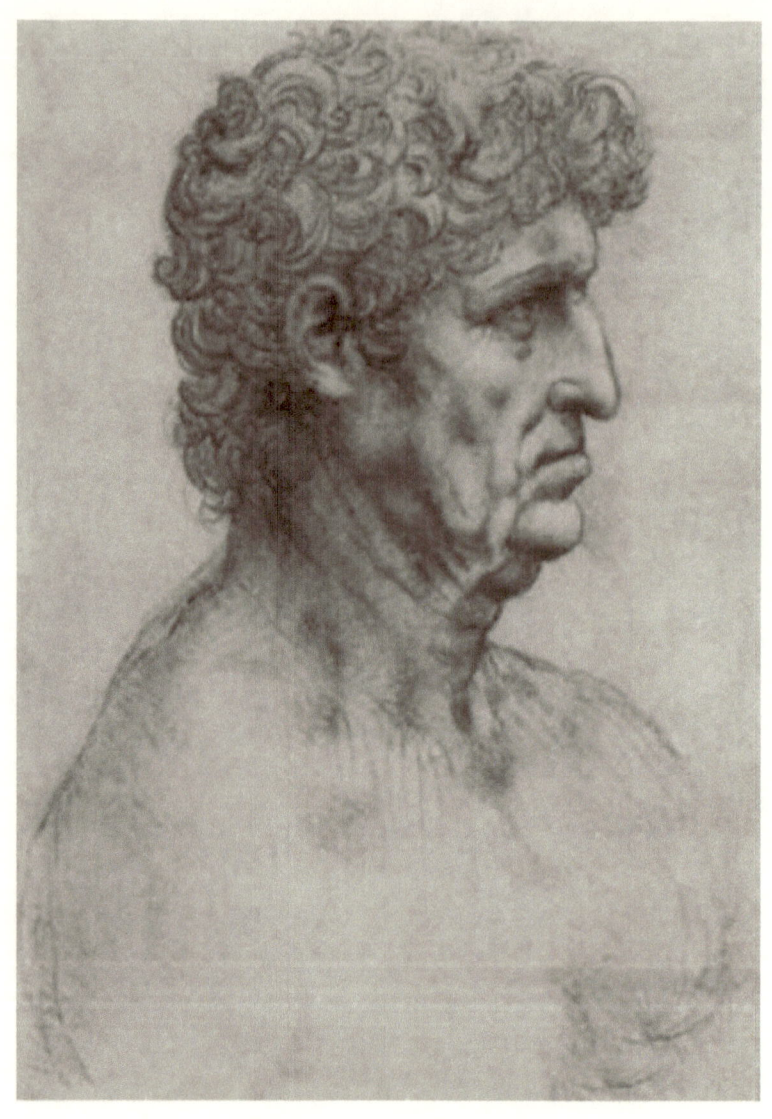

Profile of an old man

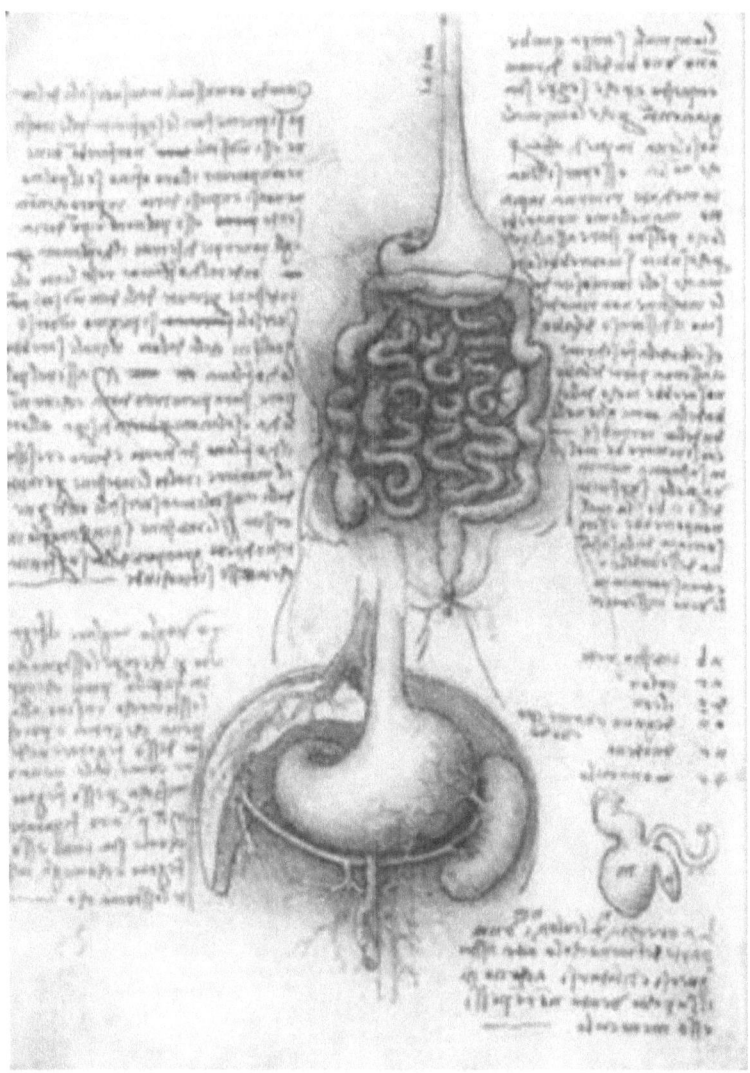

Anatomical drawing of the stomach and the intestine

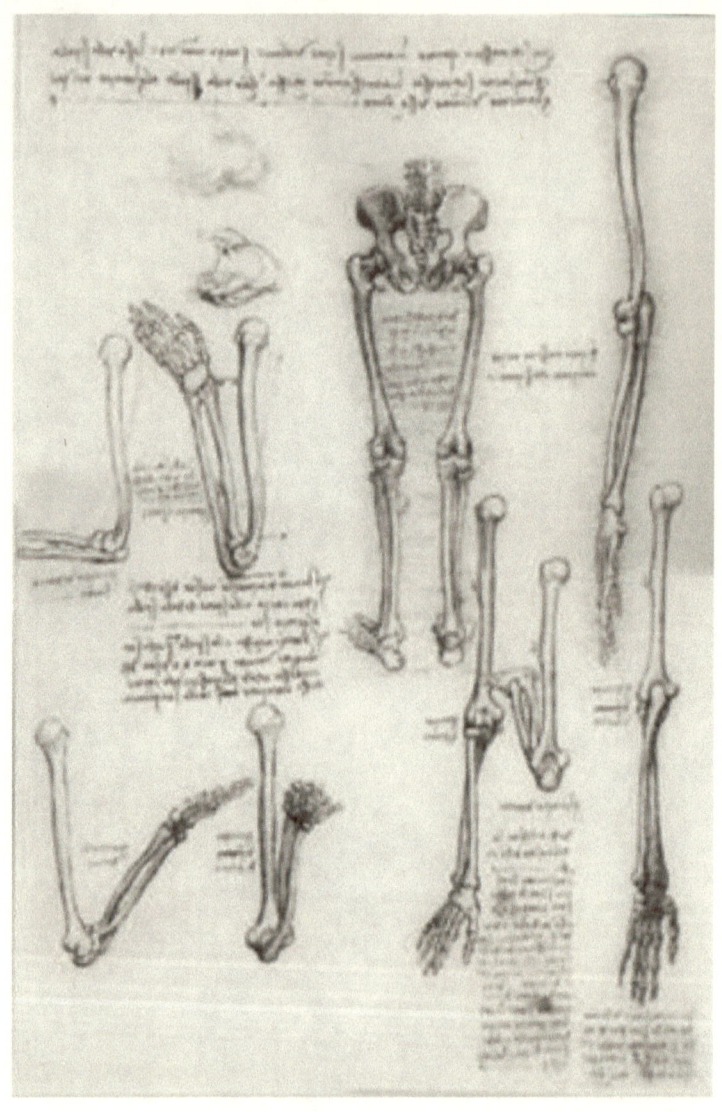

Anatomical studies of the rotation of the arms

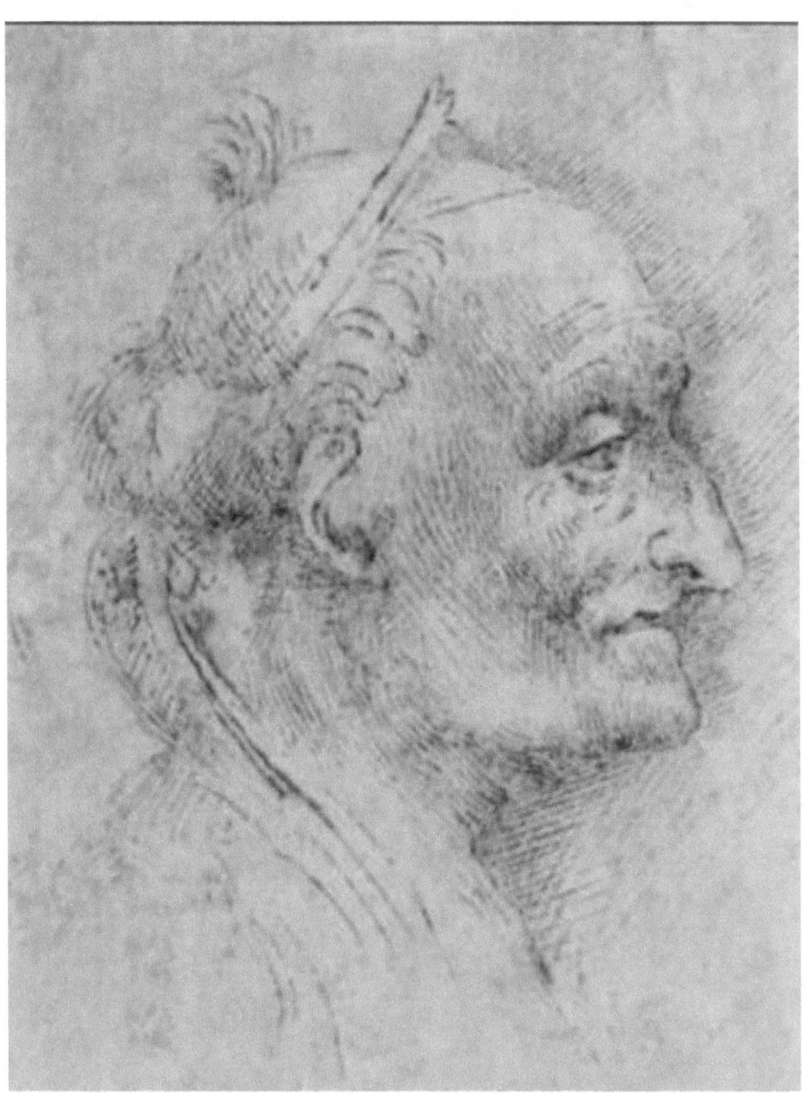

Profile of an old man

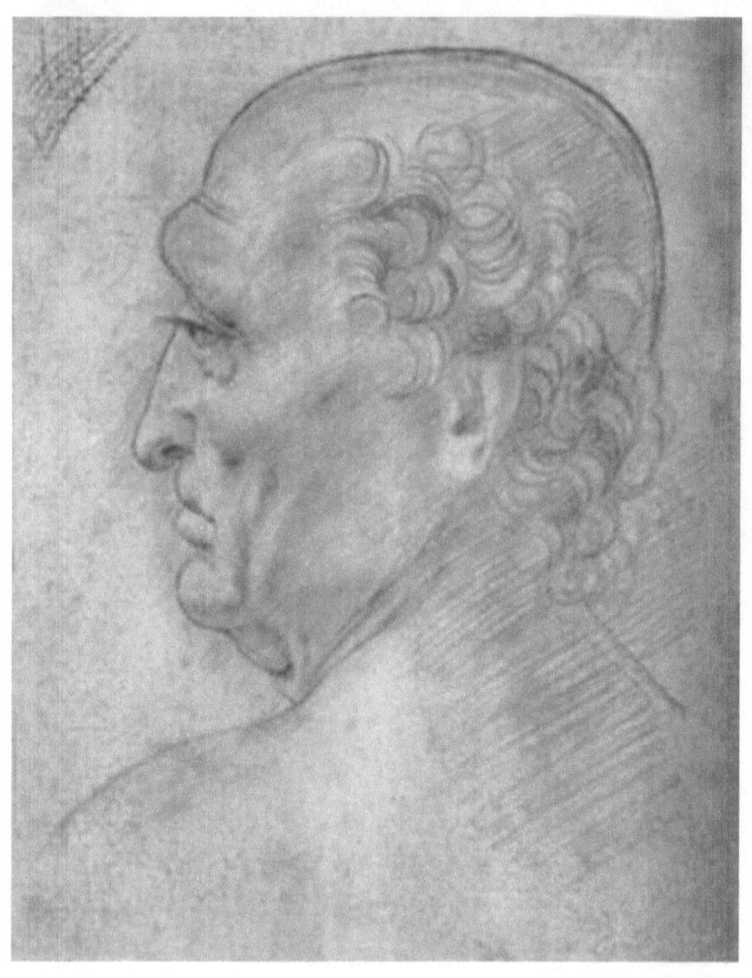

Profile of an old man

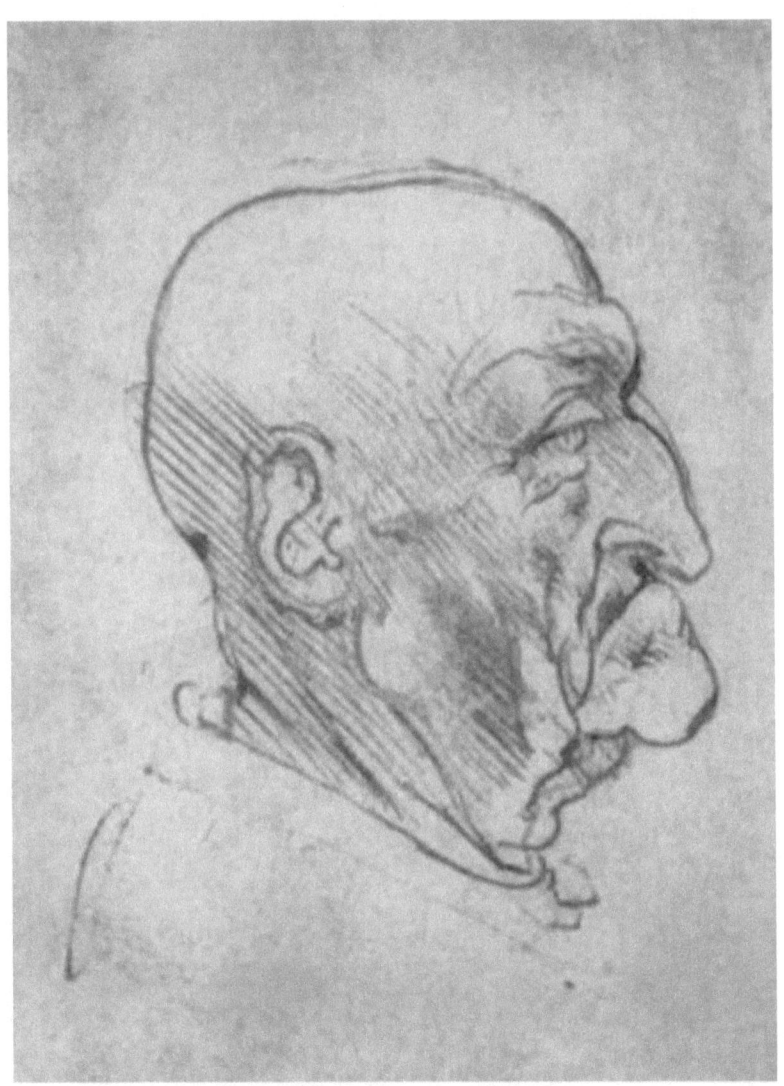

Profile of an old man

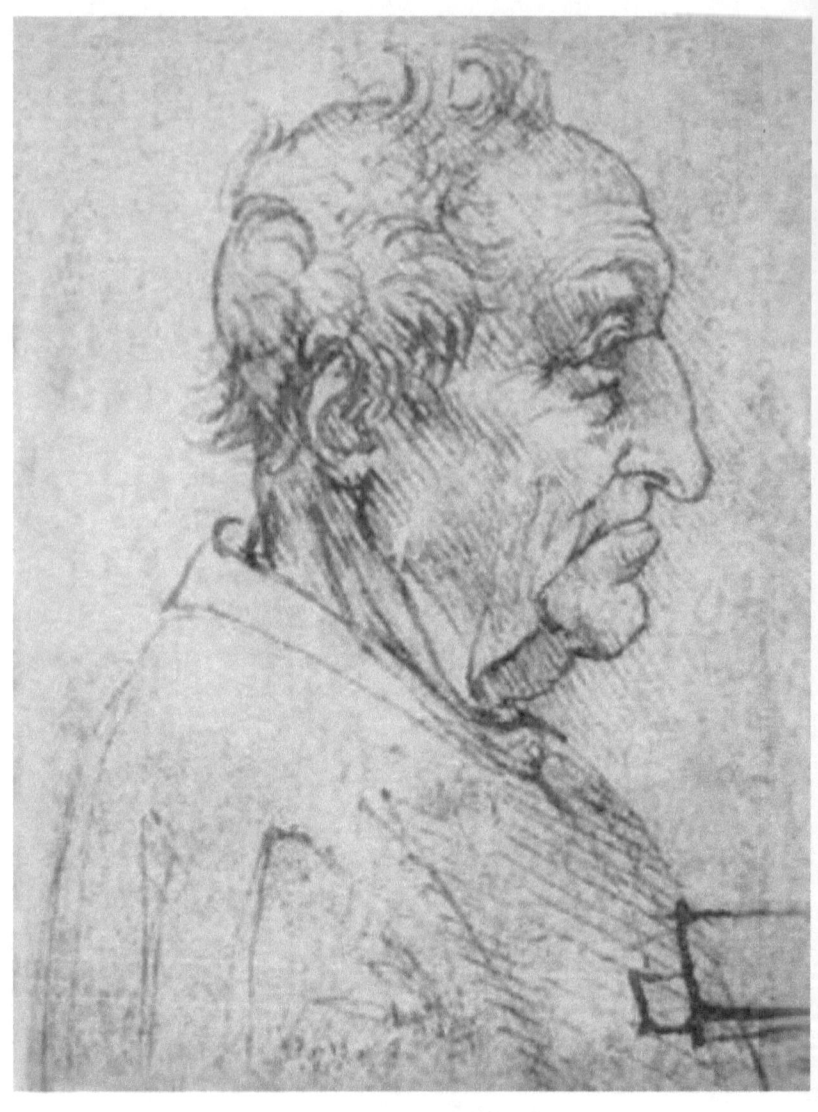

Profile of an old man

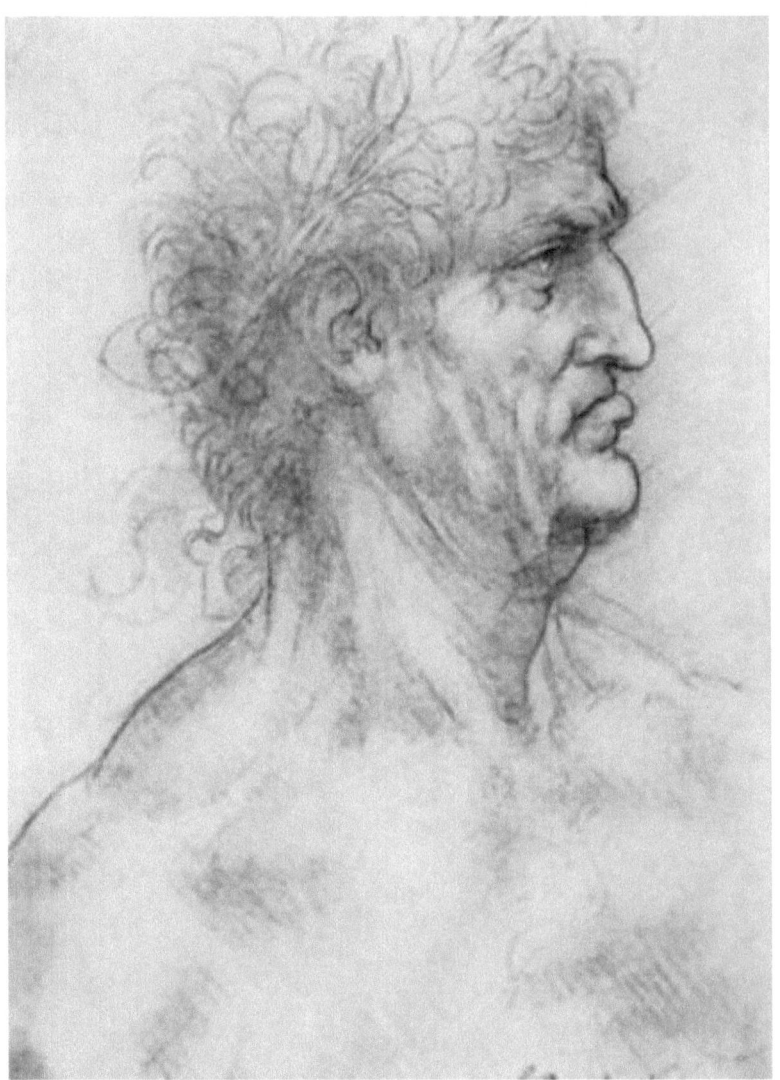

Profile of man

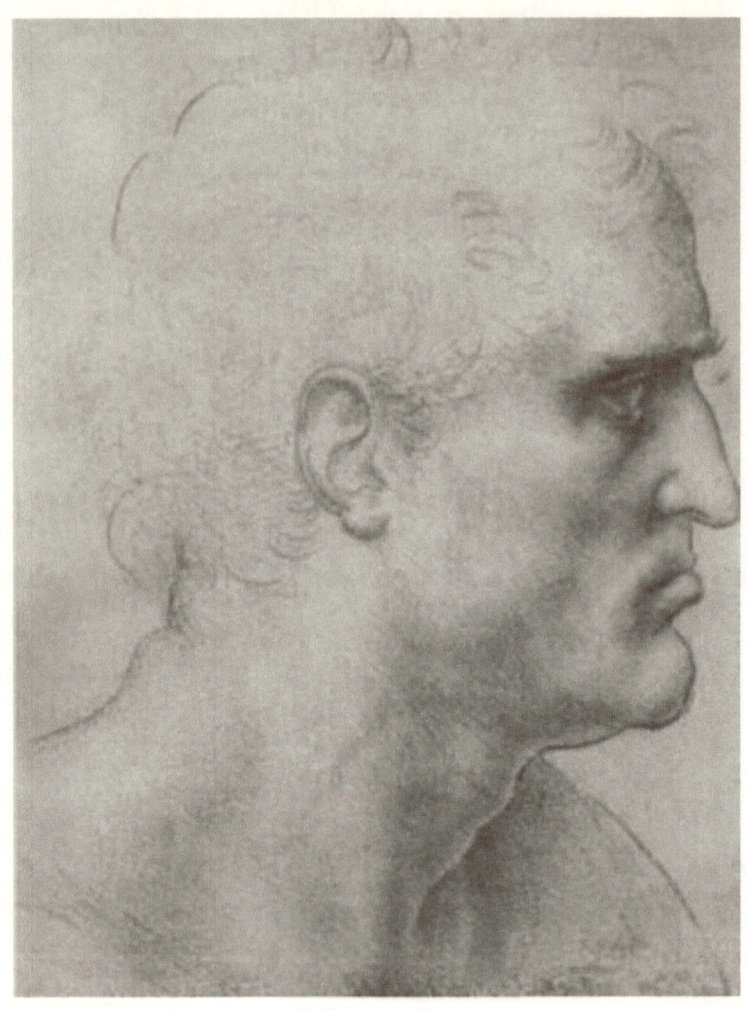

Profile of man

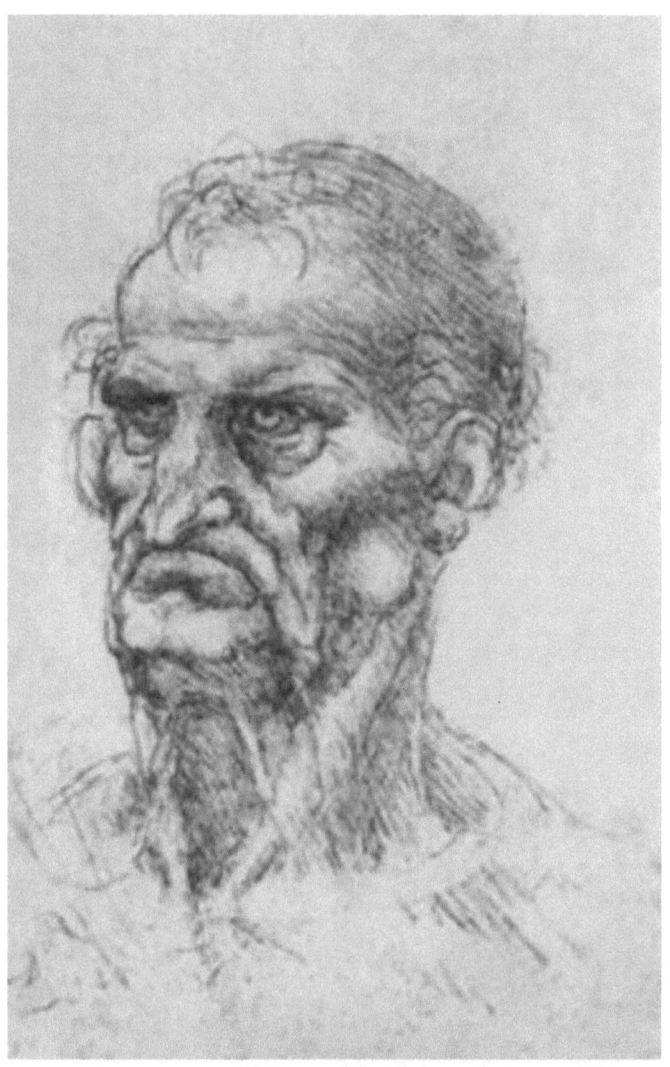

Study of an old man

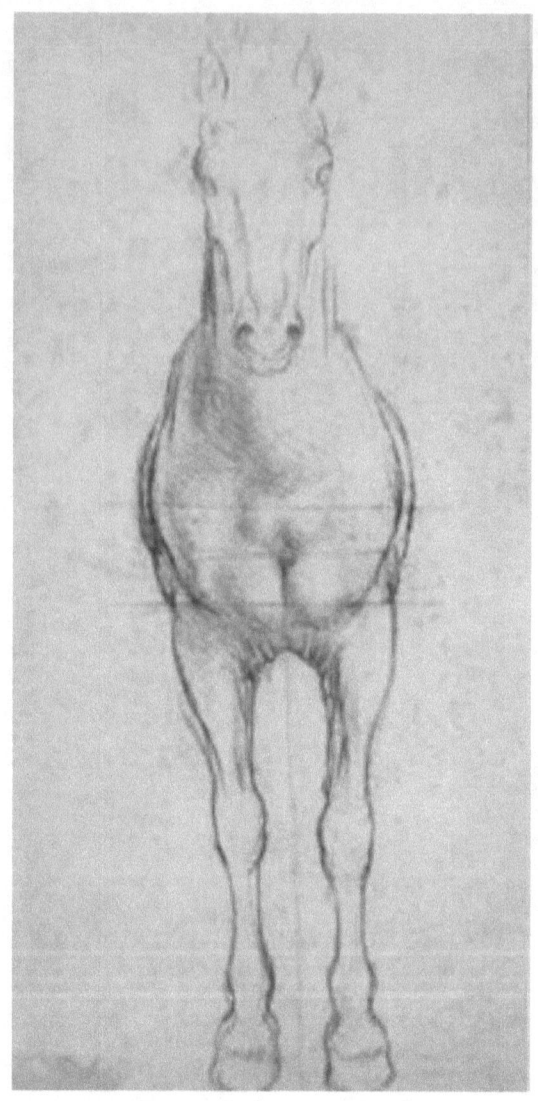

Study of the proportion of horses

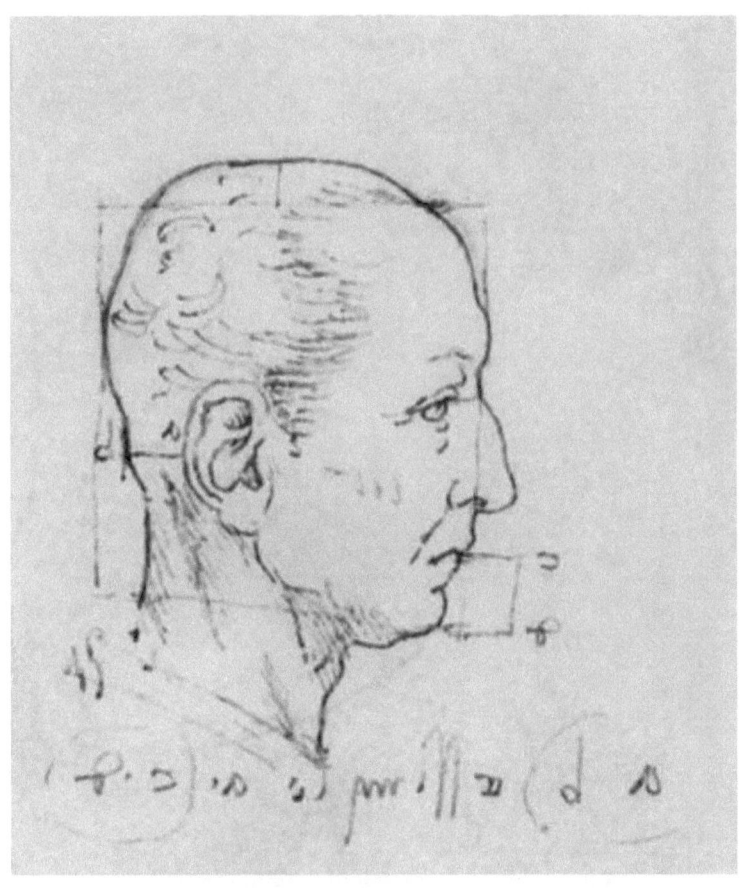

Study of the proportion of the head

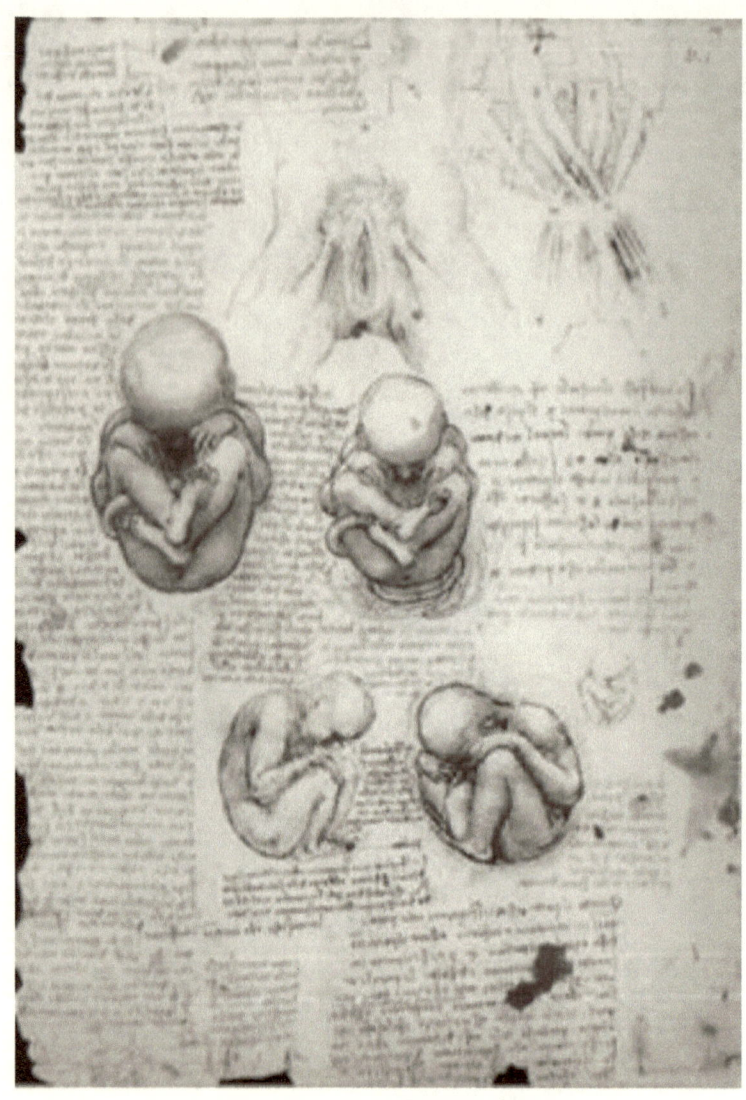

The Fotus in the Uterus

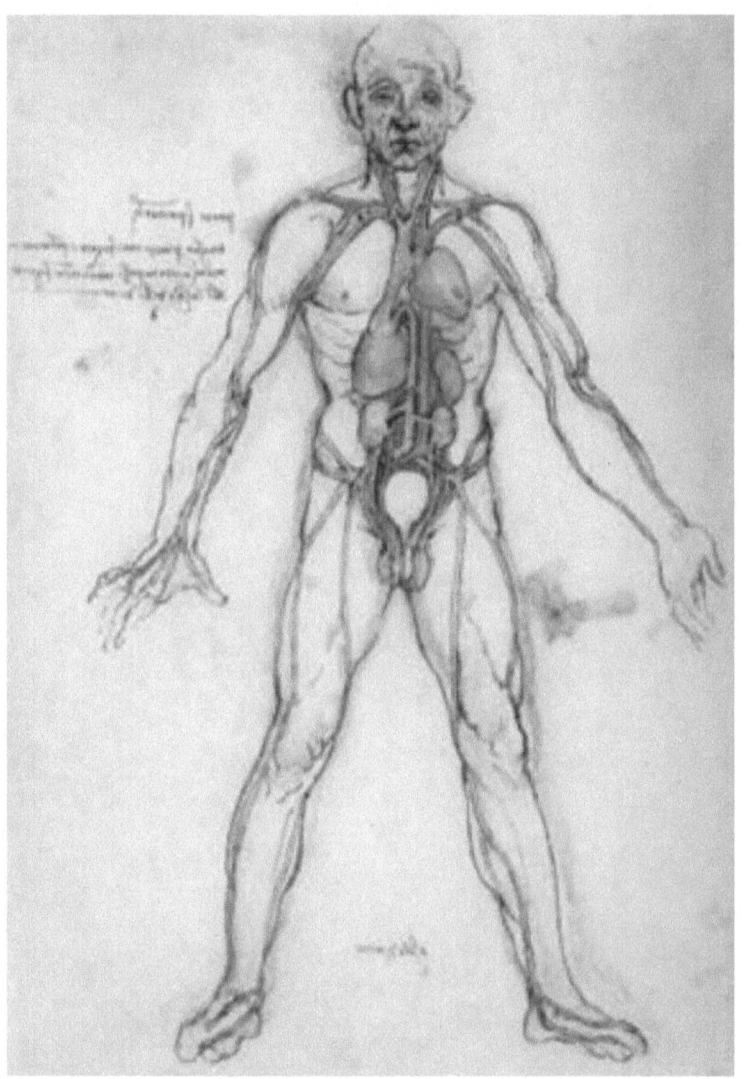

Anatomical figure

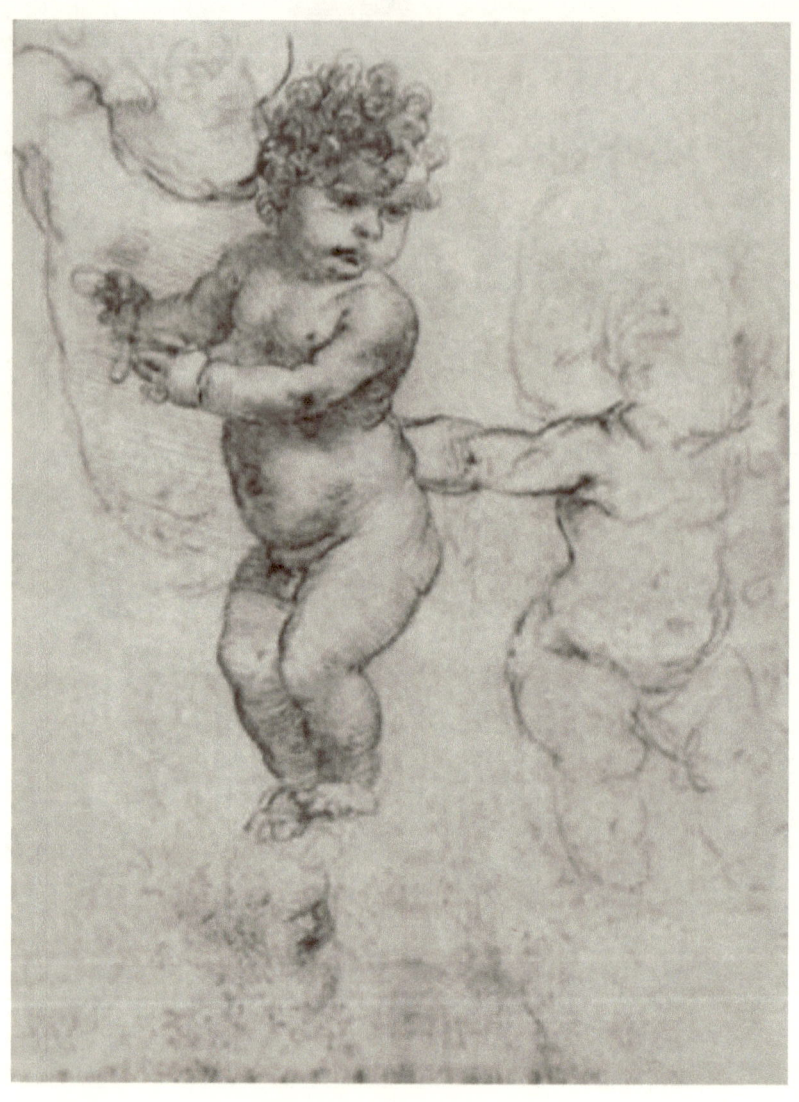

Studies of children

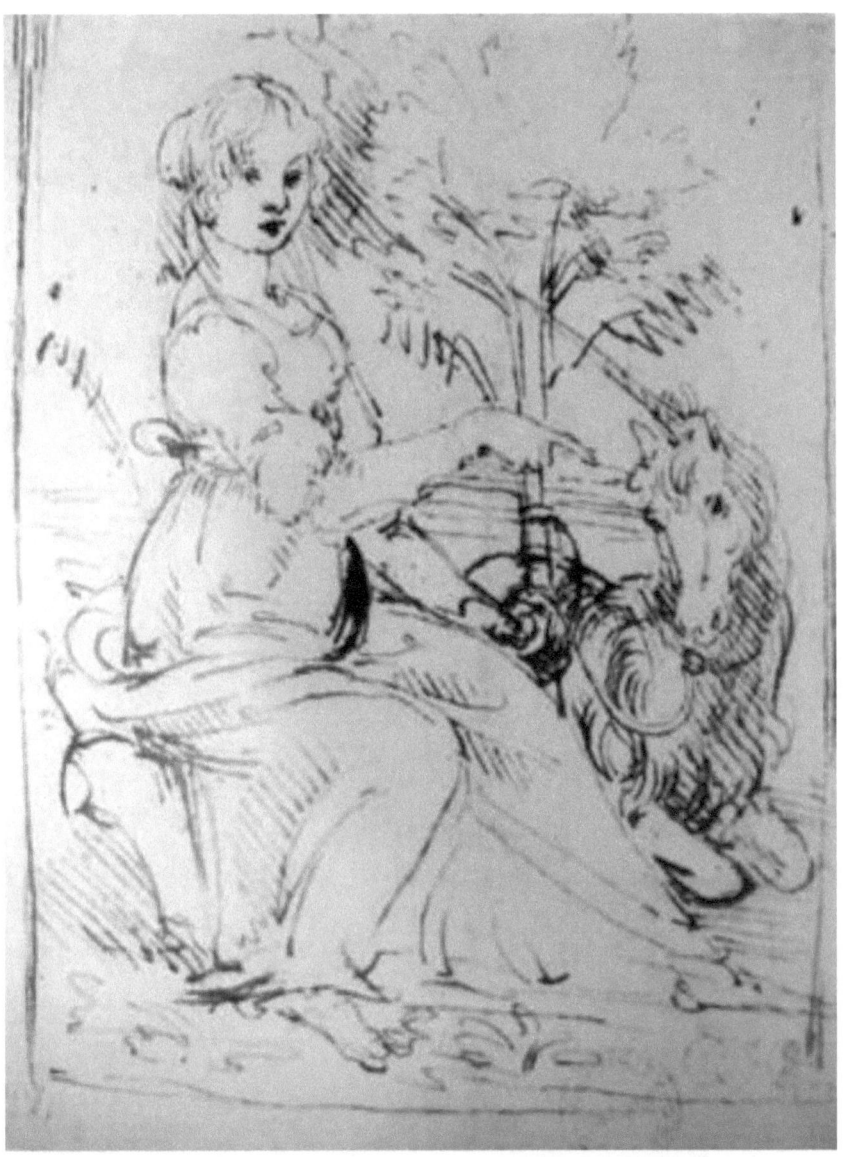

Young woman seated in a landscape and pointing at a
unicorn, n.d., Pen and dark brown ink, 94 x 74 mm

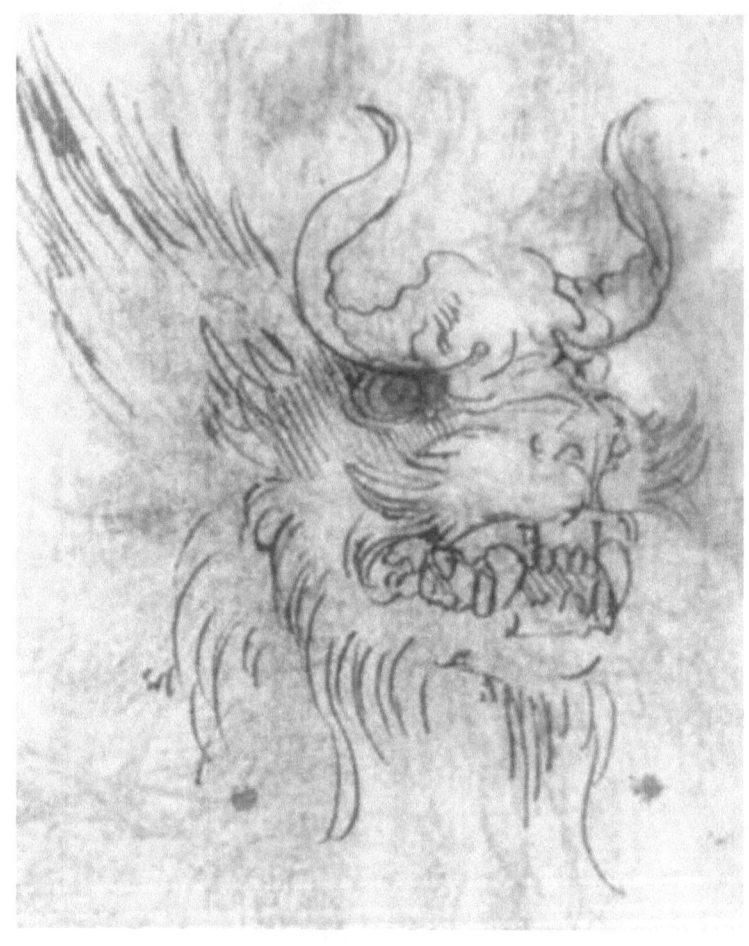

Detail from a Study of a Dragon Costume

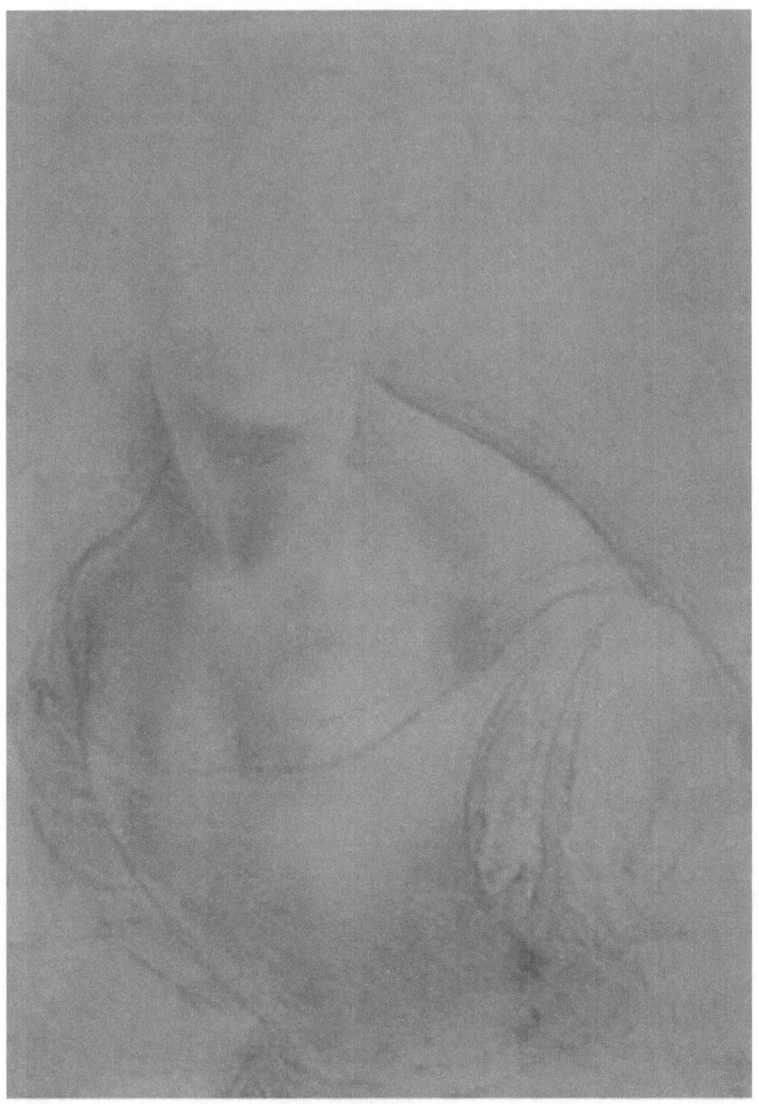

Bust of a Woman, n.d., chalk

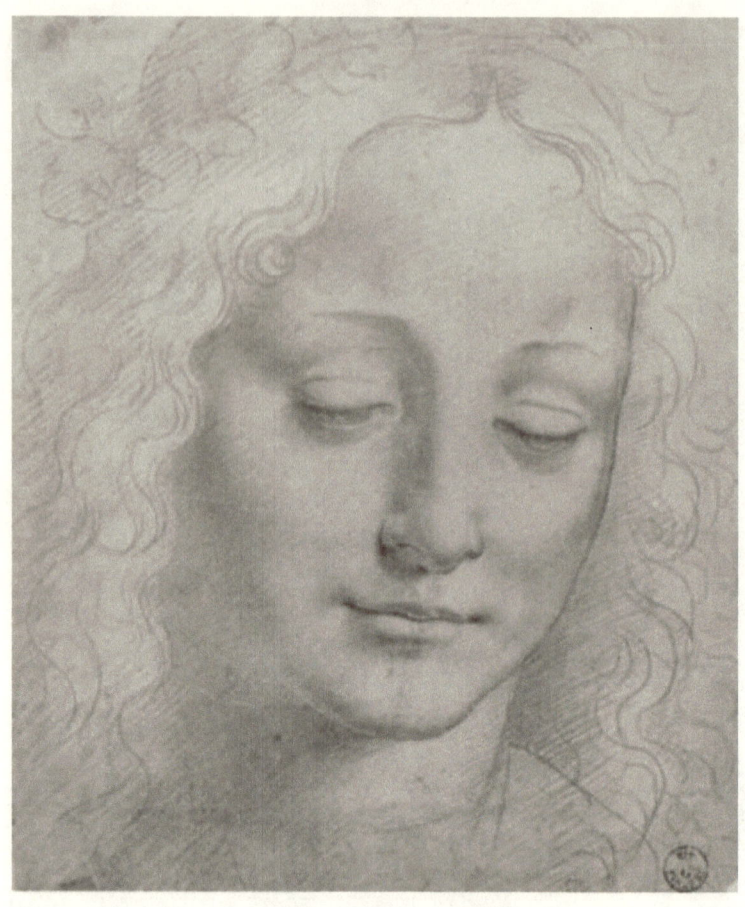

Female Head, n.d., charcoal, chalk, Galleria degli Uffizi, Florence, Italy

His Words

The Sun does not move.

Human misery Oh, how many things you surrender for the money!

All our knowledge comes from sensation.

Just as a well-spent day produces a sweet dream, so a life well used because a sweet death.

Where the soul works with his hands, there is no art.

Study the science of art and the art of science.

Anyone who thinks little errs much.

A work of art is never finished, only abandoned.

Art lives and dies limits of freedom.

Mediocre is the pupil who does not surpass his master.

Soon there will be body without shadow that virtue without envy.

That painter who has no doubts will achieve little.

Whoever else has, more afraid of losing you.

He who does not value life does not deserve it.

Just as iron rusts from disuse, inactivity also destroys the intellect.

Just as a well-spent day produces a sweet dream, so a life well used because a sweet death.

We know that mistakes are more easily detected in the work of others than yourself.

Conceiving an idea is noble, run the job is servile.

Beautiful mortal thing happens and does not last.

When Fortune comes, seize her in front firmly because behind she is bald.

When you are dealing with the water, first make consultation with the practice, and then with theory.

They will say that I not be a man of letters, well I can not express what I want to try. But they do not know that my things are to be taken, rather than the words of others, from experience, that it is the teacher who writes well, and as such I take as a teacher, and in all cases allege.

The water that you touch on the surface of a river is the last of which was happened and the first of which comes: well, it is the present moment.

Love between men is the purest from all.

Good judgment comes from good intelligence and good intelligence derived from the right, taken from the good rules, and good rules are daughters of good experience: common mother of all sciences and arts.

The studio of a painter should be a small space because a small room disciplines the mind while the distracting large.

The day will come when men will be judged by the death of an animal is judged today as the murder of a man. There will come the time in which to eat meat will be condemned as today it is condemned to eat up to our similar ones, that is to say, the cannibalism. '

The man is the victim of a sovereign dementia which makes him suffers, hoping not to suffer more. And so life escapes, without enjoying what he is already acquired.

The eye is the beautiful painted the same pleasure as the real beauty.

The noblest pleasure is the joy of understanding.

Estate eager to pay attention to the opinions of others and think hard and long if you find a missing anyone has any grounds for censure. If the answer is yes, correct the error. If the answer is no, it seems not to have heard or, if a man you respect, explain why it is wrong.

I have offended God and mankind because my work did not have the quality that should have taken.

The acquisition of any knowledge is always useful to the intellect, knows that discard the bad and keep the good.

The threat is the weapon of the threatened.

Beauty perishes in life, but is immortal in art.

The blinding ignorance confuses us. Oh miserable mortals, open your eyes! '

Most useful science is one whose fruit is the most communicable.

Consistency is started but preserve.

Inequality is the cause of all local movements.

The acquisition of any knowledge is always useful to the intellect, knows that discard the bad and keep the good.

If a person is persistent, albeit hard to understand will be intelligent, and even weak will become strong.

Wisdom is the daughter of experience.

Who really knows what he's talking, no reason to raise your voice.
Beauty perishes in life, but is immortal in art.

Life well spent is long.

A work of art is never finished, only abandoned.

The noblest pleasure is the joy of understanding.

Consistency is started but preserve.

A glass of raw clay, if broken can be repaired, but not that of fired clay.

Just as iron rusts from disuse, inactivity also destroys the intellect.

He who sows virtue, fame picks.

Painting is silent poetry, poetry blind painting.

Our greatest stupidities may be very wise.

He who does not value life does not deserve it.

Many people, after finding good seek yet and are evil.

As I thought I was learning to live, I have learned how to die.

Seek advice when you know correct itself.

I have offended God and mankind because my work did not have the quality that should have taken.

Whoever else has, more afraid of losing you.

They will say that I not be a man of letters, well I can not express what I want to try. But they do not know that my things are to be taken, rather than the words of others, from experience, that it is the teacher who writes well, and as such I take as a teacher, and in all cases allege.

Evil is not hurt me as well that I gain.

We should not desire the impossible.

Truly man is the king of beasts, for his brutality exceeds that of the latter.

Those who fall in love with practice without theory are like pilots without rudder or compass, they will never know where they're going.

Rebuke a friend in secret and praise him in public.

Mechanics is the paradise of the mathematical sciences, because it reaches the mathematical result.

He who does not punish evil commands it done.

As much as nature begins with reason and ends in experience, we must follow the march contrary, ie start with her experience and investigate the reason.

Eating reluctantly becomes repulsive food in dish.

The truth is of such excellence that when praises small things, ennobles.

Every natural action is performed by the very nature of the way and in the shortest time possible. No action may be abbreviated nature, because nature is generated as soon as possible.

Art lives and dies limits of freedom.

Justice requires power, intelligence and will, and resembles the eagle.

Where the soul works with his hands, there is no art.

The need is a teacher and tutor of nature. Is your theme and the source of his inventions, his brake and perpetual rule.

Flee the precepts of speculators whose reasons are not confirmed by experience.

Stay eager to pay attention to the opinions of others and think hard and long if you find a missing anyone has any grounds for censure. If the answer is yes, correct the error. If the answer is no, it seems not to have heard or, if a man you respect, explain why it is wrong.

Nothing deceives us as much as our own judgment.

Obstacles can not crush me; every obstacle provides a final decision.

Conceiving an idea is noble, run the job is servile.

Perspective is to painting what the bridle the horse,
which the rudder to the boat.

That painter who has no doubts will achieve little.

We know that mistakes are more easily detected in the
work of others than him.

A painter will produce pictures of little merit if he takes
the work of others as a reference.

As virtue is born, is born of envy against him, and
before the body loses its virtue shadow envy.

Thus, the study will not spoil the memory, then that
does not retain anything that takes.

I would argue that a man can not achieve excellence if
it satisfies the ignorant and not those of his own trade.

The ambitious that are not content with the benefit of
the life and beauty of the world, have the punishment
he did not understand life and be insensitive to the
value and beauty of the universe.

Sometimes I feel that my soul is in shadows, then I
bow, kiss you, and no light.

Nature is full of arguments that never had the
experience.

Even the smallest feline is a masterpiece.

The man has a great argument, but for the most part vain and false, the animals have minor but useful and true, and certainly a little better than a great deception.

If God exists, I'll ask accounts absurdity of life, pain, death, having given some other reason and stupidity ... and so many other things.

Do not disown the past.

All the elements, when out of its natural place, want to return to it, especially fire, water and earth.

It's always good to what is beautiful ... Example of this error give those who speak elegantly, but without doctrine.

Each instrument (or medium) should be tailored to the experience.

Water is the vehicle of nature.

The more you know, the more you love.

Poetry is superior to painting in the representation of words and painting is superior to poetry in the representation of the facts. For this reason I believe that painting is superior to poetry.

A good painter is to paint two main things: the man and the work of the mind of man. The first is easy, the second difficult.

Ivy has long life.

Nobody should ever imitate the style of another because, in terms of art, will be called a nephew and not a child of nature.

The threat is the threat weapon.

The mind of the painter is a copy of the divine mind as it operates freely in creating many types of animals, plants, fruits, landscapes, impressive ruins and sites.

The mind of the painter should be like a mirror that is filled with as many images as there are things in front of him.

The ratio between human work and nature is the same that mediates between man and God.

Study the science of art and the art of science.

Our greatest stupidities may be very wise.

Seek advice when you know correct itself

Who really knows what he's talking, no reason to raise your voice.

www.ingramcontent.com/pod-product-compliance
Lightning Source LLC
Chambersburg PA
CBHW020902180526
45163CB00007B/2599